T0316909

THE FLOW OF ILLICIT FUNDS

THE FLOW OF ILLICIT FUNDS

A CASE STUDY APPROACH TO ANTI–MONEY LAUNDERING COMPLIANCE

OLA M. TUCKER

GEORGETOWN UNIVERSITY PRESS / WASHINGTON, DC

The publisher is not responsible for third-party websites or their content. URL links were active at time of publication.

Library of Congress Cataloging-in-Publication Data

Names: Tucker, Ola M., author.
Title: The Flow of Illicit Funds : A Case Study Approach to Anti-Money
    Laundering Compliance / Ola M. Tucker.
Description: Washington, DC : Georgetown University Press, 2022. | Includes
    bibliographical references and index.
Identifiers: LCCN 2021035751 (print) | LCCN 2021035752 (ebook) |
    ISBN 9781647122478 (paperback) | ISBN 9781647122461 (hardcover) |
    ISBN 9781647122485 (ebook)
Subjects: LCSH: Money laundering—Law and legislation—United States. | Money
    laundering.
Classification: LCC KF1030.R3 T83 2022 (print) | LCC KF1030.R3 (ebook) |
    DDC 345.73/0268—dc23
LC record available at https://lccn.loc.gov/2021035751
LC ebook record available at https://lccn.loc.gov/2021035752

23 22   9 8 7 6 5 4 3 2   First printing

Cover design by Erin Kirk
Interior design by BookComp, Inc.

To S,
for his support, encouragement,
and patience throughout this project

CONTENTS

ABBREVIATIONS

AML	anti–money laundering
AMLA	Anti–Money Laundering Act
AMLD	Anti–Money Laundering Directive
BEC	business email compromise
BMPE	Black Market Peso Exchange
BSA	Bank Secrecy Act
BSAAG	Bank Secrecy Act Advisory Group
CDD	customer due diligence
CDD Rule	Customer Due Diligence Rule
CFT	counter-financing of terrorism
CTA	Corporate Transparency Act
CTR	currency transaction report
DEA	Drug Enforcement Administration
DOJ	Department of Justice
EDD	enhanced due diligence
FATF	Financial Action Task Force
FBI	Federal Bureau of Investigation
FFIEC	Federal Financial Institutions Examination Council
FI	financial institution
FinCEN	Financial Crimes Enforcement Network
FIU	financial intelligence unit
GTO	Geographic Targeting Order
HIFCA	High-Intensity Money Laundering and Related Financial Crime Area
IMF	International Monetary Fund
IRS	Internal Revenue Service
KYC	know your customer
ML	money laundering
MLCA	Money Laundering Control Act
MLSA	Money Laundering Suppression Act
MSB	money services business

OECD	Organization for Economic Cooperation and Development
OFAC	Office of Foreign Assets Control
PEP	politically exposed person
RICO	Racketeer Influenced and Corrupt Organizations Act
SAR	suspicious activity report
SDN	Specially Designated National and Blocked Person
SUA	specified unlawful activity
TBML	trade-based money laundering
TCO	transnational criminal organization
TF	terrorist financing
UBO	ultimate beneficial owner
UN	United Nations
UNODC	United Nations Office on Drugs and Crime
USA PATRIOT Act	Uniting and Strengthening America by Providing Appropriate Tools Required to Intercept and Obstruct Terrorism Act
WTO	World Trade Organization

INTRODUCTION

Money laundering is a serious crime that presents a heightened, yet underrated, global threat. More illicit funds are in circulation today than ever before. These funds consist of proceeds from a variety of highly lucrative and overwhelmingly harmful predicate crimes. In criminal law, *predicate crimes* are defined as those crimes that are part of a larger crime, such as money laundering. Many of these crimes, like the methods used to launder their profits, have been enabled by modern-day advances in technology (e.g., cryptocurrencies), communications (e.g., the internet), and globalization. Among these crimes, which are discussed in detail throughout the book, are human trafficking, narcotics and arms dealing, cybercrime, and the operation of illegal black markets on the *dark web* (the dark web is a collection of websites on the darknet, and the two terms are sometimes used interchangeably) that sell everything from contraband to human beings.

The anonymity resulting from recent technological innovations and the assistance of professional intermediaries are major contributors to the increasing prevalence of money laundering and related crimes. Critically, although anonymity and professional intermediaries play a key role as enablers of financial crime, the current legal and regulatory framework ineffectively addresses these two areas.

Recent scandals, high-profile investigations, and multijurisdictional enforcement actions have exposed the misuse of offshore bank accounts and anonymous shell companies that hide and secretly move wealth, have revealed the ease with which luxury real estate is used as a parking lot for criminal proceeds in exclusive zip codes, and have uncovered highly sophisticated money laundering operations known as laundromats. Reports also show that money laundering is offered as a service in exchange for a commission.[1] Corrupt politicians, powerful criminal enterprises, violent drug cartels, and even prominent financial institutions (FIs) have all been widely implicated in these and other laundering schemes.[2]

As a result, money laundering is a prevalent topic in media headlines. It has also become a part of pop culture. Commonly depicted in film, from crime dramas to comedies, portrayals of money laundering have increasingly made their way to the small screen, including several acclaimed series, such as the popular shows *Breaking Bad* (AMC, 2008–2013), *Ozark* (Netflix, 2017–), and *Narcos* (Netflix, 2015–17).

However, although awareness of money laundering has penetrated the mainstream news and entertainment media, many people don't really understand it. In fact, most would be hard-pressed to accurately define money laundering, much less explain how or even why it's done. This is not surprising, considering the number of prevailing and commonly held misconceptions and myths about money laundering, including that it must involve money (any asset can be laundered) and that it originated with Al Capone (money laundering wasn't codified as a crime until 1986). Most people also don't realize that the vast majority of money laundering is done by criminal organizations rather than by single individuals.

Further complicating the matter is that although the concept of money laundering is inherently simple, whereby ill-gotten funds are disguised to make them appear legitimate, the actual process can be extremely complex as criminals go to great lengths and use substantial creativity to hide their illegal proceeds and avoid detection. Consequently, this book aims to bring awareness to the crime of money laundering and to do so in a way that is broadly accessible to a general readership. *The Flow of Illicit Funds: A Case Study Approach to Anti–Money Laundering Compliance* first introduces the reader to the basics of money laundering and covers some of the latest money laundering methods and trends. This book also discusses the associated risks and consequences of money laundering and the development and effectiveness of applicable anti–money laundering (AML) legislation and enforcement. The book concludes by offering some suggestions about what can be done to detect and deter this illegal activity. Much of this information is presented in a historical context designed to add color and perspective and to provide the reader with a frame of reference.

The context of money laundering cases is particularly important to understand because many tend to think of financial crimes, including money laundering, as victimless. However, this could not be further from the truth. Although the effects of money laundering may not be immediately apparent, they are often shockingly destructive and devastatingly widespread. Money laundering significantly impacts the global financial system but is not limited to it. Money laundering not only leads to further crime but also contributes to some of the most serious problems confronting society, including corruption, various forms of human exploitation, and environmental degradation, among many others. Money laundering causes tremendous human suffering and disproportionately affects the most impoverished populations. It unjustly enriches kleptocrats and criminals while at the same time depriving its innocent victims of basic human needs. Money laundering results in a pernicious cycle that is more and more difficult to overcome the longer that it continues.

According to the United Nations Office on Drugs and Crime, the estimated annual amount of money laundered worldwide is approximately 2–5 percent of global GDP. This equates to between $800 billion and $2 trillion.[3] According to the US Treasury Department, $300 billion of that total amount is laundered through the United States alone.[4] However, many experts believe these numbers are grossly underestimated. The clandestine nature of money laundering makes establishing accurate figures impossible. Furthermore, its elusiveness also makes it is virtually impossible to recover laundered proceeds. As a result, less than 1 percent of laundered assets globally are ever seized.[5]

Curious general readers are not the only ones to benefit from the knowledge in this book. Even AML professionals often see a rather limited piece of an otherwise multilayered and complex puzzle. For example, in reviewing suspicious transactions, AML staffs don't always have information about the origin of the funds involved or their ultimate destination. They may not even know the purpose of the transactions in question. When such details are unavailable, it helps to have a comprehensive understanding of money laundering, including the reasons why criminals launder money, the various ways in which money can be laundered, the associated typologies, and the relevant red flags. A solid foundation of knowledge allows AML staffs to look at situations more holistically, including from different angles. This enables staffs to develop a more intelligent risk analysis as well as more effective risk management.

As any educator or instructor can attest, storytelling is an effective teaching tool. For this reason, this book uses recent case studies to illustrate major topics. These case studies and other anecdotes offer practical insights into the mechanisms criminals use to launder illicit funds. They also demonstrate specific compliance flaws that can lead to regulatory as well as criminal violations. Therefore, this book can be used as a resource in classroom and business settings. Its content can serve as a basis for academic or policy discussions about financial crime, or an organization can customize and incorporate it as part of its overall AML training program. It may even be used as a starting point in the design, development, and implementation of an AML compliance program.

Although *The Flow of Illicit Funds* is written with both novice and more seasoned financial crime and compliance professionals in mind, it is useful for anyone who wants to learn more about this evolving and often complex topic.

Regardless of their prior knowledge or experience, students and practitioners from a variety of disciplines and across a range of fields—business executives, corporate lawyers, general counsel, members of boards of directors, auditors, fraud investigators, bankers and bank personnel, law enforcement officers, policymakers, regulators, academics, researchers, and others—can gain valuable insight and practical suggestions from reading this book.

Chapter 1, "Building a Foundation: Facts, Figures, and Misconceptions about Money Laundering," begins with a brief history of money laundering and covers the origins of both the practice and the term. This distinction is critical as the two have become conflated when, in fact, they did not arise together. As the chapter illustrates, the methods the ancient Chinese used to hide plundered artifacts from their emperors follow the same basic stages in the methods criminals use to launder money today. This historical perspective is not typically covered in other books on money laundering.

The chapter also examines what constitutes money laundering and why criminals launder illicit funds—two essential questions for understanding this particular financial crime. It concludes with an overview of the leading federal statutes addressing criminal money laundering, a discussion of predicate crimes, and a description of both how money is commonly laundered through cash-intensive businesses and the limitations of this method.

Chapters 2 through 8 are devoted to some of the increasingly sophisticated methods of money laundering used today and their dominant predicate crimes. In many cases, law enforcement, policymakers, and regulators struggle to address these emerging and evolving crimes and laundering techniques. Given recent technological developments, coupled with globalization, jurisdictional boundaries are no longer the barriers they once were to moving people, funds, and goods, including commonly stolen and laundered commodities such as gold and antiques, among others. Instead, borders serve as impediments to law enforcement rather than as blockades to the flow of illegal activity. The evolution of the dark web and cryptocurrencies permits greater anonymity and decreases accountability, both of which further enable crime. These factors facilitate the ease and speed of money laundering at an unprecedented level. Consequently, it's extremely important that existing laundering techniques are analyzed in light of these circumstances and that developing ones receive more attention and study so they can be addressed and appropriately managed.

Much like money launderers, terrorists similarly exploit the financial system, and prevention efforts aimed at curbing both money laundering and terrorism generally share certain strategies and tactics as well as the uniform goal of protecting the financial system. Therefore, this book about money laundering wouldn't be complete if it failed to address the closely related topic of terrorist financing. Accordingly, the book examines the similarities and differences between terrorist financing and money laundering as well as the most common sources of terrorist income, the financial costs of acts of terrorism, and the role of economic sanctions.

To round out the discussion of money laundering, chapters 10 and 11 focus on the development and evolution of applicable AML laws and regulations. The book also discusses the role of financial institutions in laundering illegal proceeds, the requirements of AML compliance programs, and the ways in which these requirements are designed to prevent financial institutions from being used in the furtherance of financial crime. It also analyzes how AML violations stem from deficiencies in, or a lack of, one or more of these regulatory requirements.

Finally, chapter 12 concludes with some thoughts on the importance of money laundering prevention and the necessity for uniform global standards. Among other things, it includes a discussion about the central role of the gatekeeper professions, such as attorneys, financial advisers, and other professionals who serve as intermediaries between FIs and their clients and, given their specialized knowledge and/or role as fiduciaries, may function as conduits enabling the flow of criminal funds.

NOTES

1. Financial Action Task Force (FATF), "Professional Money Laundering" (Paris: FATF, July 2018), http://www.fatf-gafi.org/media/fatf/documents/Professional-Money-Laundering.pdf.

2. Graham Barrow, "Laundromats," *Financial Crimes News*, June 3, 2019, https://thefinancialcrimenews.com/laundromats-by-graham-barrow/; Enrich, *Dark Towers*; and Bullough, *Moneyland*.

3. United Nations Office on Drugs and Crime (UNODC), "Money Laundering," accessed February 22, 2021, https://www.unodc.org/unodc/en/money-laundering/overview.html#:~:text=The%20estimated%20amount%20of%20money,goes%20through%20the%20laundering%20cycle.

4. US Department of the Treasury, *National Money Laundering Risk Assessment, 2015* (Washington DC: Treasury Department, 2015), https://www.treasury.gov/resource-center/terrorist-illicit-finance/Documents/National%20Money%20Laundering%20Risk%20Assessment%20%E2%80%93%2006-12-2015.pdf.

5. UNODC, "Estimating Illicit Financial Flows Resulting from Drug Trafficking and Other Transnational Organized Crimes," August 31, 2011, https://www.unodc.org/documents/data-and-analysis/Studies/Illicit-financial-flows_31Aug11.pdf.

CHAPTER 1

BUILDING A FOUNDATION

*Facts, Figures, and Misconceptions
about Money Laundering*

Efforts to combat money laundering are fairly recent, having begun only in the late twentieth century; however, the practice of laundering illicitly derived gains has been around since ancient times. Although laundering techniques have evolved over time, the biggest changes arose in just the past few decades. These transformations have coincided with the emergence of AML legislation and increased regulatory controls at financial institutions, to which criminals responded by adapting their methods. The development of new technologies, such as mobile devices; advancements in communications, such as the rise of the internet and social media; and an increasingly global and interconnected financial system have made this evolution in money laundering possible.

Present-day laundering schemes are highly sophisticated and complex operations that span jurisdictions. They are run by powerful transnational criminal syndicates, ruthless terrorist organizations, violent drug cartels, and other organized groups that generate vast sums of illicit profits in need of legitimizing. The masterminds behind these enterprises are savvy "criminal-preneurs" who manage their illegal ventures similar to Fortune 500 corporations: they diversify, form strategic alliances, and make calculated, risk-based, and profit-driven business decisions. For example, the infamous Colombian drug lord and leader of the Medellín Cartel, Pablo Escobar, considered himself an entrepreneur and even compared himself to automobile tycoon and founder of the Ford Motor Company, Henry Ford.[1] At one point, Escobar's cartel controlled as much as 80 percent of the international cocaine trade. In fact, he was named on *Forbes'* list of international billionaires for seven years straight, from 1987 until 1993—quite an amazing feat considering his humble origins as the son of a poor Colombian farmer.[2] One of the tactical alliances Escobar formed, and that helped grow his empire, was with the Ochoa family. Escobar and the Ochoas collaborated on such deals as the manufacturing, distribution, and marketing of their cocaine, much like in the operation of a legitimate business. Similarly, criminal groups have increasingly geared this resourcefulness, ingenuity, and enterprising approach to exploit corporate structures and offshore accounts, to take advantage of financial institutions, to abuse cryptocurrencies, to collude with powerful and corrupt political figures, and to manipulate the global trade system (e.g., trade-based money laundering [TBML]).

Criminal organizations and terrorist groups occasionally even engage in philanthropic efforts, such as funding schools and hospitals, when it suits them. Besides his ruthlessness, Pablo Escobar was also paradoxically known for his charity, earning the nickname "Robin Hood" because he funded social programs and housing projects, among other things, to benefit the poor. Similarly, terrorist groups have been known to invest in social work, primarily as a means to advertise their cause and gain popular support.[3] Thus, many of the money laundering schemes that criminal and terrorist groups use reflect the same shrewd business acumen they apply to their profit-focused criminal pursuits.

Modern money launderers leverage both the legitimate and illegitimate economies to disguise their financial transactions, making it impossible to distinguish between their licit and illicit funds. They capitalize on new developments and technologies such as the dark web and virtual currencies. And they are nimble, adapting quickly and changing course as necessary to elude law enforcement and avoid detection. Critically, and perhaps most importantly, they understand the value of anonymity. As a result, the money laundering techniques they use today can be exceedingly intricate and complex, making financial trails frustratingly difficult to trace and unravel.

News reports illustrate the global scope and diversity of money laundering now. Russian hackers and other cybercriminals deploy malware on personal, company, and government computers and then launder their illicit gains, all of which is done anonymously and entirely online, with the pecuniary rewards far outweighing any perceived risk. Unscrupulous kleptocrats, oligarchs, and corrupt politicians amass vast amounts of wealth through grand corruption and then use the extensive network of resources at their disposal to launder it. Transnational criminal organizations exploit the legitimate financial and trade systems to route illegal profits across the globe undetected for their use in the furtherance of other crimes. Terrorist networks also engage in various illegal activities, from counterfeiting to narcotics and human trafficking, to fund their growing operations. To launder those funds, they then employ a similarly diverse array of methods, including using both traditional and nontraditional financial transfer systems such as shell companies, front businesses, and *hawalas* (an ancient and informal method of transferring money, particularly across borders, whereby local agents collect or disperse funds or goods on behalf of friends, relatives, or other associates and that is based on trust that any future obligations will be settled accordingly). Many of these money laundering schemes wouldn't have been possible just a few decades ago.

Notably, reports of money laundering tend to focus on the perpetrators and the funds. Such accounts rarely, if ever, mention the casualties involved. But the fact is that money laundering is far from a victimless crime. Fueled by greed and facilitated by corruption, money laundering has devastating socioeconomic consequences on developing and developed countries. It is a form of illegal capital flight that drains countries of revenue. Characterized by vast outflows of assets and/or capital from a particular country, region, or city, capital flight has negative economic repercussions in the area from which the funds dissipate. These illicit financial flows disproportionately impact those who are least able to handle it, further stripping impoverished nations and ordinary citizens of critically needed resources and leading to even greater inequality. In this manner, crime and corruption breed further crime and corruption, resulting in a devastating cycle. Therefore, money laundering presents a much bigger humanitarian threat than is initially perceived or generally recognized.

A BRIEF HISTORY OF THE ORIGINS OF MONEY LAUNDERING

Although it's impossible to pinpoint precisely when the practice of money laundering first began, it most likely dates back far longer than one would guess. In fact, an early form of money laundering has been around for millennia.

In his book *Lords of the Rim: The Invisible Empire of the Overseas Chinese*, historian Sterling Seagrave recounts how over three thousand years ago, Chinese merchants hid the wealth and spoils they acquired through trade to avoid their confiscation by rulers.[4] The methods Seagrave describes, including converting profits into more easily transferable forms, moving assets across borders, and reinvesting wealth for subsequent use, are surprisingly similar to the ones money launderers utilize in modern times.

Money did not yet exist at the time of Seagrave's account (the first known coins did not appear until somewhere around 600 BC); thus, the practice of money laundering, or at least the basic principles behind it, predates the existence of money. How is it possible to engage in money laundering if no money is involved? The answer is because anything of value that constitutes the proceeds of crime can be laundered. Even though the mention of criminal proceeds may conjure up images of suitcases full of stolen cash, criminal proceeds can take the form of any tangible good (e.g., art, antiques, diamonds, drugs, tablets) or intangible good (e.g., personally identifiable information, bank account numbers, intellectual property).

In ancient China, just as in other places, products such as tea, spices, silver, and gold, among others, were often traded through barter. Therefore, if the Chinese merchants were dealing in stolen or otherwise illicitly acquired goods or commodities, they could have theoretically laundered these goods by converting them into a different form, hiding them for later use, or otherwise disguising them while retaining control and ultimately benefiting from their ownership. Similarly, ancient people engaged in an early form of tax evasion, a crime closely related to money laundering, by concealing their ownership of certain objects or misrepresenting the true value of artifacts to avoid their taxation, or even seizure, by sovereigns.

There are also accounts dating to the Middle Ages of merchants and moneylenders evading newly enacted laws against usury by disguising their illegally obtained income from the state. Likewise, it has long been known that pirates commonly concealed their plunder and probably engaged in laundering gold and other valuable loot for centuries. However, until more recently, laundering itself wasn't considered a crime. Rather than the attempt to hide the product of a crime, it was the underlying crime—for example, theft or usury—that was the focus of punishment.[5]

In contrast to the practice of money laundering, the etymology of the phrase is much more recent, having come into modern usage less than a century ago. The term as we commonly know it today is popularly thought to have originated during the Prohibition era of the 1920s when Al Capone and other Italian mobsters were said to have used laundromats to commingle legal profits with illegal earnings from bootlegging (and other crimes such as extortion, gambling, and prostitution), thus disguising the origin of their illicit proceeds. This theory has largely been discredited, however, as it is more likely that the term was applied retrospectively. Instead, the phrase appears to have originated in a newspaper article published in 1973 in Britain's *Guardian* newspaper, which apparently used it in print for the first time in a story on the Watergate scandal. The *Guardian* article used the phrase to describe the laundering of campaign contributions that were improperly received by Nixon's reelection campaign. These donations were reportedly delivered to the White House in bags of cash and later hidden in offshore banks, outside the reach of US subpoena power.[6]

Ironically, just three years earlier, President Nixon had signed into law the Bank Secrecy Act (BSA) of 1970, which was the first piece of US legislation designed to fight money laundering and remains the primary anti–money laundering law in the United States today. Notably, although the term "money laundering" appears in later amendments to the BSA, the phrase did not appear anywhere in the act as it was originally written. Primarily a record-keeping and reporting statute, the act imposed regulatory requirements on US banks (and, through subsequent amendments, on other covered financial institutions). At the heart of the legislation was concern over illegal drug proceeds and the illicit use of foreign bank accounts in countries with banking secrecy laws, as such activities enabled organized crime in the United States.

The phrase "money laundering" first surfaced in the American judicial system in 1982 when it was referenced in the case *United States v. $4,255,625.39*.[7] That proceeding was a civil forfeiture action where, over the course of a few months, more than $4 million in drug proceeds originating from Cali, Colombia, was laundered through a single Miami bank account in a series of all-cash deposits consisting primarily of small denominations. Under today's AML regime, such activity would constitute a BSA violation on the part of the bank, which would be subject to steep fines and penalties.

Interestingly, money laundering did not become a federal offense until 1986, when the Money Laundering Control Act (MLCA) was enacted, long after Al Capone's time, and imposed record-keeping and reporting requirements on financial institutions.

MONEY LAUNDERING DEFINED

"Money laundering" is a rather generic term used to describe the process used to disguise the original source and ownership or control of criminally derived proceeds. It can be defined simply as the cleaning of dirty money. This is essentially the definition given in the 1999 movie *Office Space* as three coworkers look up the meaning of money laundering after suddenly finding themselves with a windfall of illicit cash. But what is meant by "dirty" money, and how can it be "cleaned"? Leading authorities provide several definitions that help to answer these questions. Although each definition varies in the level of detail provided, and some are quite comprehensive, they all center around legitimizing illegally derived proceeds by obscuring their criminal source.

The Financial Action Task Force on Money Laundering (FATF), the leading global AML and terrorist-financing watchdog and standards setter, gives a fairly straightforward definition of money laundering.[8] According to the FATF, money laundering is the processing of criminal proceeds to disguise their illegal origin.[9] *Black's Law Dictionary*, the preeminent legal dictionary in the United States, defines money laundering similarly as "the act of transferring illegally obtained money through legitimate people or accounts so that its original source cannot be traced."[10]

The US Treasury Department's Financial Crimes Enforcement Network (FinCEN) takes a much more comprehensive approach, defining money laundering as a three-step process. According to FinCEN, "Money laundering is the process of making illegally gained proceeds (i.e. 'dirty money') appear legal (i.e. 'clean'). Typically, it involves three steps: placement, layering and integration."[11]

Put another way, money laundering is the process used to break the link between the criminally derived funds and their criminal source. The leading federal criminal money laundering statutes, 18 U.S.C. § 1956 and 18 U.S.C. § 1957, define money laundering with more specificity than the previous definitions and help further define what constitutes dirty money by including a list of specified predicate offenses from which the tainted funds must derive.

Essentially, however, the term "money laundering" is derived from the premise that funds generated from illegal activity are tainted and must be "washed" to distance them from their criminality. Perhaps Jeffrey Robinson, the financial crime expert and author of *The Laundrymen: Inside Money Laundering, the World's Third-Largest Business*, put it best when he wrote, "'Laundering' perfectly describes what takes place: illegal, or dirty, money is put through a cycle of transactions and comes out the other end as legal, or clean, money. In other words, all traces of illegality are scrubbed away by a succession of transfers or deals, so that those same funds reappear as legitimate income."[12]

WHY DO CRIMINALS LAUNDER MONEY?

Laundering dirty funds separates the illegal proceeds from their illicit source so that they cannot be traced back to crime. Once the funds are washed, they can be used just as if they were legally earned, without arousing suspicion of their origin or otherwise drawing attention to the crime that generated the funds. This also helps the criminal avoid detection for having committed an illegal act. Consequently, the goal of money laundering is to provide ill-gotten gains with the appearance of legitimacy so that they can be used freely.

An individual who possesses illicit funds can't simply go out and spend the money openly, particularly if it is inconsistent with his (or her) financial standing. (In most cases, money launderers, at least those who are caught and prosecuted, are overwhelmingly male.[13]) Eventually, such spending will draw the attention of law enforcement, tax officials, and others, who will start questioning the individual's acquisition of the newfound wealth and its source. Consequently, he or she must have a plausible explanation for where the money came from.

Therefore, criminals launder money for two main reasons: The first is to avoid being connected with the crime(s) that gave rise to the criminal proceeds; the second is to be able to use the proceeds as if they were legally acquired. Disguising the criminal source of the funds makes it appear as though they rightfully belong to the spender by providing a cover for their origin.

THE THREE STAGES OF MONEY LAUNDERING

Although each money laundering case is unique, and such details as the source of funds and the parties involved will differ, the basic process generally remains the same. Thus, in accordance with FinCEN's definition, the process of money laundering consists of three steps or stages: placement, layering, and integration. (In the first season of the Netflix series *Ozark*, the lead character, Marty Byrde, aptly summarizes these steps.)

Placement is the first stage of the laundering process. As the term suggests, it involves putting ill-gotten cash into a legitimate financial institution to start the process of cleaning it, thus equating it to inserting dirty laundry into a washing machine. This step represents the initial entry of dirty funds into the financial system and relieves the criminal of holding large amounts of illicit cash.

Placement is considered the riskiest step for the launderer as it is the point at which the criminal is most prone to detection. This is because banks are required to establish and maintain a customer identification program (CIP), which includes identifying and verifying clients when opening accounts as well as various other know your customer (KYC) procedures that consist of basic background checks, sanctions screening, and inquiries into wealth and funding sources. Furthermore, customers who are generally considered to pose a higher risk of money laundering (ML) and/or terrorist financing (TF)—such as politically exposed persons (PEPs)—are subject to additional scrutiny, which is called enhanced due diligence (EDD).

While banks are not required to definitively prove that their customers' funds are clean, these AML internal controls, as well as others (e.g., monitoring), are meant to detect potential ML/TF activity and weed out those who may be attempting to misuse the financial institution. As a result, the compliance procedures that banks conduct at the customer onboarding phase, when funds are first put into the financial institution, expose the launderer to the greatest possibility of detection.

Layering is the second and most substantive stage of money laundering during which the dirty money is washed. Using the washing machine analogy, this stage is the equivalent of the spin cycle. It often entails the first movement of the dirty funds within the financial system. It is also the most complex phase of the laundering process, typically consisting of multiple and convoluted transactions to disguise the funding source, obscure the financial trail, and confuse auditors and investigators. In fact, the more complicated the transactions, the more difficult it is to trace the origin and the ultimate ownership of the funds.

Transactions during this stage generally involve multiple banks and accounts while converting cash into traveler's checks; changing currency; conducting multiple wire transfers; routing funds across jurisdictions; moving funds among a network of anonymous shell companies, trusts, or foundations; and investing in businesses requiring minimal paperwork. Such transactions may be done multiple times and across diverse products, hence the reason that this stage is called layering.

Integration, the third and final stage in the money laundering process, is the point at which the ill-gotten gains reenter the mainstream financial system and are considered to have been legitimized. It is analogous to removing clean laundry from the washer. During this phase, the launderer may undertake a legal transaction, such as the sale, transfer, or purchase of real estate, securities, or other high-end assets that were acquired during the layering stage, to secure ownership of the funds in the formal economy. By this point, it is nearly impossible to distinguish licit from illicit funds. Therefore, of the three stages, integration is considered the least risky and consequently the least prone to detection.

Although money laundering is described as consisting of three separate and distinct stages, in practice it is a continuous and fluid process. In fact, the three-stage illustration is a simplified depiction of an otherwise much more dynamic and complex scheme. Additionally, the stages of the laundering process don't necessarily have to occur sequentially. Rather, the stages can occur in numerous combinations or overlap and blur together.

Furthermore, the length of time it takes to launder illicit proceeds can vary significantly from case to case. For example, even though criminals generally want prompt access to laundered funds so that they can use the money immediately, they can also park illicit proceeds in real estate or leave money sitting in other investments for years. There's no requirement that the ill-gotten gains must be immediately integrated into the legitimate financial system.

Illicit funds can then be laundered in countless different ways. In fact, wire transfers, one of the most common means of moving money, are initiated more than 500,000 times daily (totally over $2 trillion USD).[14] That transactions used in the money laundering process are nearly indistinguishable from legitimate transactions makes it very difficult to identify money laundering by reviewing transactions alone, especially without considering any additional information. Because the transactions appear so similar, it is also difficult, if not impossible, to determine whether an illegal financial transfer is related to money laundering, tax evasion, or even terrorist financing, especially in the early stages of the laundering process.[15] These facts further highlight the complexity of money laundering and the difficulty in detecting and combating it.

A BROADER VIEW OF THE MONEY LAUNDERING PROCESS

Describing money laundering as a process that occurs in three stages is a useful illustration but provides a rather narrow view of how money is actually laundered. More specifically, it limits money laundering to what happens with the funds as they circulate within the financial system. However, it's just as important to look at where the illicit funds originated and where they are ultimately destined. Looking at the process more broadly can help AML professionals and investigators identify various money laundering typologies. Therefore, it's helpful to think of money laundering as an activity that starts not with the initial placement of funds into the legitimate financial system but with the predicate crime that generated the illegal funds (e.g., theft, embezzlement, illegal trade in wildlife). Likewise, the laundering operation does not end at the point at which the funds are integrated into the financial system (e.g., purchasing a yacht, making investments). Rather, it's equally as important to keep tracing the funds to their final destination—the individual or criminal group that ultimately derives the monetary benefit. For instance, do the integrated funds flow to a terrorist group in Afghanistan that then uses the money to fund its operations, or does the money end up in the coffers of a Colombian drug cartel that then uses it to purchase weapons?

Just as predicate crimes differ, so do the techniques used to launder the illicit proceeds generated from these crimes. In the AML and counter-financing of terrorism (CFT) context, the various techniques, methods, and trends used to launder money and finance terrorism are referred to as typologies. *Typologies* generally differ by location and are shaped by variables such as the economy, the financial markets, and the legal system (including the AML/CFT regime) in a particular jurisdiction. As a result, methods used to launder criminal proceeds and finance illicit activities will vary from one place to another as well as over time.[16]

For instance, in Afghanistan, the Taliban, the most active terrorist group in the country, is the driving force behind the cultivation of poppies, which are used to make heroin. The Taliban once relied largely on the formal banking sector to move and launder funds from drug trafficking, but when Afghan banks implemented more stringent rules, the group turned to informal money or value transfer systems such as hawalas (discussed in chapter 9). The laundered proceeds from heroin trafficking were then used to further finance terrorist activity and fund the group's resurgence.[17] But with the withdrawal of US armed forces from Afghanistan in August 2021 and the Taliban's subsequent control of the government, the terrorist group will have nearly unfettered access to banks and state resources for potential use in the furtherance of drug smuggling and money laundering.[18]

Like the Taliban, the triads, China's large organized crime syndicates, are also involved in the international drug trade and generate significant illicit revenue that needs to be laundered. However, the triads employ methods that are vastly different from those of the Taliban to launder their drug proceeds. The criminality begins in the Chinese province of Guangdong, where the chemical factories that manufacture the synthetic opioid fentanyl and the chemical precursors used to make the drug are located. The narcotics are then smuggled to Vancouver, British Columbia, where the triads have had a stronghold since the 1990s. After the drugs are sold, the triads launder their proceeds through shell companies, luxury real estate, and other expensive assets such as high-end automobiles.[19]

Similar to these criminal groups, Colombian drug cartels must also launder illicit drug proceeds but have their own distinct methods of doing so. In fact, Colombian drug cartels use a variety of techniques to launder money and have been diversifying the ways they previously laundered funds to account for their increased profits from record cocaine production. Traditional techniques included investing in land, real estate, and construction as well as other cash-intensive front businesses and the black market peso exchange (BMPE, discussed in chapter 3). The newer techniques include the same methods of investing but with a new focus on smaller cities rather than major urban centers, such as Medellín and Colombia's capital city of Bogotá. The cartels have also been increasingly using cryptocurrencies.[20]

Money laundering typologies reflect the various unique and evolving methods, techniques, and schemes criminals use to conceal, launder, and move illicit funds. As the preceding examples illustrate, typologies differ widely among criminal groups and geographic areas as criminals adapt their money laundering strategies to best suit the dynamics of their trade. Predicate offenses and geographic locations are among the indicators that can help identify money laundering typologies. Recognizing these typologies can help identify specific ML/TF threats and enable the development of strategies to combat them. Although the presence of any one indicator by itself may not necessarily point to criminal activity, indicators can serve as red flags to trigger further review, such as enhanced due diligence and additional monitoring. Compliance officers, in particular, should continuously look to update and learn new and emerging typologies while focusing on those most relevant to their industry, product, or service. Identifying these typologies can also help compliance personnel be more effective in their fight against financial crime as well as assist institutions in ensuring their regulatory compliance.[21]

PREDICATE CRIMES

Money laundering is distinctly different from most other crimes, including other financial crimes, in one important aspect: unlike other criminal offenses, where the underlying act itself is considered criminal (e.g., murder, theft, rape, embezzlement), the activity (i.e., financial transactions) involved in laundering money would not otherwise be illegal if no prior crime generated the illicit proceeds. (One noteworthy exception would be *structuring*, or the practice of breaking up large sums of cash into multiple smaller deposits to avoid detection. Structuring constitutes a separate criminal offense in the United States and several other jurisdictions. See chapter 6.) In other words, one cannot launder lawfully earned money (although it would constitute a felony to knowingly launder the unpaid taxes on those funds; in that case, the unpaid taxes would constitute illicit proceeds). Therefore, money laundering constitutes the series of transactions that take place following a criminal act known as a predicate crime or a predicate offense.

In criminal law, a *predicate crime* is defined as a crime that provides the resources for, or contains some of the elements of, a larger or more serious crime. Stated another way, a predicate crime is the underlying criminal offense that gives rise to the criminal proceeds that are the subject of a money laundering charge. As one may guess, the predicate crime must generate some pecuniary benefit or financial gain. In fact, courts have ruled that some sort of profit-producing criminal activity must precede money laundering.

When it comes to money laundering legislation, there are many variations in the definition of predicate offense as well as regarding which crimes constitute a predicate offense. Some countries limit predicate offenses to drug trafficking and related crimes. Others maintain an exhaustive list of predicate offenses, while still others define predicate offenses more generically to include all crimes, all serious crimes, or all crimes subject to a specified penalty threshold.[22] Over time, the scope of predicate offenses has generally broadened mainly due to the changing character of money laundering offenses. The international anti–money laundering community now generally agrees that the scope of predicate offenses should be expanded to include all serious crimes, a position that is reflected in the various AML-related conventions and directives.

In the United States, the federal money laundering statute contains a lengthy list of crimes, known as specified unlawful activities (SUAs), that are considered predicate offenses for money laundering.[23] The more than 250 SUAs encompass foreign, federal, and state crimes. For a money laundering charge, the actual source of the funds must be one of the specified forms of criminal activity identified by the statute in 18 U.S.C. § 1956(c)(7) or those incorporated by reference from the Racketeer Influenced and Corrupt Organizations Act (RICO).[24] (The RICO statute is discussed further in chapter 10.)

The crimes enumerated in the federal statute as SUAs consist of a wide range of white-collar crimes, different varieties of fraud, racketeering activity, acts constituting a criminal enterprise, drug-related offenses, human trafficking, cybercrimes, environmental crimes, terrorism financing, sanctions offenses, and crimes against foreign nations, among many others. Notably, the government can prosecute a defendant for money laundering even if it cannot obtain a conviction for the SUA, or the predicate crime, itself.

In the first few decades following the criminalization of money laundering in the United States, illegal drug sales and related drug offenses made up the majority of predicate crimes charged in connection with money laundering. In fact, anti–money laundering legislation and the "war on drugs" developed in parallel in the United States. During this period, law enforcement was faced with the growing threat caused by the Colombian drug cartels, particularly the Cali and Medellín Cartels.[25] The Netflix series *Narcos* presents a fairly accurate, historical depiction of the rise and fall of Colombia's Cali and Medellín Cartels and the various crimes carried out by these groups.

Since the 1980s, drug proceeds make up the bulk of illicit cash because illegal drugs, whether purchased on the street or elsewhere, are paid for in cash. Even mid-level drug distributors and wholesalers deal in cash.[26] As a result, an abundance of illicit cash has coursed through the US financial system. Consequently, law enforcement efforts to combat money laundering have historically focused on illegal narcotics and, more specifically, on targeting drug traffickers and criminal organizations where it would have the most impact—their profits. Since criminal organizations must use the financial system to transfer and disguise their illicit funds, it was considered the point of greatest weakness for the criminals and the point at which they were most vulnerable to detection. Additionally, tracing the laundering process through the financial system was a more cost-effective and less dangerous means for law enforcement to meet its objectives. Hence, by imposing AML regulations on banks and other financial institutions, the onus was put on them to detect and deter money laundering.

A much wider array of crimes, besides narcotics-related offenses, are now considered predicate offenses for money laundering. Although the available federal court data regarding money laundering convictions is limited (for example, defendants charged with money laundering may plead to lesser charges), broadly speaking, various types of fraud—including bank fraud, consumer fraud, health-care fraud, securities fraud, and tax refund fraud—along with drug crimes now make up the greatest majority of predicate crimes charged.[27] Other crimes that contribute to a large amount of the illicit proceeds in the United States are human smuggling, human trafficking, organized crime, and corruption.

MONEY LAUNDERING AND CORRUPTION

There have been many studies and much has been written about the intrinsic link between money laundering and corruption, and several international organizations, including the FATF and the World Bank, recognize this interrelationship.[28] Corruption, such as the bribery of government officials and the theft of public funds, generates huge profits to be laundered. Corruption also facilitates many methods of money laundering and terrorist financing as well as predicate offenses. Furthermore, systemic corruption undermines the effectiveness of the legal and regulatory framework underlying AML/CFT efforts, including their enforcement. Consequently, the connection between money laundering and corruption results in an ongoing cycle whereby corruption enables money laundering, which, in turn, furthers corruption.

But just as money laundering and corruption are inextricably linked, so too are anti–money laundering and anti-corruption strategies. For example, as noted in an anti-corruption strategy report published by the World Bank in March 2007, effective customer due diligence (CDD) under AML/CFT requirements plays a key role in combating corruption and promoting greater overall financial transparency. The report goes on to note that increased cooperation among financial intelligence units (FIUs), anti-corruption agencies, law enforcement, and the private sector is necessary to maximize the effectiveness of the AML regime in the fight against corruption. Finally, the World Bank report further documents that law enforcement agencies in many surveyed countries identified corruption as the main underlying offense for money laundering. Therefore, AML/CFT policies serve a dual purpose wherein they also function as critical anti-corruption tools.[29]

MONEY LAUNDERING AND TAX EVASION

Money laundering is often associated, and sometimes even confused with, tax evasion. To a certain extent, the two have a lot of similarities and frequently occur together.

Tax evasion is an illegal activity whereby a person or entity deliberately avoids paying duly owed taxes. It typically involves the misrepresentation of income to the Internal Revenue Service (IRS) and may include underreporting actual income, inflating deductions, or concealing earnings in offshore accounts.[30] People evade paying taxes in various ways, ranging from filing tax forms with false information to illegally transferring property.

Money laundering and tax evasion share several commonalities. To start, both crimes are categorized as felony offenses: money laundering is codified in 18 U.S.C. § 1956 and § 1957; tax evasion is codified in 18 U.S.C. § 7201 and § 7206. Additionally, both crimes are financially motivated and involve concealing or disguising monetary proceeds. Due to their pecuniary and nonviolent nature, money laundering and tax evasion have traditionally been considered white-collar crimes that are primarily committed by businesses and government professionals.[31] However, both crimes can be and increasingly are committed by criminal organizations and others involved in illegal or illicit businesses.

The scandal involving a high-end brothel operated by Heidi Fleiss illustrates the relationship between an illicit enterprise, tax evasion, and money laundering. Fleiss, infamously known as the Hollywood Madam, ran an upscale escort service in Los Angeles, California, in the late 1990s. Catering toward wealthy and famous clients, she reportedly earned $300,000 a week in illicit proceeds.

Engaging in a business enterprise involving prostitution falls within the numerous predicate offenses for a money laundering charge under 18 U.S.C. § 1952. In addition to money laundering, Fleiss was also convicted of tax evasion and sentenced to thirty-seven months in prison. Interestingly, she received a prison term that was far less than the maximum suggested by the federal sentencing guidelines, which prescribed a sentence at least twice as long. Explaining the sentencing decision, the presiding judge noted expert witness testimony that stated the sentencing guidelines for money laundering were meant to target criminal organizations and drug cartels rather than madams.[32] Considering the evolution of money laundering law and its corresponding perceptions over the past few decades, a sentence that lenient would unlikely be handed down today.

Another noteworthy similarity between money laundering and tax evasion is that the proceeds involved in these offenses frequently entail significantly large sums of money. This is because the trouble and risk of laundering a small amount of illicit funds or evading a minimal tax payment are not worthwhile.

Both offenses also often involve the illicit movement of funds globally, particularly to offshore tax havens and jurisdictions known for strict bank secrecy rules. As a result, money laundering and tax evasion are forms of *illicit financial flows*, which are defined as the illegal movement of money or capital from one country to another.[33] These capital flows negatively impact all economies but are disproportionately problematic for developing countries, as they funnel money away from much-needed resources and contribute to instability by encouraging criminal activity and undermining the rule of law.

Further linking the two crimes is the fact that launderers, and others involved in criminal enterprises, typically also engage in tax evasion since reporting illegally earned income is likely to draw the attention of law enforcement and result in criminal charges. Paradoxically, according to the IRS, individuals are required to report and pay taxes on all earnings regardless of how the earnings were derived.[34] It may sound comical (and criminals rarely do it), but the US government explicitly requires that criminal proceeds be reported to the IRS and taxed just like legitimate income. The official IRS instructions specifically state that "income from illegal activities, such as money from dealing illegal drugs, must be included in your income."[35]

Although popular culture has long associated Al Capone with money laundering, tax evasion landed him in federal prison in 1931. Despite living a publicly lavish lifestyle, Capone did not file a single tax return, providing the basis for his tax evasion charges. Also, money laundering wasn't finally codified as a federal offense until 1986. The 1987 crime film *The Untouchables* details the pursuit of Al Capone (played by Robert De Niro) by a team of special agents that builds a tax evasion case against him upon discovering that he hasn't filed his tax returns.

Notably, although tax evasion is considered a predicate offense to money laundering in some countries, such as the United Kingdom and Canada, it is not listed as an SUA in the US government's money laundering statute. However, prosecutors have used mail and wire fraud offenses as an indirect route to charge money laundering arising out of a tax crime.[36]

Because it derives the bulk of its revenue from taxes, the US government closely monitors financial activity for purposes of tax collection.[37] It also keeps a close eye on financial activity for purposes of law enforcement. Correspondingly, money laundering and tax evasion schemes both use the same mechanisms, including nominees, foreign currencies, multiple bank accounts, wire transfers, and international tax havens, to avoid detection from tax and law enforcement authorities.

MONEY LAUNDERING AND FRAUD

Fraud is a general term that refers to deliberate misrepresentation. *Black's Law Dictionary* defines fraud as "a knowing misrepresentation of the truth or concealment of a material fact to induce another to act to his or her detriment."[38]

Fraud encompasses a wide and diverse range of criminal activity and includes tax fraud, health-care fraud, Ponzi and pyramid schemes, identity theft, various types of cyber fraud, and even the widespread mortgage fraud that contributed to the financial crisis between 2007 and 2010. Individuals (as in the case of Bernie Madoff's multibillion-dollar Ponzi scheme) as well as corporations (as in the case of the infamous Enron, Tyco, and WorldCom accounting scandals of 2001 and 2002) can be the victims of fraud.

Fraud is used to deprive another of money or property (or, in some cases, a legal right). Like tax evasion and money laundering, fraud is largely motivated by financial gain. Because fraud generates illicit funds that need to be legitimized, money laundering often accompanies fraudulent activity. Given the various types of fraud, a high percentage of money laundering predicate offenses are fraud related.[39] Consequently, an increase in fraud is generally accompanied by a corresponding rise in money laundering activity.

Furthermore, fraud often proliferates during times of economic uncertainty and instability as fraudsters capitalize on opportunities to exploit vulnerabilities. Hence, money laundering, and other financial crimes, increases as well. The global pandemic of coronavirus disease 2019 (COVID-19) provides a stark example of this connection between fraud, money laundering, and economic instability, whereby multiple national and international law enforcement agencies, including Europol and the Federal Bureau of Investigation (FBI), have noted a rise in fraud-related activities against individuals, businesses, and even governments. These illicit activities include various types of fraud, including health-care fraud, credit card fraud, trafficking in counterfeit medicines, investment scams, scams involving fake charities, fraudulent cybercrimes, and many others.[40] In fact, FinCEN, the Financial Industry Regulatory Authority, the Securities and Exchange Commission, and the Commodity Futures Trading Commission have all issued warnings, specially aimed at financial institutions, to be on the lookout for an increase in illicit financial activity due to the COVID-19 pandemic.[41]

Many of the red flags indicative of financial fraud, such as irregular account activity and suspicious customer behavior, may also signify money laundering. As a result, many of the same methods and resources, particularly the investigative tools, used to detect and combat money laundering can also be used to ferret out and fight fraud.

Despite this relatedness between fraud and money laundering, anti-fraud and anti–money laundering functions have historically existed in separate departments in organizations, with the AML function overseen by a chief compliance officer and the fraud function overseen by a chief risk officer or equivalent role. However, in recent years, thinking of these two functions as separate and distinct has shifted, and the two areas are increasingly being combined within the broader sphere of anti-financial crime. Collaborating and sharing data and resources among the two functions provide many advantages, including the reduction of redundancies. Regulators, including FinCEN and the European Banking Federation, encourage this trend of harmonization, collaboration, and communication among areas. This enhances effective cooperation not just in the AML and anti-fraud departments but also in the cybersecurity units.[42]

MONEY LAUNDERING INVESTIGATION, ENFORCEMENT, AND PENALTIES

The United States was one of the first countries to criminalize money laundering with the passage of the Money Laundering Control Act in 1986. Congress has since amended the MLCA several times, and it is now codified in Title 18 of the US Code. It consists of the two principal federal criminal money laundering statutes—18 U.S.C. § 1956 and its companion, 18 U.S.C. § 1957.

Specifically, section 1956 pertains to the laundering of monetary instruments—for example, currency, personal checks, and money orders. It prohibits anyone from conducting or attempting to conduct a financial transaction that involves the proceeds from a number of specified unlawful activities.

Section 1957 pertains to engaging in monetary transactions in property derived from specified unlawful activity. This section is frequently referred to as the "money spending statute" because it makes knowingly spending (or taking) money derived from an illegal source a felony. The purpose of section 1957 is to make the criminal proceeds worthless, thereby discouraging the criminal act.[43] This is consistent with the overall objective behind the criminalization of money laundering generally—that is, to take the profit out of the commission of crime.

In addition to being one of the first criminal money laundering laws in the world, the MLCA is also one of the strongest. Unlike the Bank Secrecy Act, which generally has no extraterritorial jurisdiction, the provisions of the MLCA have extensive extraterritorial jurisdiction. Section 1956 applies extraterritorially to US citizens involved in money laundering anywhere in the world as well as to noncitizens if any part of the offense takes place in the United States. Similarly, under section 1957, there is extraterritorial jurisdiction over money laundering conducted outside the United States, by both Americans and non-US persons, as long as any part of the transaction occurs in the United States. Furthermore, a number of foreign crimes are listed among the predicate offenses for money laundering.

Several federal agencies can conduct criminal money laundering investigations. These include the FBI, the US Immigration and Customs Enforcement, the US Secret Service, the Drug Enforcement Administration (DEA), the Criminal Division of the IRS, and the Postal Inspection Service. Even the Environmental Protection Agency is involved in cases of money laundering linked to environmental crime.

A special unit in the Criminal Division of the US Department of Justice (DOJ) called the Money Laundering and Asset Recovery Section handles prosecutions of money laundering. Additionally, any of the ninety-four US Attorneys' offices can undertake money laundering prosecutions. Furthermore, federal agencies may work together, as well as with state and local authorities, in cases where their jurisdiction overlaps.

According to the MLCA, there is no de minimis amount for the charge of money laundering, and the law applies no matter how small the transaction.[44]

The applicable statute of limitations for money laundering crimes is five years.[45]

Both individuals and legal entities can be convicted of money laundering under the MLCA. The penalties for violations of the act can be civil or criminal in nature and may include prison terms, fines, civil penalties, restitution, and forfeiture (confiscation of property by the government). Separate penalties are outlined for violations of section 1956 and section 1957.[46]

The penalty for violations of section 1956 can be a fine of up to either $500,000 or double the amount of money that was laundered, whichever is greater. The court is also authorized to sentence the defendant to a prison term of not longer than twenty years. Additionally, any property involved in the transaction or traceable to the proceeds of the underlying criminal activity is subject to forfeiture.

Section 1957 has a lower penalty than section 1956. The maximum prison sentence for a violation of section 1957 can be no more than ten years. The reason for the lesser penalty is that this offense has a lesser mental state, whereby the prosecution does not have to show the defendant knew the money was coming from criminal activity. In contrast, under section 1956, prosecutors must prove beyond a reasonable doubt that the defendant knew where the money originated. Essentially, section 1957 is designed to prevent individuals from being willfully ignorant of the source of illicit funds.

Conspiracy, attempt, aiding, and abetting are also outlawed under the MLCA. The conspiracy section of the federal money laundering statute is not complicated, making it easier to prove conspiracy than it is to prove money laundering. Interestingly, violations of section 1957 and conspiracy to violate section 1957 carry the same fines and prison terms. Therefore, prosecutions of white-collar crimes frequently include money laundering conspiracy charges. Oftentimes, money laundering cases will also include tax evasion counts, as they can help strengthen the prosecution's case.

In addition to the federal statute, money laundering is also criminalized under state laws, which largely parallel federal law. Over half of the states in the United States criminalize money laundering.[47] At the state level, local district attorneys' offices are tasked with investigating and prosecuting money laundering offenses. Notably, an individual can be prosecuted at both the state and federal level for the same conduct without the risk of double jeopardy, as the Double Jeopardy Clause of the Fifth Amendment does not apply to prosecution of the same crime under both federal and state laws.[48]

Given that the United States was one of the first countries to pass legislation criminalizing money laundering, perhaps it is not surprising that it also prosecutes money laundering more aggressively than any other nation.[49] There are three reasons for this. First, drug trafficking has been an outstanding problem in the United States, perhaps more so than in any other industrial-ized country. Hence, measures targeting drug trafficking have been central to the formation of money laundering legislation in the United States. Second, beginning in the 1970s, the United States has had great success prosecuting organized crime, and that led to the creation of the legislative framework and law enforcement expertise required to go after money laundering. Third, the United States has a strong and long-standing law enforcement culture, which extends into the anti–money laundering sphere.[50]

THE THREE MAIN METHODS OF MONEY LAUNDERING

Illicit proceeds can be laundered in myriad ways, limited only by the crim-inal's imagination. Furthermore, money laundering methods are constantly changing as the dynamics of criminal enterprises shift and as criminals adapt to new technologies and attempt to get around the latest laws and regula-tions. Therefore, covering all the potential ways to launder money is impos-sible. Ultimately, however, money laundering boils down to moving money around, which can be broken down into three main methods:

1. Using the financial system (e.g., making wire transfers between banks)
2. Physically moving money (e.g., shipping cash across borders)
3. Physically moving goods through the trade system (e.g., misrepresenting the price or the quantity of exports or imports in trade transactions)[51]

Each of these three methods can be simple to exceedingly complex. The typical scheme involves moving illegally obtained funds through a series of transactions to conceal their source. Although one transaction may be suf-ficient to distance illicit funds from their criminal source in some cases, it generally does not suffice in others. More often, multiple complex transac-tions are needed to obfuscate the financial trail. The laundering process can involve a very high level of sophistication and may require moving money across jurisdictions, using various financial and nonfinancial institutions, and involving other witting or unwitting participants, such as company forma-tion agents, lawyers, accountants, and others.

THE LIMITATIONS OF CASH-INTENSIVE BUSINESSES

Perhaps one of the most straightforward ways in which illegal proceeds have commonly been laundered is by commingling them with legitimately earned funds in cash-intensive businesses, such as laundromats, restaurants, convenience stores, or car washes, to name just a few. Sometimes referred to as front businesses, these cash-intensive business are otherwise lawful businesses that run primarily on cash transactions and encompass a variety of industries. Due to the cash-based nature of such businesses, determining how much money they actually generate may be difficult. Consequently, it's easy to misrepresent profits, inflate earnings, and manipulate invoices as well as provide numerous plausible explanations for increased funds. These factors also make it difficult for financial institutions to identify unusual activity associated with such businesses. Therefore, criminals and criminal organizations have historically favored cash-intensive businesses as a means to legitimize illicit proceeds and continue to use them for money laundering today. Banks and other financial institutions also widely consider them to be high-risk customers.

However, particularly in today's economy, where electronic transfers are increasingly the norm and many other options for laundering money quickly have less risk of detection, the use of cash-intensive businesses for money laundering comes with some significant drawbacks and limitations. Notably, the amount of profit brought in by a single cash-intensive business is generally limited to what would be reasonable for a business of that type. For example, a pizza parlor or a restaurant can report profits only up to a certain amount before the IRS, and eventually law enforcement, takes notice and starts to question the reported revenue. Therefore, someone with vast amounts of money to launder would need to own multiple restaurants or car washes (or both), all of which would be subject to scrutiny. This is both time and effort intensive, particularly when more efficient options are available.

As chapters 2–8 show, other methods and techniques are available to launder far greater sums of money at a much quicker rate and, perhaps even more importantly, in ways that provide anonymity, allowing the criminal to stay under the radar while retaining control of his or her funds. Some of these methods include misusing anonymous legal entities and networks of untraceable shell companies; engaging in TBML; purchasing real estate, particularly luxury real estate in high-end markets; using virtual or cryptocurrencies; and undertaking cyber-laundering schemes, such as those involving online money mules and the dark web.

RED FLAGS ASSOCIATED WITH MONEY LAUNDERING

Red flags are warning signs or indictors of suspicious activity that may signal money laundering. The presence of a red flag is not conclusive evidence that money laundering is taking place; likewise, the absence of red flags is not confirmation that financial crimes aren't occurring. The existence of a red flag is an alert that a transaction should be carefully reviewed before proceeding to prevent a potentially illicit transaction from passing through an institution. Generally, the likelihood of money laundering activity increases as the number of red flags increases.

Red flags merely signify the potential involvement of illicit activity and represent only part of the picture. Not every activity that deviates from the norm constitutes money laundering. Therefore, each situation should be looked at as a whole rather than be limited to reviewing a single transaction. Additionally, the specific facts and circumstances of each case must be considered and evaluated carefully before making any decision, such as whether to accept or decline a potential customer, process a transaction, or file a suspicious activity report (SAR). This includes considering what constitutes normal and expected activity for that particular customer or in that specific situation. For example, CDD reviews should closely scrutinize such details as the parties and jurisdictions involved, the past activity associated with the account, and the overall business purpose of the transaction as well as whether the activity in question makes sense in light of all the facts. Obtaining additional information may be necessary to complete the assessment.

Furthermore, lists of red flags are not exhaustive. Such lists also need to remain flexible and need to be continuously reviewed and updated as money laundering methods evolve and as the circumstances of the institution and its corresponding risks change.

Red flags will typically differ by the industry (e.g., finance, construction), the sectors within a particular industry (e.g., banking, securities, insurance), the methods or techniques used to launder money (e.g., TBML, money laundering through real estate), the customer type (e.g., individual or entity), the transaction type (e.g., wire transfers, automated clearinghouse transactions), and the jurisdiction (i.e., low-risk versus high-risk jurisdictions). Red flags may be further grouped into specific categories. These categories may include suspicious customer behavior, efforts to avoid reporting requirements, insufficiency regarding the quality or completeness of information provided, activity inconsistent with customer's business, and unusual activity related to transactions involving fund transfers, bank-to-bank transactions, bulk currency shipments, trade finance, insurance, and shell companies, among many others.

Various standard-setting organizations, and other groups dedicated to anti–money laundering efforts—such as the Financial Action Task Force, the Financial Crimes Enforcement Network, and the Federal Financial Institutions Examination Council, among many others—publish on their websites lists of red flags tied to money laundering and terrorist financing. While not exhaustive, these lists provide helpful examples that can be used to identify suspicious activity; to deter money laundering, terrorist financing, and other financial crime; and to ensure compliance with AML requirements. One of the simplest and most cost-effective measures that a financial institution can take to detect and deter money laundering is to educate its employees about the potential risks and their associated warning signs.

CONCLUSION

Money laundering schemes are often purposely designed to be complex and elusive. Considering the ever-evolving and clandestine nature of criminal activity and of money laundering in particular, it's important that anyone working in the AML field stay abreast of the various money laundering typologies and the applicable developments in related laws and regulations. They should also keep up with enforcement actions and recent cases, such as those covered in this book. Although a basic awareness and general knowledge of the money laundering landscape is useful, a broader perspective, such as what this book provides, can assist in formulating mitigation strategies, enabling more effective detection and deterrence, and helping ensure regulatory compliance.

NOTES

1. Shelley, *Dark Commerce*, 153.
2. Amanda Macias, "10 Facts Reveal the Absurdity of Pablo Escobar's Wealth," *Insider*, September 21, 2015, https://www.businessinsider.com/10-facts-that-prove-the-absurdity-of -pablo-escobars-wealth-2015-9.
3. Pierre-Emmanuel Ly, "The Charitable Activities of Terrorist Organizations," *Public Choice* 131, no. 1/2 (2007): 177–95, https://www.jstor.org/stable/27698091.
4. Nigel Morris-Cotterill, "Money Laundering," *Foreign Policy*, no. 124 (May–June 2001): 16–20, 22, https://doi.org/10.2307/3183186.
5. Rodolfo Uribe, "Changing Paradigms on Money Laundering," *Observer News*, 2003, http://www.cicad.oas.org/oid/new/information/observer/observer2_2003/ml paradigms.pdf.
6. Safire, *Safire's New Political Dictionary*, 398.
7. United States v. $4,255,625.39, 551 F.Sup.314 (S.D.Fla. 1982).
8. FATF, "About: Who We Are," accessed August 8, 2020, https://www.fatf-gafi.org/about/.
9. FATF, "FAQs about Money Laundering," accessed August 8, 2020, https://www.fatf -gafi.org/faq/moneylaundering/.
10. Garner, *Black's Law Dictionary*, 889.

11. Financial Crimes Enforcement Network (FinCEN), "History of Anti-Money Launder- ing Laws," US Treasury Department, accessed October 29, 2020, https://www.fincen .gov/history-anti-money-laundering-laws#:~:text=Money%20laundering%20is%20the %20process,into%20the%20legitimate%20financial%20system.

12. Robinson, *Laundrymen*, 4.

13. United States Sentencing Commission, Commission Datafiles: FY 2015 through FY 2019, USSCFY15-USSCFY19, accessed October 29, 2020, https://www.ussc.gov /research/datafiles/commission-datafiles.

14. FinCEN, "FinCEN Issues Amendments to the Funds Transfer Rules," US Treasury Department, March 26, 1996, https://www.fincen.gov/news/news-releases/fincen-issues -amendments-funds-transfer-rules.

15. Sullivan, *Anti-Money Laundering*, 5.

16. International Monetary Fund, "Anti-Money Laundering/Combating the Financing of Terrorism: What Are Typologies?," accessed March 2, 2021, https://www.imf.org /external/np/leg/amlcft/eng/aml1.htm#typologies.

17. FATF, *Financial Flows Linked to the Production and Trafficking of Afghan Opiates* (Paris: FATF, June 2014), http://www.fatf-gafi.org/media/fatf/documents/reports/Financial -flows-linked-to-production-and-trafficking-of-afghan-opiates.pdf.

18. "Taliban Vow to Ban Heroin, but Can They Survive without It?," *France News 24*, August 19, 2021, https://www.france24.com/en/live-news/20210819-taliban-vow-to -ban-heroin-but-can-they-survive-without-it.

19. Jeff Burbank, "Mob News & Notes: Chinese Triads Launder Billions through Van- couver, Buying Luxury Real Estate, Cars," *The Mob Museum* (blog), May 31, 2019, last updated June 5, 2019, https://themobmuseum.org/blog/chinese-triads-launder -billions-through-vancouver-buying-luxury-real-estate-cars/.

20. Parker Asmann, "Money Laundering Tactics Adapting to Colombia Cocaine Boom," *InSight Crime*, October 10, 2018, https://www.insightcrime.org/news/analysis/money -laundering-adapting-colombia-cocaine-boom/; and Adriaan Alsema, "Laundering Colombia's Drug Money: Part 1: How to Do It," *Colombia Reports*, July 19, 2020, https:// colombiareports.com/laundering-colombias-drug-money-part-1-how-to-do-it/.

21. FAFT, *Global Money Laundering and Terrorist Financing Threat Assessment* (Paris: FAFT/ OECD, July 2010), https://www.fatf-gafi.org/media/fatf/documents/reports/Global %20Threat%20assessment.pdf.

22. UNODC, *Toolkit to Combat the Trafficking in Persons* (New York: United Nations, 2008), https://www.unodc.org/documents/human-trafficking/HT_Toolkit08_English.pdf.

23. Money Laundering Control Act, 18 U.S.C. § 1956 (1986).

24. Lisa Gregory, Peter S. Spivack, and Rupinder K. Garcha, "In Brief: Money Laundering Offences in USA," *Lexology*, June 26, 2020, https://www.lexology.com/library/detail .aspx?g=fbb52d9f-a7a6-4c3c-8517-742a9b9c73e4.

25. Jean-François Thony, "Money Laundering and Terrorism Financing: An Overview," *Cur- rent Developments in Monetary and Financial Law* 3 (April 29, 2005), article 15.

26. Steven M. D'Antuono, section chief, Criminal Investigative Division, Federal Bureau of Investigation (FBI), "Combating Money Laundering and Other Forms of Illicit Finance: Regulator and Law Enforcement Perspectives on Reform: Statement before the Senate Banking, Housing, and Urban Affairs Committee," Washington, DC, November 29, 2018, https://www.fbi.gov/news/testimony/combating-money-laundering-and-other -forms-of-illicit-finance.

27. Peter Reuter and Edwin M. Truman, "Combating Predicate Crimes Involved in Money Laundering," in *Chasing Dirty Money: The Fight against Money Laundering* (Washington, DC: Peterson Institute for International Economics, 2004), 109–11, https://www.piie .com/publications/chapters_preview/381/5iie3705.pdf.

28. FATF, *Corruption: A Reference Guide and Information Note on the Use of the FATF Recommendations in the Fight against Corruption* (Paris: FATF, 2012), https://star.worldbank .org/sites/star/files/corruption_reference_guide_and_information_note_2012.pdf.

29. World Bank, *Strengthening World Bank Group Engagement on Governance and Anticorruption* (Washington, DC: World Bank, March 14, 2007), http://www1.worldbank.org /publicsector/anticorrupt/corecourse2007/GACMaster.pdf.

30. Legal Information Institute, Cornell Law School, "Tax Evasion," accessed August 4, 2020, https://www.law.cornell.edu/wex/tax_evasion.

31. FBI, "What We Investigate: White-Collar Crime," accessed March 9, 2021, https://www .fbi.gov/investigate/white-collar-crime.

32. Shawn Hubler, "Fleiss Sentenced to 37 Months for Tax Evasion," *Los Angeles Times*, January 8, 1997, https://www.latimes.com/archives/la-xpm-1997-01-08-me-16452-story .html; and Seth Abramovitch, "Heidi Fleiss Reflects on 25th Anniversary of Her Arrest, Ex Tom Sizemore and What Charlie Sheen Really Spent on Girls," *Hollywood Reporter*, June 7, 2018, https://www.hollywoodreporter.com/news/heidi-fleiss-her-arrest-macaw -cause-drug-addict-tom-sizemore-1117449.

33. Global Financial Integrity, "Illicit Financial Flows," accessed August 4, 2020, https:// gfintegrity.org/issue/illicit-financial-flows/.

34. Internal Revenue Service (IRS), "Forms and Instructions: Tax Form 1040," accessed August 4, 2020, www.irs.gov/Form1040.

35. IRS, "Publication 17 (2020), Your Federal Income Tax," accessed August 4, 2020, https://www.irs.gov/publications/p17#en_US_2019_publink1000171197.

36. Ian M. Comisky, "May Tax Evasion Be Charged as a Money Laundering Offense? The Times Are a-Changing," *ABA Practice Point* 39, no. 4 (August 25, 2020), https://www .americanbar.org/groups/taxation/publications/abataxtimes_home/20aug/20aug-pp -comisky-money-laundering/.

37. Tax Policy Center, "Briefing Book: A Citizen's Guide to the Fascinating (Though Often Complex) Elements of the US Tax System," updated May 2020, https://www .taxpolicycenter.org/briefing-book/what-are-sources-revenue-federal-government).

38. Garner, *Black's Law Dictionary*, 670–71.

39. Sal Jadavji, "Fraud and Money Laundering: What's the Connection?," *ACAMS Today*, September 2, 2011, https://www.acamstoday.org/fraud-and-money-laundering-whats -the-connection/#:~:text=Criminal%20activity%20related%20to%20fraud,money%20 laundering)%20for%20money%20laundering.

40. FBI, "FBI Urges Vigilance during COVID-19 Pandemic," accessed March 9, 2021, https://www.fbi.gov/coronavirus; and Europol, "COVID-19: Fraud," accessed March 9, 2021, https://www.europol.europa.eu/covid-19/covid-19-fraud.

41. Richard Summerfield, "Heightened Vigilance: COVID-19 Creates Fraud and Money Laundering Vulnerabilities," *Financier Worldwide*, accessed March 9, 2021, https://www .financierworldwide.com/heightened-vigilance-covid-19-creates-fraud-and-money -laundering-vulnerabilities#.YEf75ulKjfY.

42. FinCEN, "FinCEN Advisory to Financial Institutions on Cyber-Events and Cyber-Enabled Crime," US Treasury Department, FIN-2016-A005, October 25, 2016, https://

www.fincen.gov/resources/advisories/fincen-advisory-fin-2016-a005; and Kevin W. Toth, "The Convergence of Cyber, Fraud, and AML: How the Puzzle Pieces Fit Together to Solve the Emerging Cyber Risk" (Chicago: ACAMS, June 11, 2019), https://www.acams.org/en/media/document/9481.

43. Stefan D. Cassella, "The Forfeiture of Property Involved in Money Laundering Offenses," *Buffalo Criminal Law Review* 7, no. 7 (2004): 583, 614.

44. Money Laundering Control Act, 18 U.S.C. § 1956 (1986).

45. Crimes and Criminal Procedure, 18 U.S.C. § 3282(a).

46. Congressional Research Service, "Money Laundering: An Overview of 18 U.S.C. § 1956 and Related Federal Criminal Law," CRS Report no. RL33315 (Washington, DC: Congressional Research Service, 2017), https://www.everycrsreport.com/files/20171130_RL33315_a7fb09655852a4a57b91fc3fa500ad82a3158c34.pdf.

47. Congressional Research Service.

48. Gregory, Spivack, and Garcha, "Money Laundering."

49. Reuter and Truman, "Improving the Global AML Regime," in *Chasing Dirty Money*, 188.

50. Reuter and Truman, 188.

51. FATF, "Trade Based Money Laundering" (Paris: FATF, June 23, 2006), https://www.fatf-gafi.org/media/fatf/documents/reports/Trade%20Based%20Money%20Laundering.pdf.

CHAPTER 2

ANONYMOUS

The Role of Shell Companies

Shell companies are a curious legal fiction because they generally lack a physical presence and exist mainly on paper, yet they can own assets and conduct transactions. Shell companies are lawful to own and operate but have come under considerable scrutiny because they can be formed anonymously, which makes them prone to significant misuse while simultaneously serving as substantial roadblocks for investigators and authorities.

Lax regulations and a lack of uniform global standards for professional intermediaries who assist with the formation and operation of corporate entities, including the provision of various legal, business, and financial services, enable the manipulation and exploitation of anonymous shell companies. Consequently, the illicit use of shell companies facilitates corruption, tax evasion, money laundering, and other financial crimes that have far-reaching and devastating consequences, particularly for poor and developing countries.

WHAT ARE SHELL COMPANIES?

Shell companies are legal entities and, as such, have certain rights and obligations, including the ability to enter into contracts, own property, engage in transactions, and be parties in lawsuits. However, rather than having a physical address or other physical presence, such as an office, factory, or distribution center, as is common with more traditional companies, shell companies merely have a mailing address. Typically, it is simply a rented post office box that is used for the receipt of service of process and corporate documents (and can easily be changed at any time).

Furthermore, shell companies do not offer any products or services, generally do not have any employees, and consequently do not run any other business operations. In fact, most shell companies have limited or no assets. Additionally, shell companies are nontraded entities and therefore are not listed on any stock exchange.

Shell companies can be formed as corporations, limited liability companies (LLCs), or limited partnerships and are recognized as lawful corporate vehicles in almost all parts of the world, including every major financial center. As a result, shell companies can be used in transactions internationally and serve an important role in global markets.

LEGITIMATE USES AND BENEFITS OF SHELL COMPANIES

Shell companies, including anonymous shell companies, have many legitimate uses. They are most often used as transactional vehicles for various financial and other business matters. What makes shell companies particularly useful is that they can hold bank and brokerage accounts; wire funds; own and transfer assets, including stock and real estate; and otherwise engage in various transactions.[1] Shell companies can also engage in financial and estate planning, facilitate corporate mergers, and serve as holding companies. A shell company can even take on the role of a trustee for a trust.

The benefits associated with owning a shell company come in the form of business, legal, regulatory, and tax advantages. They allow investors to pool resources, immunize the business and the owner from certain kinds of business and financial risk, provide protection against litigation, limit personal liability for business debts and claims, safeguard both tangible (e.g., real estate) and intangible assets (e.g., intellectual property, copyrights, royalties, and trade secrets), and offer favorable tax treatment, which can amount to significant savings in some cases. Moreover, anonymous entities can provide owners and directors with privacy and protection from those who might want to get at their wealth, including disgruntled business partners, competitors, and ex-spouses. Shell companies have even been used to guard against potential kidnapping and ransom requests.

A simple illustration of the many uses and benefits of shell companies is in establishing LLCs to hold real estate. For example, an individual who owns multiple rental properties may find it advantageous to establish a different LLC for each property. Furthermore, each LLC could also have its own bank account for such transactions as accepting rental income and paying any associated fees and expenses of the rental property. As long as the owner keeps his or her personal funds separate from the rental property money, this structure provides the advantage of effectively separating the owner's personal and business assets, thereby reducing personal liability risk should an accident occur on one of the properties and a resulting lawsuit arise. Moreover, any claim or judgment levied on a particular LLC would be limited only to that LLC, thereby insulating the other properties from costly damages. Additionally, this business structure also provides the benefit of pass-through taxation.

ILLEGITIMATE USES OF SHELL COMPANIES

Although the vast majority of shell companies are used for legal purposes, they are also highly susceptible to abuse, particularly in cases where the identity of the individual who owns or controls the shell company is hidden. Such anonymity is possible because most countries do not collect or maintain updated documentation on corporate owners. This constitutes a huge gap in the global legal framework whereby almost anyone can set up an anonymous shell company and thereafter use it for a host of nefarious purposes, including various illicit transactions. Without records of who owns the entity, it is virtually impossible for authorities to track the company or trace its transactions back to their true owner. As a result, there is no accountability, essentially allowing corrupt and criminal corporate owners to engage in illegal activity without any fear of retribution or risk of getting caught. Therefore, due to their legal standing as corporate entities, combined with the anonymity surrounding their formation and operation, shell companies have the capacity to move vast sums of illegal wealth without notice. Yet forming and operating these anonymous shell companies remain legal in many parts of the world.

While some uses of shell companies may be ethically or morally dubious or otherwise fall into a legal gray area (e.g., some tax avoidance strategies), other uses of shell companies are clearly illegal (e.g., tax evasion). In addition to tax-related crimes, shell companies are used in a wide variety of illicit activities, including sanctions dodging, terrorist funding, and money laundering, and in connection with numerous other crimes: drug trafficking, human trafficking, weapons smuggling, fraud schemes, cybercrimes, and many others. In fact, as confirmed by the Financial Action Task Force, the World Bank, and other organizations, shell companies constitute one of the most common methods for laundering illicit funds resulting from corruption, whereby they are used to give or receive bribes or to embezzle state funds.[2]

For example, the notorious Russian arms dealer Viktor Bout, also known as the "Merchant of Death" (portrayed by Nicholas Cage in the 2005 movie *Lord of War*), used a global network of anonymous shell companies—some of which were incorporated in Delaware, Florida, and Texas—to hide assets, evade international sanctions, and sell contraband. The anonymity that the shell companies provided enabled Bout to sell weapons to some of the most ruthless criminals in the world, including dictators and guerrilla forces in Africa, South America, and the Middle East. As a result, Bout has been accused of arming some of the most violent conflicts around the globe and of conspiring to kill Americans.[3]

Another ubiquitous illegal use of shell companies is for purposes of tax evasion. In fact, research demonstrates that the extremely wealthy most commonly engage in offshore tax evasion, which is not surprising considering that they have the most to benefit from it. For example, in a 2016 study focusing on the growing divide between the richest 1 percent and all other taxpayers, researchers found that the top wealthiest households in Norway, Sweden, and Denmark evaded paying approximately 25 percent of their duly owed taxes, whereas all other households earning less money underpaid their tax bills by less than 5 percent.[4]

Certainly, tax evasion isn't limited to the Nordic countries. According to the Brookings Institution, a nonprofit public policy organization based in Washington, DC, approximately one out of every six tax dollars owed to the US government in federal taxes is not paid.[5] As a matter of fact, Jeffrey Winters, a professor of political science at Northwestern University who specializes in the topic of oligarchy, notes that when strategically configured, shell companies, which are used predominantly by the rich, can make $30 million in gains appear like a $10 million loss to the IRS.[6]

The Panama Papers scandal, which came to light in April 2016 and involved a data leak of over 11 million documents containing confidential financial and attorney-client information for over 200,000 offshore entities, revealed how the wealthy, powerful, and politically connected from all over the world used the offshore finance industry to engage in shady and outright illegal activity. The scandal was also notable because of the size of the data leak and the highly public figures involved, including numerous politicians, world leaders, celebrities, prominent businessmen, sports figures, and other ultra-wealthy and well-known individuals from more than two hundred nations. The 2019 Netflix film *The Laundromat*, starring Meryl Streep, Antonio Banderas, and Gary Oldman, is based on the Panama Papers and details the collapse of Mossack Fonseca, the Panamanian law firm and corporate service provider at the heart of the scandal.

But Panama is certainly not the only secrecy jurisdiction. Nor are the Panama Papers the only document leak to expose the extent of illicit and questionable practices rampant within the offshore finance industry. The magnitude of shell company abuses in different tax and financial secrecy havens have been unveiled in other similar data disclosures: the Offshore Leaks in 2013, the Lux Leaks in 2014, the Swiss Leaks in 2015, the Bahamas Leaks in 2016, and the Paradise Papers in 2017. In 2020 the Luanda Leaks involved the release of financial documents detailing how the daughter of the former Angolan president amassed a fortune at the expense of her country with the assistance of shell companies and professional intermediaries, and the FinCEN Files exposed thousands of confidential suspicious activity reports that showed how major global banks facilitate money laundering.

THE EASE OF FORMING A SHELL COMPANY

Shell companies are generally associated with places that have reputations as offshore tax havens, such as the island nations in the Caribbean, and countries such as Switzerland that have well-known bank secrecy laws. In more recent years, however, shell companies have been increasingly linked to major international financial centers, such as London, New York, Hong Kong, Singapore, and Dubai. The fact is a shell company can be formed in almost any country in the world, with formation requirements, including those pertaining to the ease of formation and the level of secrecy, varying by jurisdiction. Similarly, the existence and strength of AML regimes and AML enforcement also differ from place to place. Therefore, prospective corporate owners are free to shop around for the jurisdiction that best meets their goals, whether that be an onshore or offshore jurisdiction. As the various document leaks that have emerged over the past several years clearly show, a litany of intermediaries, including lawyers, accountants, and other advisers, offer a host of services to assist with the company formation process.

In the United States, company formation is relatively easy and straightforward. Until recently, companies could be formed anonymously, leading to the country's emergence as a leading financial secrecy haven in recent decades.

The corporate formation process, which includes the formation of corporations, LLCs, and partnerships, is governed by the individual states rather than at the federal level. Therefore, the incorporation laws (applicable to corporations) and formation requirements (applicable to other types of business entities, such as limited partnerships and LLCs), as well as their associated fees, vary considerably. Additionally, the laws governing the management and conduct of business entities following their establishment also differ by state.

Furthermore, no state requires that an entity must be established in the owner's home state or in the state in which the business will operate (although some states require that businesses name a registered agent with a physical address in the state). Individuals are free to create a shell company in any state of their choice (or in another country, if they prefer), depending on whether they are looking for tax savings, lax filing requirements, strong privacy laws, or a business-friendly legal system to govern potential disputes.[7]

Significantly, each state derives revenue, to differing degrees, from the various registration and filing fees associated with company formation. Some states have adopted more lenient company formation requirements to compete for clients in what has been referred to as a "race to the bottom" in terms of lax incorporation standards. They widely vary in how much, or how little, information they collect about company owners. Consequently, a small number of states—namely, Delaware, Nevada, and Wyoming—have developed reputations, whether fairly or not, as secrecy havens.

Delaware in particular offers extreme flexibility when incorporating in the state, making the incorporation process more efficient there than almost anywhere else in the world. Moreover, its tax system provides multiple ways for businesses to legally lower their tax bills. Finally, Delaware has a long-standing and well-reputed legal system specializing in matters of corporate law. As a result, more than half of the publicly traded companies in the United States and over 65 percent of Fortune 500 companies are incorporated in Delaware.[8]

In the United States, one can establish a shell company in person or remotely. One can employ a corporate service provider; work through an attorney, accountant, or another third party; or simply do it on his or her own. In fact, shell companies can also be set up entirely online by completing a few forms and providing payment information. For example, over the internet, an individual located across the world can set up a shell company in the United States without ever having to physically enter the country.[9]

Prior to the passage of the Corporate Transparency Act (CTA) in January 2021, a federal law that requires private companies to disclose their beneficial owners to FinCEN, the AML/KYC processes, including customer identification and verification requirements, were not mandated at either the federal or state level. Accordingly, not a single state in the United States required the collection of beneficial ownership information for the creation of a corporate entity.

Since a shell company is a legal entity that can sue and be sued, a registered agent must be named to accept a subpoena or other legal documents pertaining to a lawsuit. Depending on the requirements of the state where the entity is formed, the registered agent can be the beneficial owner, a friend or family member, or a commercial registered agent.

Most states charge an annual fee to maintain a company in the state. A few states, including Delaware, further require the submission of an annual report. The entire process to form a legal entity, including registration with the state and receipt of the final documents, takes approximately two weeks. The average total cost is typically around a few hundred dollars but can be more depending on the state and whether the company purchases additional services, such as having someone draft an operating agreement or register for a federal tax ID number (both of which can otherwise be done on one's own for free). Although lawyers and others can assist with part or all of the company formation process, anyone can create a legal entity on his or her own. Therefore, although it may not make sense for the average person to establish a shell company absent some business-related purpose, it certainly would be worth the comparatively minimal effort, time, and expense for someone with a lot of (legally or illegally earned) money to safeguard.

BENEFICIAL OWNERSHIP

Primarily as a result of steadfast and rigorous investigative journalism by the International Consortium of Investigative Journalists (ICIJ), by other organizations, and by individual reporters, shell companies, the lack of transparency around beneficial owners, and the role of the financial sector in facilitating illicit transactions have all come under increased scrutiny from the public, regulators, and law enforcement. Policymakers and legislators appear to have taken notice because a recent wave of AML laws, regulations, and directives has focused on beneficial ownership, including requirements concerning beneficial ownership registries. Some of the most notable ones include the European Union's Fourth and Fifth AML Directives (AMLD4 and AMLD5), which require the implementation of a publicly accessible central register of beneficial ownership information; FinCEN's Customer Due Diligence Rule (CDD Rule), which obligates covered financial institutions to identify the beneficial owners of their legal entity customers; and the Corporate Transparency Act, which mandates that US-registered corporate entities disclose their beneficial owners to FinCEN.

A *beneficial owner*, sometimes also referred to as the ultimate beneficial owner (UBO), is a natural person (i.e., not a legal entity) who receives the benefits of owning some form of property even though the legal title of that property may be in the name of another individual, of a group of individuals, or even of another entity. For example, publicly traded securities are often registered in the name of a broker rather than in the name of the individual who ultimately will benefit from their financial value. Therefore, beneficial ownership is different from legal ownership, although in many cases, the legal owner is also the beneficial owner. A beneficial owner should also be distinguished from a *beneficiary*, who can be a natural person or a legal entity and gains some sort of advantage or benefit, usually monetary in nature, from another. For example, an individual or an LLC could be the beneficiary of a life insurance policy, a trust, or a will and is thus eligible to receive the corresponding benefits.

The FATF defines beneficial owner as "the natural person(s) who ultimately owns or controls a legal entity and/or the natural person on whose behalf a transaction is being conducted. It also includes those persons who exercise ultimate effective control over a legal person or arrangement."[10]

Regarding its CDD Rule, FinCEN defines beneficial ownership using a control prong and an ownership prong. The *control prong* focuses on a single individual, such as the chief executive officer (CEO) or the president, with the significant responsibility to manage, direct, or control a legal entity customer. (Note that *legal entity customer* is defined in 31 CFR § 1010.230 as "a corporation, limited liability company, or other entity that is created by the filing of a public document with a secretary of state or similar office, a general partnership, and any similar entity formed under the laws of a foreign jurisdiction that opens an account."[11] The *ownership prong* focuses on the equity interests, whether direct or indirect, of a legal entity customer and can be anyone who owns 25 percent or more of the entity and even a pooled vehicle of up to five people. If no one owns at least 25 percent, then the beneficial owner will be defined only under the control prong.[12]

To illustrate the concept of beneficial ownership, let's say that Jane Doe is the beneficial owner of a particular rental property. However, rather than titling the property in her own name, Jane lists her shell company as the owner of the rental property. In that case, the legal title of the rental property is in the name of Jane Doe's shell company, but Jane Doe still (indirectly) owns and controls the property and thus makes major decisions with respect to the property, such as whether to sell it. Jane, as the beneficial owner, also ultimately reaps the benefits of ownership through the receipt of the rental payments, which constitute her profits.

The Jane Doe example is a rather simplistic one. Criminals go to great lengths to obscure their ownership in shell companies that are used for illicit purposes. They can do so by intricately layering a series of shell companies and using nominees to stand in as the actual owners. Such structures may even span jurisdictions, particularly ones with strict privacy laws. Therefore, the identity of the beneficial owner behind a carefully configured legal arrangement can be impossible to uncover.

Although definitions of the term "beneficial owner" vary, all require that it be a natural person (as opposed to an entity or another type of legal arrangement). Peeling back the layers of the corporate entity to reveal the individual controlling it prevents anonymity and the corresponding misuse it enables. The identification of beneficial owners is critical for law enforcement purposes, where lack of transparency serves as a roadblock in investigations. Therefore, beneficial ownership is an important concept in the fight against financial crime as well as for tax transparency and financial reporting. Collecting, verifying, and maintaining beneficial ownership information are key ways to address illicit financial flows and the criminal misuse of the global financial system.

CASE STUDY: WHERE THERE'S GRAND CORRUPTION, THERE'S RAMPANT MONEY LAUNDERING

Anyone who works in the field of financial crime, and AML in particular, knows that where there's large-scale corruption, there's also rampant money laundering. This is especially the case with grand corruption, which has the potential to generate millions, and even billions, of dollars in illegal funds.

Grand corruption is the abuse of high-level power. It involves public figures, such as high-ranking government and political officials, and entails the theft or diversion of public funds. As a result, the individuals typically involved in grand corruption schemes are ones whose actions are subject to public scrutiny. How can public figures pilfer and then launder large sums of wealth without anyone noticing? They use anonymous shell companies. And they often enlist the assistance and advice of professional intermediaries and middlemen, such as lawyers, accountants, and various consultants, in what has come to be known as the gatekeeping professions.

Studies undertaken by the Stolen Asset Recovery Initiative—a partnership between the World Bank Group and the United Nations Office on Drugs and Crime—and the FATF confirm that along with wire transfers, shell companies are the most common means used to launder money in major corruption cases, particularly in those involving more than a million dollars.[13] The Luanda Leaks, a series of investigative reports named after the capital of Angola and published by the ICIJ in January 2020, illustrates this all-too-common link between corruption and money laundering. The reports also show how the corrupt and powerful misuse corporate vehicles and other legal arrangements as well as offshore secrecy jurisdictions. Additionally, the accounts highlight the critical role of the minimally regulated professional services industry and how this group of professionals is responsible for enabling corruption, money laundering, and other financial crimes.

At the center of the Luanda Leaks scandal is Isabel dos Santos, the oldest daughter of José Eduardo dos Santos, the autocratic former president of Angola who was in power from 1979 to 2017. A whistleblower leaked a comprehensive collection of detailed documents, including thousands of business and financial records, that show how over the course of her father's rule and at the expense of her nation's people, Isabel corruptly amassed a fortune that left Angola—rich in oil, diamonds, and other natural resources—one of the most destitute countries in the world. According to data from the World Bank, Angola currently has one of the highest infant mortality rates in the world, the average life span of its citizens is only about sixty years, a large percentage of Angolans don't have access to clean water, and nearly half of the country's population lives on less than two dollars per day.[14] Yet *Forbes* has noted that Isabel is the wealthiest woman in Africa and the first African female billionaire.[15]

Although Isabel insists that her fortune is self-made and that she never took any public funds, a wealth of documents reveals an entirely different story, supporting widespread allegations of corruption, embezzlement, insider deals, nepotism, tax evasion, and money laundering—all of which was enabled in large part through otherwise legally formed corporate structures. The picture that emerges is of a global empire built on corruptly acquired state funds that Isabel and her husband, a Congolese businessman named Sindika Dokolo, amassed and that comprises over four hundred companies and subsidiaries as well as properties all over the world. The couple's combined commercial interests are extensive and varied, spanning multiple industries. In addition to interests in oil and diamonds, the couple also held stakes in the telecommunications, media, retail, finance, and energy industries.

Since the governing family controlled nearly all the public institutions in Angola, corruption was virtually inevitable. During his nearly forty-year term as president, José dos Santos appointed relatives and friends to prominent positions, allowing a small elite group to profit from Angola's natural resources as the rest of the country's people became more and more impoverished. Dos Santos also granted his daughter stakes in several Angolan companies and numerous lucrative deals, public contracts, tax breaks, licenses, and even diamond-mining rights. Furthermore, he appointed Isabel as the head of Sonangol, the state oil company and primary oil exporter, and he gave her a seat on the board of Unitel, Angola's largest telecommunications company.

The rampant corruption necessitated money laundering, both of which would not have been possible without the use of otherwise legitimately created corporate entities. It was facilitated by various professional intermediaries, including a cadre of lawyers, accountants, financial advisers, corporate services providers, consultants, and other middlemen—all of whom also profited. Through a vast web of shell companies located across the globe, Isabel and her husband were able to launder their illegitimately acquired wealth and evade taxes while avoiding scrutiny.

Records show that Angolan state companies transferred huge amounts of foreign currency to shell companies in foreign jurisdictions whose ultimate beneficiaries were Isabel and Dokolo. Consulting fees, loans, and contracts were directed from the couple's businesses to shell companies they controlled in various secrecy jurisdictions around the world, including the British Virgin Islands (BVI), the Netherlands, Malta, and Mauritius, among others. Shell company invoices show extraordinarily large payments for ambiguous work described simply as "consulting services," a classic red flag for money laundering and financial crime. Isabel and Dokolo also owned a luxury penthouse apartment located in Lisbon, Portugal, through a shell company incorporated in Delaware. In many of these cases, nominees were used to ensure that the couple's names did not appear on public documents. The nominees were either individuals they knew well or other companies that the couple owned. This arrangement allowed Isabel and Dokolo to conceal their identities yet still guaranteed them full control of the shell companies and access to their assets.

Emails and other documents reveal that accountants, attorneys, and other consultants advised the couple on how to move money, get around banking compliance requirements, secure their anonymity, and avoid paying taxes even after banks became less willing to do business with the pair, whose status as PEPs marked them as high risk and whose increasingly complex financial arrangements and links to jurisdictions with poor AML controls raised concerns.[16] While banks are subject to stringent requirements and strict regulatory oversight, professional services firms, lawyers, accountants, financial advisers, and others providing business services generally have far less regulatory burdens and don't face nearly as much scrutiny. While these professions may have codes of conduct or standards for membership in professional organizations, these criteria are generally self-created, and the professions are usually self-regulated. In other words, unlike financial institutions, governments do not regulate or oversee these gatekeeper professions.

For example, the United States has either very limited or no legal requirements at all, depending on the profession, mandating the assessment or the vetting of clients. Although the European Union has stricter rules, studies by the European Commission found that compliance with client vetting requirements is inconsistent. Furthermore, an analysis by Transparency International and other similar studies have found that financial intermediaries, whether deliberately or not, facilitate money laundering.[17] Moreover, a 2018 FATF report examining how criminals launder money and evade taxes found that the gatekeeper professions played a critical role in a great majority of the cases.[18] Accordingly, professional intermediaries possess a specialized knowledge and skill set that, if left unchecked, may be exploited to manipulate legal and financial systems and regulations.

Meanwhile, Isabel and her husband were charged with embezzlement and money laundering, and their assets were frozen. (Several months after the charges were brought, Sindika Dokolo died in a diving accident in Dubai.[19]) Cases such as theirs tend to drag on for years. Even if prosecutors prevail, asset recovery is unlikely, and Angola will probably never obtain the stolen funds.

BEYOND ANGOLA

No country is immune from corruption or the resulting cycle of financial crime. Scenarios similar to the one in Angola have played out in many resource-rich countries across the African continent and elsewhere. Corruption is one of the biggest impediments to economic and social development. Furthermore, corruption is enabled by financial secrecy, which results from the use of anonymous corporate structures.[20] Opaque entities make it all too easy for corrupt officials to divert money from the state and into their own pockets. For example, investigations by Global Witness revealed how anonymous companies incorporated in the BVI bought copper and cobalt mines in the Democratic Republic of Congo for a small fraction of their actual value and later resold them at a huge gain. An unknown individual (or individuals) behind the deal unjustly profited while billions of dollars in state funds that rightly belonged to the Congolese people were diverted.[21]

Likewise, the Obiang family of Equatorial Guinea has been linked to many illicit activities, including money laundering through US financial institutions and shell companies.[22]

Like Angola, Equatorial Guinea is another natural resource–rich African country with an extremely high wealth disparity and is positioned at the bottom of the human development index. The ruling Obiang family, including President Teodoro Obiang and his eldest son, Vice President Teodoro Nguema Obiang Mangue, have been accused of plundering their country's oil wealth and using it to lead an extremely extravagant lifestyle. For example, Nguema Obiang owned multiple expensive homes, including a $30 million mansion in Malibu, California, and a 101-room penthouse in Paris. He also owned a fleet of luxury sport cars and a Gulfstream jet, all of which are grossly inconsistent with his official salary as vice president. Many of his lavish purchases were done through anonymous shell companies, including one in Delaware and one in BVI.[23]

Anonymous shell companies were the primary factor in enabling the diversion and laundering of government funds in all of these cases. Additionally, the shell companies in these scenarios were misused by people in privileged and powerful positions. Although this isn't always the case—anyone can misuse a shell company, and, conversely, not everyone in a position of power or privilege does so—the fact is that wealthy and well-connected people are more likely to have access to the group of professionals, such as lawyers, accountants, and wealth advisers, who can assist with forming shell companies and can facilitate their transactions.

Therefore, preventing the misuse of anonymous companies by demanding greater corporate transparency will help prevent the misuse of anonymous companies and tackle corruption in all its forms. Consequently, it will also combat the resulting poverty, resource depletion, environmental degradation, and host of other abuses involved in corruption.

RED FLAGS ASSOCIATED WITH SHELL COMPANIES

A review of the documents in the Luanda Leaks reveals numerous transactions scattered with classic red flags that are commonly associated with shell companies and that the financial institutions and those groups providing corporate, legal, and financial services to the dos Santos family largely, if not completely, ignored. To detect and deter financial crime and other illicit transactions enabled by the misuse of opaque corporate structures, financial institutions and other businesses that conduct transactions with shell companies, as well as the professional intermediaries that provide various corporate services, must recognize the potential that these structures can be exploited, must understand the specific risks that shell companies pose, and must be able to identify suspicious activity and its corresponding red flags. The degree of risk presented will vary depending on the particular transaction at issue, the type of corporate entity involved and its ownership structure, the nature of the customer, the purpose of the account, the location and type of services provided, and other related factors. Therefore, each shell company transaction should be assessed based on its unique characteristics.

Some examples of red flags that commonly indicate the misuse of shell companies include the purpose of the company is unknown or unclear; the payments associated with the company have no apparent purpose and reference vague or ambiguous terms or services, such as "consulting fees"; and the transactions include funds that pass through jurisdictions considered to be high risk or involve beneficiaries in *high-risk jurisdictions* (which the FATF defines as countries or jurisdictions having significant strategic deficiencies in their frameworks to counter money laundering, terrorist financing, and financing of proliferation and thereby present a risk to the international financial system[24]) or known financial secrecy havens. Both the FATF and FinCEN have published extensive lists of red flags related to shell companies.

CONCLUSION

Anonymous shell companies enable financial secrecy and the flow of illicit funds globally. The lack of transparency around who owns and controls shell companies creates a paradox whereby criminals can remain hidden behind a corporate entity while operating in plain sight. This causes significant challenges and insurmountable obstacles that impede law enforcement efforts.

The unregulated corporate services industry and the complicity of various professional intermediaries foster the formation and illicit use of anonymous legal entities. Currently, it is all too easy to establish an anonymous shell company; to use it to gain access to the international financial system; to route illicit funds across the world; to circumvent laws, regulations, and international sanctions; and to conduct a host of other illegitimate financial transactions with impunity and without accountability.

This results in far-reaching and long-lasting consequences that impact innocent individuals who are otherwise far removed from the illicit activity and unconnected to the nefarious actors involved. Empirical and anecdotal evidence clearly demonstrates that the illicit use of shell companies is not without victims, although some of the harmful effects caused by the illegal use of shell companies may not be obvious or even readily apparent. In some cases, such as those involving environmental degradation, resource depletion, and the aggravation of poverty, the ramifications take years to fully emerge.

Many studies show that the unlawful use of shell companies contributes to the ever-widening economic divide between the wealthiest segment of the population and everyone else.[25] Using these entities enables the covert diversion of critical resources away from those who need them most. This ultimately results in capital flight, which shell companies further enable by moving money out of developing countries. Like other forms of money laundering, the misuse of shell companies furthers the cycle of corruption, leads to political instability, and contributes to the denigration of democratic systems as well as the erosion of trust in financial markets and the rule of law. Consequently, the abuse of shell companies impacts the entire global community.

Thus, given globalization and the increasing interconnectedness of the world and its internationally accessible financial system, the only way to effectively combat the illicit use of anonymous corporate entities is at the international level through cooperative efforts among countries committed to financial transparency, including around corporate beneficial ownership. At a bare minimum, ready access to information regarding the owners and controllers of legal entities contained in beneficial ownership registries must be made available to law enforcement and financial institutions internationally. Having access to previously unavailable information would improve law enforcement investigations significantly and allow investigators to connect the dots. Transparency would also help financial institutions conduct more effective customer due diligence, monitoring, and suspicious activity reporting. This also includes improved communications and enhanced sharing of information among law enforcement and financial institutions as well as between jurisdictions.

Cross-border cooperation is crucial as criminals increasingly act without regard to borders. In fact, research shows that borders serve as greater barriers to law enforcement than to criminal activity because law enforcement efforts are hindered by extraterritorial limitations (such as the territorial application of criminal legislation).[26] Therefore, a robust collaborative international effort is necessary to remedy this impediment.

NOTES

1. Tucker, "Understanding the Risks."
2. Findley, Nielson, and Sharman, *Global Shell Games*, 100.
3. "'Merchant of Death' Viktor Bout Sentenced to 25 Years," BBC News, April 6, 2012, https://www.bbc.com/news/world-us-canada-17634050; and Stefanie Ostfeld, "Shell Game: Hidden Owners and Motives," CNN, September 11, 2012, https://www.cnn.com/2011/10/26/opinion/ostfeld-shell-companies/index.html.

4. Annette Alstadsæter, Niels Johannesen, and Gabriel Zucman, "Tax Evasion and In-equality," *American Economic Review* 109, no. 6 (2019): 2073–2103, DOI: 10.1257/aer.20172043.

5. William G. Gale and Aaron Krupkin, "How Big Is the Problem of Tax Evasion?," *Up Front* (blog), Brookings Institution, April 9, 2019, https://www.brookings.edu/blog/up-front/2019/04/09/how-big-is-the-problem-of-tax-evasion/.

6. Joe Pinsker, "Are Shell Companies Useful for People Who Aren't Ludicrously Rich?," *The Atlantic*, April 8, 2016, https://www.theatlantic.com/business/archive/2016/04/how-rich-do-you-have-to-be-for-a-shell-company-to-be-useful/477384/.

7. "After Incorporation or Formation, What's Next? (What's the Difference between Incorporation and Licensing?)," Delaware Corporate Law, Delaware.gov, accessed August 14, 2020, https://corplaw.delaware.gov/after-incorporation-formation/.

8. Elaine Zelby, "How Delaware Became the State Where Companies Incorporate," *Medium*, January 30, 2019, https://medium.com/useless-knowledge-daily/why-most-companies-incorporate-in-delaware-b8eae1e528a3#:~:text=Over%2050%25%20of%20all%20publicly,(198%2C450%20in%202017%20alone).

9. Tucker, "Understanding the Risks."

10. FATF, "FATF Guidance: Transparency and Beneficial Ownership" (Paris: FATF/OECD, October 2014), https://www.fatf-gafi.org/media/fatf/documents/reports/Guidance-transparency-beneficial-ownership.pdf; and Secretariat of the Global Forum on Transparency and Exchange of Information for Tax Purposes and the Inter-American Development Bank, "A Beneficial Ownership Implementation Toolkit" (Washington, DC: Inter-American Development Bank and OECD, March 2019), https://www.oecd.org/tax/transparency/beneficial-ownership-toolkit.pdf.

11. "31 CFR § 1010.230—Beneficial Ownership Requirements for Legal Entity Customers," Legal Information Institute, Cornell Law School, accessed September 30, 2020, https://www.law.cornell.edu/cfr/text/31/1010.230.

12. Beneficial Ownership Requirements for Legal Entity Customers, 31 CFR § 1010.230(d)(2); and 31 CFR § 1010.230(d)(1).

13. Findley, Nielson, and Sharman, *Global Shell Games*, 100.

14. World Bank, "Poverty and Equity Brief: Sub-Saharan Africa: Angola" (Washington, DC: World Bank, April 2020), https://databank.worldbank.org/data/download/poverty/33EF03BB-9722-4AE2-ABC7-AA2972D68AFE/Global_POVEQ_AGO.pdf.

15. Sydney P. Freedberg et al., "Luanda Leaks: How Africa's Richest Woman Exploited Family Ties, Shell Companies and Inside Deals to Build an Empire," International Consortium of Investigative Journalists, January 19, 2020, https://www.icij.org/investigations/luanda-leaks/how-africas-richest-woman-exploited-family-ties-shell-companies-and-inside-deals-to-build-an-empire/?gclid=CjwKCAiAzNj9BRBDEiwAPsL0d3vzQL4bDQFKNvxa3_kEB3qsECh_GaXaW4dqvrC7lbsA06LHHB5O9RoC5KYQAvD_BwE.

16. Freedberg et al.

17. Ben Hallman, Kyra Gurney, Scilla Alecci, and Max de Haldevang, "Western Advisers Helped an Autocrat's Daughter Amass and Shield a Fortune," International Consortium of Investigative Journalists, January 19, 2020, https://www.icij.org/investigations/luanda-leaks/western-advisers-helped-an-autocrats-daughter-amass-and-shield-a-fortune/.

18. Hallman, Gurney, Alecci, and de Haldevang.

19. Kerry A. Dolan, "How Isabel dos Santos, Once Africa's Richest Woman, Went Broke," *Forbes*, January 22, 2021, https://www.forbes.com/sites/kerryadolan/2021/01/22/the-unmaking-of-a-billionaire-how-africas-richest-woman-went-broke/?sh=5b4a62b86240.

20. "Corruption," Tax Justice Network, accessed March 15, 2021, https://www.taxjustice.net/topics/corruption/.

21. Global Witness, "Anonymous Companies: How Hidden Company Ownership Is a Major Barrier in the Fight against Poverty and What to Do about It" (London: Global Witness, May 2013), https://cdn.globalwitness.org/archive/files/library/anonymous_companies4b.pdf.

22. Office of Public Affairs, US Department of Justice, "Justice News: Second Vice President of Equatorial Guinea Agrees to Relinquish More than $30 Million of Assets Purchased with Corruption Proceeds," press release no. 14-1114, October 10, 2014, https://www.justice.gov/opa/pr/second-vice-president-equatorial-guinea-agrees-relinquish-more-30-million-assets-purchased.

23. Global Witness, "Anonymous Companies."

24. FATF, "High-Risk and Other Monitored Jurisdictions," accessed September 24, 2020, https://www.fatf-gafi.org/publications/high-risk-and-other-monitored-jurisdictions/?hf=10&b=0&s=desc(fatf_releasedate).

25. Global Witness, "Anonymous Companies."

26. Krstin M. Finklea, *The Interplay of Borders, Turf, Cyberspace, and Jurisdiction: Issues Confronting U.S. Law Enforcement*, R41927 (Washington, DC: US Library of Congress, Congressional Research Service, 2013).

CHAPTER 3

GAPS IN THE SUPPLY CHAIN

The Rise of Trade-Based Money Laundering

Trade and the practice of bartering for goods and services date to prehistoric times, long before paper currency and banks were invented. Back then, as now, goods were also smuggled and plundered, and their value was misrepresented. As commerce and trade developed over time, regulations were established to protect consumers and the market. Yet those who wanted to, always found new ways to circumvent these rules. Therefore, practices involving the transfer of value based on trade have been in existence for thousands of years, as have methods to exploit trade for financial gain and other illicit purposes.

WHAT IS TRADE-BASED MONEY LAUNDERING?

The money laundering method referred to as *trade-based money laundering* is based on the abuse or manipulation of the trade system. More specifically, TBML is the process whereby money is laundered by exploiting trade transactions and the financing of such transactions. As the name implies, TBML relies on trade to convert illicit financial proceeds into revenue that appears legitimate. It involves such methods as falsely documenting goods and services to move value. In this manner, large sums of money may be moved internationally or domestically.

TBML constitutes one of the three main methods by which criminals hide, move, and place illicit funds into the legitimate economy.[1] Both Fin-CEN and the FATF identify TBML as a high risk for money laundering and terrorist financing because the trade system has numerous inherent vulnerabilities that present many opportunities for criminals to launder money as well as transfer funds to terrorist groups. In fact, hundreds of billions of dollars are laundered through TBML globally every year. According to US

Customs and Border Protection, on a typical day in 2019, nearly seventy-nine thousand shipping containers and $7.3 billion worth of goods entered the country through various ports of entry.[2] This report presents the figures only for the United States; these numbers jump exponentially when considering imports worldwide. Therefore, the sheer volume of goods being transferred around the globe presents numerous opportunities for exploitation. That multiple participants are also involved in trade transactions further complicates detection and presents additional risks and challenges. Notably, multinational institutions as well as private banks have been found to play a significant role in facilitating wealth transfer through illicit trade.

The FATF did not provide an official definition for TBML until 2006. According to the FATF, TBML is "the process of disguising the proceeds of crime and moving value through the use of trade transactions in an attempt to legitimize their illicit origins."[3] Similarly, the US Department of Homeland Security defines TBML as "the process of disguising criminal proceeds through trade to legitimize their illicit origins."[4] This is accomplished through the misrepresentation of the price, quantity, or quality of both imports and exports. In this manner, criminals manipulate commercial transactions to transfer monetary value across both international and domestic borders. Therefore, rather than being a single activity, TBML refers to a variety of schemes used in combination to disguise criminal proceeds.

For example, a general TBML scheme may involve the movement of merchandise, the falsification of its value, and the misrepresentation of trade-related financial transactions. This process is generally accomplished with the assistance of complicit merchants. The overall purpose of the scheme is to disguise the origin of the illicit funds and to integrate them into the market. Once the illicit cash and the goods are exchanged, it is difficult for law enforcement to trace the source of the illicit funds.

Four specific features of TBML distinguish it from other types of money laundering and help explain the risks associated with it as well as shed light on its complexity. First, TBML generally involves international trade that spans several jurisdictions, while other forms of ML may involve only one jurisdiction. Conducting transactions across borders provides additional opportunities for criminals to take advantage of differences in the legal systems of various jurisdictions. For example, some countries may have less restrictive customs checks and less stringent AML regimes than others. Characteristics associated with modern trade, such as its high volume and speed, enhance these vulnerabilities.

Second, TBML involves intersections involving the trade sector and the finance sector; thus, criminals can take advantage of vulnerabilities in both sectors. To be effective, AML regimes must cover these sectors, and TBML investigations should involve checks and cross-referencing of data from both areas.

Third, due to its nature, international trade is inherently exposed to the vulnerabilities of the foreign exchange market. The conversion of currencies increases the opportunities for criminals to launder illegal proceeds.

Finally, another aspect of international trade that makes it more vulnerable to TBML is the interconnected supply chain. Its length and scope are exposed to numerous significant risks and threats.[5]

RECOGNITION AND SCOPE OF TBML

Not only has international trade grown in recent decades but it has done so at a much faster pace than ever before. This rapid growth in global trade has greatly increased the potential opportunities for TBML. According to many AML experts, TBML is the largest money laundering methodology in the world.[6] Yet, surprisingly, TBML does not get nearly as much attention as its counterparts. As a result, significantly more resources and countermeasures are focused instead on combating money laundering through financial institutions and via bulk cash smuggling than through TBML. Consequently, as efforts to hinder money laundering through these better-known means have become more effective in recent years, criminals have turned their attention to TBML, an ML method that has proven both effective and relatively easy to disguise, thus hindering detection. As with other potential threats to the financial system, TBML continues to evolve with financial markets and practices.

TBML hasn't been generally recognized as a significant threat for several reasons. One reason is that TBML is extremely broad, operating at both the domestic and international levels. It can involve real, completely fictitious, or simply slightly falsified trades and transactions. It also varies across supply chains and can apply to both goods and services. Furthermore, it can take many forms, including the manipulation of the price, the quality, and the quantity of such goods or services.

Another reason that TBML isn't more widely recognized is that although TBML operates in plain sight, it is very difficult to detect (as well as difficult to know the true extent and pervasiveness of the problem). Also, customs agencies have limited resources to detect suspicious trade transactions. Therefore, with the sheer number of trade transactions occurring daily, it is easy to disguise the illicit trade transactions among the legitimate ones. This chicanery becomes further complicated when legitimate and illegitimate transactions are combined and when licit and illicit funds are commingled.

According to the World Trade Organization (WTO), the value of world merchandise exports in 2018 was US$19.48 trillion, and the value of world commercial services exports was US$5.77 trillion in 2018.[7] Considering that TBML activities are hidden among these massive volumes of trade activity, it is no surprise that TBML is difficult to uncover. Moreover, even though TBML occurs in every country in the world, jurisdictions differ in their understanding, approaches, categorizations, and enforcement of TBML, further complicating efforts to establish true figures regarding its actual prevalence.

Finally, TBML techniques vary in complexity and are becoming increasingly sophisticated, thus further complicating their detection. TBML is frequently used in combination with other money laundering techniques and other crimes to further obscure the money trail. For example, TBML can involve the use of anonymous shell companies, adding greater layers of opacity. It can also implicate customs and other types of fraud, tax evasion, capital flight, export and import control laws and regulations, international sanctions, terrorist financing, and others.

COMMON TBML TECHNIQUES

As previously mentioned, TBML can take many forms. Sometimes the distinction between TBML and other forms of money laundering may not be clear. TBML practices can also differ by jurisdiction and may be based on local business practices and customs. In general, however, TBML schemes involve the following activities:

- *Over- or under-invoicing*: This involves misrepresenting the price of goods or services to transfer additional value to either the importer or the exporter. In the cases of collusion with the importer and/or the exporter, there may not be any inconsistencies between the trade documents and the shipped goods, making it virtually impossible to detect the transaction as TBML. This is one of the most common methods for laundering funds across borders, according to the FATF.
- *Multiple invoicing*: This involves invoicing one shipment several times to justify multiple payments for the same shipment of goods or delivery of services. Furthermore, using different financial institutions to make the additional payments increases the complexity of the transactions and complicates detection efforts.

- *Over- or under-shipping*: This involves shipping more or fewer goods than are invoiced. Over-shipment is often used to avoid import duties. In extreme cases, importers and exporters may collude and not ship anything at all but still proceed with falsifying documents for the non-existent transaction. This is referred to as phantom shipping.
- *Phantom or ghost shipping*: This involves "empty" shipments accompanied by false invoices and usually includes collusion with the importer. Banks and other financial institutions may unknowingly get involved with the trade financing of such shipments.
- *Obfuscation or fraudulent shipping*: This involves shipping something other than what is invoiced and includes misrepresenting either the quality or the type of goods (rather than the price of the goods). This technique can also be used with services, such as financial advice or consulting.[8]

One of the more typical TBML schemes involves using illicit proceeds to purchase goods for export, the subsequent sale of which effectively launders the proceeds.[9] To accomplish this, physical US currency is converted into a commodity, which is then exported or imported typically to another jurisdiction. Thus, no actual currency is physically moved across borders. This technique usually involves over- or under-invoicing or over- or under-shipping, where the price, quality, or quantity of the goods sold are manipulated. For example, in the case of over-invoicing, Company A ships ten laptops with a market value of $1,000 each to Company B but invoices Company B $2,000 per laptop. Company B then has a seemingly legitimate reason to transfer $20,000 to Company A, half of which is "dirty money" to be laundered. Company A thereby makes a profit of $10,000, and these criminal proceeds are now "clean." Additionally, Company A could further benefit by seeking tax incentives when exporting certain goods. Furthermore, it can evade capital controls by putting the excess proceeds in an offshore account.[10]

Likewise, the same can be done in reverse by using the TBML technique of under-invoicing. For example, Company A ships ten trucks with a market value of $100,000 each (market value of $1,000,000) to Company B but invoices Company B for just $50,000 per truck (half the market value). Company B transfers $500,000 to Company A but then sells the trucks to a dealer for $1,000,000 (market value). In this way, Company A can transfer $500,000 of dirty money to Company B. This transaction appears legitimate and would be difficult to prove otherwise. To further evade scrutiny, however, the companies would likely limit the under-invoicing to a margin of 10 percent or less.[11]

The products most often used in TBML activities include highly taxed products (such as cigarettes, alcohol, and electronics) and products having large price differentials between countries (such as pharmaceuticals and consumer goods). Therefore, legitimate companies operating in these sectors experience the greatest loss of sales and profits.[12]

Other products that are particularly susceptible to TBML are *dual-use goods*, which encompass an array of products that can be used for both civilian purposes and military applications. For example, the common chemical ammonium nitrate is used in fertilizer and in explosives. Another example is defense articles, which encompass a broad range of items that can be adapted, configured, designed, developed, or modified for military, missile, satellite, or other controlled use and may include firearms, parts and accessories, models, or software and other related technical data.[13]

TYPES OF ACTORS INVOLVED IN TBML

According to the Financial Threats Council of the Intelligence and National Security Alliance, a nonprofit organization that seeks to advance intelligence and national security priorities through public-private cooperation and information sharing, TBML generally involves three types of actors: transnational criminal organizations, terrorist groups, and corrupt foreign officials. All three groups manipulate the same weaknesses in the financial and trade systems to use them toward their own advantage, including raising and laundering funds to support their illegal activities.

Transnational criminal organizations (TCOs) and drug-trafficking organizations both frequently make use of TBML to legitimize the proceeds from their illegal activities. They do so by purchasing products for export and then selling them by way of legitimate-seeming businesses, thus cleaning their illegally acquired revenue. The frequently significant differences between the transactional price and the actual value of the product are used to pay bribes and fund continued operations. This illicit practice ultimately serves to fuel not only the illegal drug industry but also other criminal activities such as human trafficking.

Likewise, terrorist organizations, such as the Taliban, are known to utilize specific TBML techniques, including inaccurate invoicing, falsifying documents, and tax evasion. In this way, they can covertly move their assets out of the countries in which they were derived and into the countries in which they plan to carry out their operations.[14]

Finally, corrupt government officials play a significant role in the trade-based movement of funds generally and in TBML specifically. In fact, corrupt officials are key facilitators of TBML because their unique positions allow them to access the necessary information, procedures, and resources to succeed. They also have influence over law enforcement and decision-makers.

BLACK MARKET PESO EXCHANGE

The United States is the world's largest importer of illegal drugs, much of which come from Latin America. In fact, the United States is the largest cocaine market in the world.[15] This trafficking generates tens of billions of dollars annually in illicit profits that must then be laundered. This is where the Black Market Peso Exchange comes in. The BMPE is a common scheme used to launder drug proceeds from Latin America and works by combining two or more TBML techniques.

This complicated system of money laundering was initially utilized by Colombian narcotics traffickers and was subsequently adopted by Mexican cartels. It is a great example of how money launderers and other criminals adapt their methodologies to circumvent laws and regulations. In fact, the BMPE emerged after Colombia banned the US dollar in the 1960s and imposed higher taxes on imported goods. As a result, peso brokers became more common as people purchased goods with pesos they obtained from peso brokers and paid for them in foreign currency. By the 1980s, the demand for cocaine in the United States and the resulting proceeds from cocaine sales were so high that the drug cartels had a difficult time getting the money back into Colombia. Thus, peso brokers were adopted into BMPE schemes to launder drug profits and convert them into pesos. Drug traffickers today continue to use this technique, which allows them to pay their suppliers in another country without physically having to move currency across borders.

In addition to laundering dollars, the BMPE also enables Latin importers to avoid extensive import fees and taxes by smuggling products into the country. More specifically, using this system, a money broker in the United States accepts the drug dollars from a US-based agent and then provides Colombian pesos to the supplier in Colombia through Colombian merchants seeking to import US goods. The agent then uses the drug dollars to purchase those goods and ships them back to Colombia, thus allowing US-based drug traffickers to avoid the dangers of smuggling large amounts of cash across borders.[16] Broadly speaking, this system enables drug cartels in the United

States to exchange their dollars for pesos already in Colombia by selling the dollars to Colombian businessmen who seek to buy US goods for export.[17]

The following example illustrates a simplified black market peso scheme in which different trade-based money laundering techniques can be combined. Note that each successive step in this process makes proving the nexus between US dollars and narcotics ever more difficult.[18]

The arrangement begins with the smuggling of illegal drugs into the United States, typically by a Latin American drug cartel (usually based in Colombia or Mexico), that are then sold for cash (US dollars). This first step, which constitutes the riskiest one in the criminal scheme, creates an excess of cash (generally in small denominations of US currency) that cannot be easily transported or deposited without drawing attention. Since this cash would be more useful in pesos, a peso broker (or money trader), who serves as the backbone of the scheme, is needed to help convert the dollars into pesos.[19]

Next, the drug cartel must arrange with agents in the United States to sell the US dollars (at a discount) to a peso broker located outside the country (typically in Colombia). The peso broker then pays the drug cartel with pesos from his bank account in Colombia, and for this work, he receives a commission. This step effectively eliminates any further involvement of the drug cartel from the arrangement. At this point, the drug cartel has avoided the risk and costs of attempting to smuggle cash across the border and has converted its illegal drug profits into usable pesos.[20]

Furthermore, the peso broker, through his agent in the States, must "structure" the US currency—that is, break it up into smaller deposits (by using smurfs)—to avoid bank reporting requirements that are triggered when making deposits exceeding $10,000. (Structuring and smurfs are covered in detail in chapter 6.) The peso broker then deposits all this money into a US bank account.

To convert the US dollars back to pesos again, the peso broker works with a Colombian importer (who may or may not be in on the scheme) who needs US dollars to purchase goods from a US-based exporter. The peso broker's function here is to pay the US exporter (on behalf of the Colombian importer) from his US bank account. The US exporter then ships the goods to Colombia, and, finally, the Colombian importer sells the goods (which often consist of high-value items, such as electronics, auto parts, and household appliances) for pesos and repays the peso broker. Thereby, the peso broker replenishes his supply of pesos.

Even Fortune 500 corporations, including Ford, General Electric, General Motors, Hewlett-Packard, Sony, and Whirlpool, have been implicated in BMPE schemes. In these instances, appliances, cars, electronics, and other goods were first purchased with drug profits without knowledge of the sellers and then shipped to Colombia, where they were resold for pesos. Thus, drug proceeds in US dollars were converted into usable assets.[21]

The BMPE therefore is not just an effective means of money laundering but also a way for drug cartels to avoid certain risks. They can dodge those associated with having large sums of cash at international borders and bypass making large cash deposits that can trigger bank reporting requirements (such as those mandated by the Bank Secrecy Act).[22]

Although the term "Black Market Peso Exchange" once referred to a money laundering technique that was originally associated with Colombian narcotics trafficking, people in many countries now widely use its arrangements to repatriate the proceeds of various types of crimes.

CASE STUDY: USING TOYS AND PESOS TO LAUNDER DRUG MONEY

In 2012 two sisters, co-owners of a California-based toy manufacturing company called Angel Toy Company (ATC), were found to be involved in a widespread and long-running BMPE scheme. They helped launder profits for drug-trafficking organizations by structuring cash deposits under the $10,000 currency reporting requirement to avoid filing currency transaction reports (CTRs).[23]

As part of the money laundering scheme, the Los Angeles–based toy company received several million dollars in cash payments generated from Colombian narcotics trafficking. In some cases, cash payments were simply dropped off at the ATC's offices located in downtown Los Angeles; in other cases, cash deposits were made directly into the ATC's bank account. The illicit cash was broken up into smaller deposits, in a process known as structuring, to avoid bank reporting requirements and put into the financial system through smurfing. The investigation into the case revealed that over $8 million in cash was deposited into the ATC's bank account during a four-year period, with not a single transaction being more than $10,000.[24]

The drug cartel's illicit funds, which were held in the toy company's bank account, were wired to China to buy toys for import into the United States, thereby converting the proceeds of narcotics trafficking into goods. The toys, which primarily included teddy bears and other stuffed animals, were then reexported from the United States to Colombia and sold, thus moving value to the desired jurisdiction through trade in legitimate goods (in lieu of transporting US currency across the border). The proceeds from the sale of the toys in Colombia were used to reimburse the cartels in Colombian pesos. Using this method, dirty drug money in the United States was converted into clean Colombian pesos through the international purchase and sale of legitimate goods—in this case, toys. Thus, the criminals used international trade to layer and integrate their proceeds into the legitimate economy and disguise their illicit origin.[25]

Ultimately, the ATC's two co-owners and a complicit Colombian businessman were convicted and fined. The toy company was also found guilty of conspiracy to launder money.

Interestingly, a similar BMPE scheme involving another California-based toy company, Woody Toys, Inc., occurred around the same time. In that case, the husband and wife co-owners of the toy store also helped launder money for drug cartels and engaged in structuring currency transactions. Just as in the case of Angel Toy Company, the owners of Woody Toys structured bank deposits consisting of illicit drug funds into smaller payments to avoid the filing of a CTR.[26] Likewise, Woody Toys also used drug proceeds to purchase and import toys that were then shipped to merchants in Colombia and Mexico. After selling the toys, the Colombian and Mexican pesos, now clean, were remitted to the drug-trafficking organizations. In this manner, the toy company laundered approximately $3 million for the Mexican and Colombian drug cartels.

Both BMPE schemes used a common TBML method in which goods were exported at overvalued prices in return for inflated payments from importers overseas. Such strategies benefit drug cartels and other criminal organizations by giving them a means to launder illicit funds through the international trade system. These maneuvers also give foreign retailers access to discounted US currency, thus enabling the foreign retailers to avoid steep exchange rates and other fees. Additionally, complicit companies benefit from such ventures through increased sales volume and cash flow.[27]

Trade-based methods of money laundering are incredibly difficult to detect in part because customs officials cannot possibly check and verify every shipment. Also, customs officials have no way of knowing the fair market value of all the various goods that enter and leave a country daily. For example, they have no way of knowing if the toy companies' plush teddy bears are worth ten, thirty, or a hundred dollars.

RED FLAGS ASSOCIATED WITH TBML

Given the nature of TBML activity, including the type and variety of transactions involved, mitigation of TBML risk is particularly tricky for financial institutions. Banks and other financial institutions are at a further disadvantage because they have limited information about trade transactions. Furthermore, a bank has no way to physically check shipments or confirm services, so it ultimately is left to rely on documents. Therefore, banks, including seasoned banking professionals, often find it very difficult to verify whether a documented deal is falsified, the price or quantity of goods is mispresented, or a customs declaration is forged.

Numerous regulatory authorities, standard-setting organizations, and industry associations across the globe—including the FATF, the Wolfsberg Group, and FinCEN, among others—have published red flags that are indicative of TBML. In some cases, red flags have been grouped according to different categories of TBML, reflecting the complexity of the problem.

To mitigate TBML risk, banks, other financial institutions, and companies must be especially vigilant to warning signs and aggressively scrutinize all transactions that appear to be trades in various goods. It's particularly important to look for signs of overpricing and underpricing, especially with respect to those transactions between shell companies or those involving high-risk jurisdictions. Inconsistencies or discrepancies in documentation, including receipts, invoices, and contracts, are another big indicator that something is amiss. Ignoring warning signs could expose an organization to inadvertent wrongdoing, potential fines and penalties, and reputational damage.

Some examples of red flags that commonly occur in TBML include inconsistencies between the company's line of business and the background of the parties involved or the type of products sold; shipments of goods that are inconsistent (either in size, frequency, destination, or type of goods) with the exporter's or importer's regular business activity or that exceed the known capacity of the shipping container, tanker, or other vessel; and shipping routes (including origin, destination, or pass-through countries) that are abnormal, or inconsistent with expected routes, or involve high-risk jurisdictions.[28]

Finally, legal entities, such as anonymous shell companies, are frequently used in trade-based money laundering schemes to provide a facade of legitimacy to trade transactions and money transfers. As a result, red flags associated with the illicit use of shell companies may also be indicative of TBML activities.

CONCLUSION

The US Treasury Department, in its "2018 National Money Laundering Risk Assessment," identified TBML as one of the most commonly used and one of the most difficult to detect methods of money laundering. Although TBML schemes vary greatly, the basic mechanism remains the same—the misuse of the trade system to transfer value and disguise the source of illicit wealth.

As with the other money laundering methods described in this book, the large transfers of wealth that occur with TBML, and that typically flow out of developing and emerging economies and into more developed nations, are especially harmful to those nations with weaker economies and already high levels of corruption and other crime. According to a PwC report pub- lished in January 2015, 80 percent of illicit financial flows from developing countries are accomplished through TBML. Furthermore, a 2013 study con- ducted by Global Financial Integrity focusing on fifty-five developing coun- tries found that illicit financial outflows, most of which were in the form of trade mis-invoicing, came to an estimated $947 billion in 2011 alone. That figure constitutes approximately 3.7 percent of the combined GDP in these countries.[29] Such TBML-enabled capital flight, which occurs when money rapidly flows out of a country, ultimately results in devastating costs and losses for these countries, which can least handle them, and reduces funds for critical domestic investment and other economic activity.

TBML doesn't just affect developing countries. This illicit practice neg- atively impacts wealthier nations, including the United States, as well. For example, these schemes create barriers to entrepreneurship, rob legitimate companies of profits, and disrupt product supply chains, further harming lawful businesses and the consumers that rely on them.[30] Furthermore, TBML undermines national foreign policy objectives and national security by enabling the corruption of government officials and by eroding revenues that would otherwise go to legitimate government activities. TBML is also used to provide financial support to many governments' biggest foes— terrorists and TCOs.

Threats to the financial system will continue to evolve, and TBML is no exception. Trade-based money laundering exists in every country. In fact, its effectiveness increases when it is conducted across borders. Therefore, TBML is very much a global problem that requires a global response. According to a research report by the Organization for Economic Cooperation and Devel- opment (OECD), global markets offer criminal organizations new means to reduce their overall risks by diversifying into profitable activities with a low probability of being detected.[31] Although attention to TBML has increased somewhat after the FATF published its initial report on the topic, *Trade Based Money Laundering*, in 2006, much more remains to be done.

A lack of information is a major obstacle in the fight against TBML and other forms of money laundering and financial crime. Transparency and greater access to applicable information, such as trade data, shipping records, other pricing information, and relevant information on exporters, importers, and company ownership, would prove immensely useful.

Any strategy to combat and prevent TBML, while still permitting genuine trade to continue unfettered, must start with a thorough understanding of TBML methods, practices, and associated risks. Thus, as with other money laundering methodologies, a coordinated international effort that includes increased global transparency, more effective communications, and data sharing among regulatory bodies, law enforcement, and financial institutions is required to effectively address this highly complex and destructive global problem.

NOTES

1. FATF, "Trade Based Money Laundering" (see chap. 1, n. 51).
2. Sheldon Whitehouse, Bill Cassidy, and Marco Rubio, *Trade-Based Money Laundering: U.S. Government Has Worked with Partners to Combat the Threat, but Could Strengthen Its Efforts*, GAO-20-333 (Washington, DC: Government Accountability Office, April 2020), https://www.gao.gov/assets/710/705679.pdf.
3. Whitehouse, Cassidy, and Rubio.
4. US Department of Homeland Security (DHS), "Trade Transparency," accessed September 22, 2020, https://www.dhs.gov/trade-transparency.
5. Asia/Pacific Group (APG) on Money Laundering, *APG Typology Report on Trade Based Money Laundering* (Sydney: APG on Money Laundering, July 20, 2012), https://www.fatf-gafi.org/media/fatf/documents/reports/Trade_Based_ML_APGReport.pdf.
6. US Congress, Senate, Caucus on International Narcotics Control, *The Buck Stops Here: Improving U.S. Anti-Money Laundering Practices*, 113th Congress, 1st sess. (Washington, DC: US Senate, April 2013), https://www.drugcaucus.senate.gov/sites/default/files/Money%20Laundering%20Report%20-%20Final.pdf; and US Treasury Department, *2018 National Money Laundering Risk Assessment* (Washington, DC: Treasury Department, 2018), https://home.treasury.gov/system/files/136/2018NMLRA_12-18.pdf.
7. WTO, *World Trade Statistical Review, 2019* (Geneva: WTO, 2019), 17, https://www.wto.org/english/res_e/statis_e/wts2019_e/wts2019_e.pdf, accessed September 25, 2020.
8. Bankers Association for Finance and Trade (BAFT), *Combatting Trade Based Money Laundering: Rethinking the Approach* (Washington, DC: BAFT, 2017), https://www.amlc.nl/wp-content/uploads/2018/11/baft17_tmbl_paper.pdf.
9. US Treasury Department, *2018 National Money Laundering*.
10. Paul Hamilton, "Trade-Based Money Laundering—and How to Combat It," *AML Knowledge Centre* (blog), accessed September 24, 2020, https://aml-knowledge-centre.org/trade-based-money-laundering-and-how-to-combat-it/.
11. Hamilton.
12. Intelligence and National Security Alliance (INSA), Financial Threats Council, *Using Intelligence to Combat Trade-Based Money Laundering* (Arlington, VA: INSA Financial

Threats Council, April 2020), 6, https://www.insaonline.org/wp-content/uploads/2020
/04/INSA_WP_TBML.pdf.

13. University of Pittsburgh, Office of Trade Compliance, "Export of Defense Articles
and Services (ITAR)," rev. September 9, 2021, https://www.tradecompliance.pitt.edu
/manual-guidelines/guidance-documents/export-defense-articles-and-services-itar#:
~:text=Defense%20Article%20means%20any%20item,technical%20data%20related
%20to%20items, accessed September 30, 2021.

14. INSA Financial Threats Council, *Using Intelligence*.

15. US Treasury Department, *2018 National Money Laundering*.

16. US Senate, *Buck Stops Here*.

17. US Treasury Department, "FinCEN Advisory: Colombian Black Market Peso Exchange,"
9 (November 1997), https://www.fincen.gov/sites/default/files/shared/advisu9.pdf.

18. US Treasury Department.

19. Lane Powell, "Money Laundering through the Black Market Peso Exchange," *Lexology*,
June 12, 2018, https://www.lexology.com/library/detail.aspx?g=acf393a5-7fea-49ac-a51f
-17afab60a75a.

20. Powell.

21. Shelley, *Dark Commerce*, 144–45.

22. Powell, "Money Laundering."

23. US Immigration and Customs Enforcement (ICE), "LA Toy Company Owners Sentenced
in International Money Laundering Scheme," Newsroom, US Department of Homeland
Security, January 31, 2012, https://www.ice.gov/news/releases/la-toy-company-owners
-sentenced-international-money-laundering-scheme.

24. ICE.

25. Asia/Pacific Group, *APG Typology Report*.

26. ICE, "Co-owner of Los Angeles-Area Toy Company Sentenced in Drug Money Laundering Case," Newsroom, US Department of Homeland Security, May 6, 2013, https://
www.ice.gov/news/releases/co-owner-los-angeles-area-toy-company-sentenced-drug
-money-laundering-case.

27. ICE.

28. FinCEN, "Advisory to Financial Institutions on Filing Suspicious Activity Reports
Regarding Trade-Based Money Laundering," US Treasury Department, FIN-2010-A001,
February 18, 2010, https://www.fincen.gov/resources/advisories/fincen-advisory-fin
-2010-a001; and Asia/Pacific Group, *APG Typology Report*.

29. Shelley, *Dark Commerce*, 143.

30. INSA Financial Threats Council, *Using Intelligence*.

31. Rena S. Miller, Liana W. Rosen, and James K. Jackson, *Trade-Based Money Laundering:
Overview and Policy Issues*, CRS Report no. R44541 (Washington, DC: Congressional
Research Service, June 22, 2016), 4, https://fas.org/sgp/crs/misc/R44541.pdf.

CHAPTER 4

PRICEY PARKING FOR ILLICIT FUNDS

*Money Laundering through
Luxury Real Estate*

As with just about anything of value, real estate—be it in the form of land or buildings, either residential or commercial in nature—can be misused to launder dirty money. However, the high-end real estate sector is most prone for use in money laundering. Penthouses in Manhattan, luxury condos in Miami, stately residences in London, vineyard estates in the south of France, and even gleaming shopping centers in Dubai—all have been used to launder illicit funds. The higher the price of the real estate, the more money can be laundered through it. Therefore, although all real estate markets are vulnerable to money laundering and experience negative consequences as a result, high-end properties in major real estate markets around the world, such as London, Toronto, and New York, are the prime targets.

Real estate comes with many benefits, making it as attractive to criminals as it is to any investor. As a result, real estate constitutes a widely used means of moving illicit funds. In fact, it is one of the oldest known ways to launder criminal proceeds. The FATF in the last few years has noted the real estate sector is one of the many vehicles criminals and criminal organizations use to launder their ill-gotten gains.[1] According to one of its reports, real estate made up approximately 30 percent of criminal assets that were confiscated globally between 2011 and 2013.[2]

Real estate investments have been used for nefarious purposes by a wide range of actors, from the governing elite looking to launder the proceeds of grand corruption to transnational criminal organizations seeking to hide their illicit gains offshore. Paul Manafort, Teodoro Obiang, the Russian mob, and corrupt Venezuelan officials have all made headlines laundering money through real estate in recent years.

The lack of information regarding the beneficial ownership behind substantial financial transactions facilitates real estate laundering. The ease with which anonymous companies, trusts, and foundations can acquire property and launder money correlates with the insufficient rules and enforcement practices in major markets.[3]

Certainly not all offshore ownership is illicit, and not all people who purchase real estate through companies are criminals. However, foreign investment in real estate by corporate entities established in secrecy jurisdictions has been found especially problematic.

Although perhaps seemingly benign, money laundering through real estate is another form of capital flight that has significant negative impacts, both at the local level and internationally. It contributes to the ever-widening income disparities that affect all communities globally.

WHY LAUNDER MONEY THROUGH REAL ESTATE?

Several characteristics about the real estate sector make it attractive for potential misuse by both money launderers and terrorist financiers. Laundering illicit funds through real estate is not complicated to do and does not require any specific expertise. Therefore, it provides a relatively easy and straightforward means of integrating criminal proceeds into the legitimate economy.

Real estate can be bought with cash or purchased through a variety of other financing and credit options as well as via opaque corporate structures, including trusts, foundations, and shell companies. Many of these methods provide anonymity and can be used to disguise true ownership. Since real estate transactions are subject to far less scrutiny than their financial sector counterparts, this money laundering method provides an overall low risk of detection for those seeking to remain under the radar.

Real estate constitutes a generally safe investment and has the potential of increasing in value over time. Large amounts of money can be parked in a high-end property and then reinvested elsewhere, presenting a low risk of capital loss. Real property can be used as a second residence or a vacation home, or improved and sold for a profit, or rented out to generate income, making it very functional. One can also simply hold on to it and bequeath it in a will. In some instances, investing in real estate in another jurisdiction can bestow residency or a path to citizenship. Moreover, purchasing real estate in wealthy countries, such as the United States, allows criminals from corrupt jurisdictions to transfer their illicit capital into a more stable economy.

Furthermore, real estate can provide many tax advantages, legal, illegal, and otherwise. In addition to serving as a tax shelter, real estate can also be used to evade paying taxes. Also, the high value of luxury properties and the investment potential in high-end real estate projects enable the laundering of large sums of wealth, sometimes in a single transaction.

Additionally, owning real estate in desirable zip codes, such as Beverly Hills or Notting Hill, or possessing expensive leisure properties, such as a vineyard or a ski resort, can increase one's social status and confer prestige. Such attributes may be desirable even for criminals, including socially conscious and status-seeking money launderers. Moreover, real estate provides the veneer of legitimacy for the owner.

For all these reasons, illegal profits have effectively been laundered through land, expensive homes, and other businesses for centuries. As long as the advantages pertaining to real estate remain, criminals will continue to use it as a means of laundering dirty funds.

FACTORS THAT ENABLE MONEY TO BE LAUNDERED THROUGH REAL ESTATE

In addition to the features that make real estate an attractive and convenient ML vehicle, the real estate sector has many vulnerabilities, including legal and regulatory gaps, that make it particularly susceptible to money laundering. Most vulnerabilities stem from the fact that the real estate sector is not subject to the same strict AML/KYC requirements that banks are. As a result, real estate professionals generally do not perform due diligence checks on parties to real estate transactions, including enhanced due diligence checks on parties that may pose a higher risk, such as PEPs. Additionally, sanctions screening is not required, nor are SARs mandated. This results in a huge gap whereby corrupt funds can easily enter the US economy through the real estate sector.

Furthermore, there is no comprehensive regulation or supervision of real estate professionals regarding AML, even though these associated businesses are considered high risks in facilitating ML. Consequently, real estate professionals may end up as witting or unwitting middlemen in transactions involving illicit real estate purchases.

This lack of regulation has made the US real estate market a big destination for corrupt funds from abroad. In fact, *New York Magazine* characterized

Manhattan real estate as the new "Swiss bank account."[4] A prime example is Columbus Circle's former Time Warner Center, now known as Deutsche Bank Center, in Manhattan, a favorite among foreign nationals. More than a dozen overseas owners of multimillion-dollar condos in the building became the subjects of foreign government investigations. One of these individuals was the former Russian senator and banker Vitaly Malkin, who owned a $15.6 million condominium in the building through an anonymous corporate entity. Malkin later was investigated in multiple countries for his involvement in a number of significant financial crimes.[5] Additionally, he owned a ski chalet in France that he had purchased through an anonymous entity and for which he was ultimately brought to court and ordered to pay millions of dollars in unpaid back taxes.

Similarly, Miami is considered a go-to real estate destination for wealthy international buyers from Russia, China, Venezuela, and Brazil. In Florida, newly constructed luxury condos were the property of choice for stashing illicit wealth.

Most recently, however, London has taken the "global top spot" for the sale of luxury residential real estate, with wealthy foreigners buying more homes there than in any other city in the world, according to the *Financial Times*. In fact, even coronavirus travel restrictions and lockdowns have not decreased the demand for so-called super-prime properties, which are properties listed at $10 million and greater. Of these properties, the average sale price was a hefty $18.6 million, and most went to Russian, French, and Chinese purchasers.[6] Thus, it is no coincidence that London also happens to be a hot spot for real estate laundering.[7]

Real estate professionals often meet face-to-face with clients and are therefore in a prime position to collect identification information from their clients and to conduct basic background checks and screenings. They are also in a unique position to identify and report unusual and suspicious transactions relating to real estate purchases. Therefore, subjecting the real estate sector to AML/KYC requirements, such as CDD and SARs, would not only help identify criminals seeking to launder their funds through US real estate but also stem the flow of illicit funds into the country's economy.

HOW IS MONEY LAUNDERED THROUGH REAL ESTATE?

As noted in chapter 1, the three stages of money laundering are placement, layering, and integration. When real estate is used in the laundering process, it generally constitutes the final stage of the laundering cycle because purchasing real property is one way to integrate criminal funds into the formal economy. The income derived from the sale or rental of the property then appears as though it is from a legitimate source.

An analysis of domestic and international money laundering cases demonstrates ten common, although by no means exhaustive, methods by which illicit funds have been laundered through real estate.[8] Criminals can also use a combination of these techniques to further disguise the money trail. An understanding of these strategies helps identify how money launderers use real estate and can assist in detecting and deterring future money laundering activity.

Method One

This method incorporates two distinct techniques—cash purchases, whether for partial or full payment, and the concurrent structuring of cash deposits—in the easiest and most common way to launder money through the real estate sector. Although it's entirely possible to buy a property entirely with cash, a launderer is more likely to arrange for several smaller payments, all less than the currency reporting threshold, and often from various bank accounts.

Method Two

Obtaining loans and mortgages is another common method used in real estate laundering because these financial transactions can serve as cover for illegal funds. Furthermore, the repayment of a mortgage or loan allows the payer to mix licit and illicit funds. This method simply involves applying for a mortgage and then settling the mortgage in full shortly thereafter. Although taking out a mortgage is itself not a red flag, banks and other lenders consider settling a large mortgage after a short period a red flag.

Method Three

Launderers can also use third parties, such as friends, business associates, or family members, to buy real estate on their behalf. In this case, the launderer supplies the funds for the property's purchase to a third party, which then purchases the property and becomes the legal owner of the property; however, the launderer ultimately controls the property. Money launderers who have a criminal record or whose name appears on a sanctions or blacklist would use this route. This method permits the launderers to avoid any direct involvement in the transaction and in the money laundering process.

Method Four

Shell companies, front companies, trusts, foundations, and other entity structures (established either in the United States or overseas) can also be used to purchase real estate and launder illicit funds. This laundering method works similar to using third parties: the properties are held in the name of the legal entities, allowing the launderers to distance themselves from ownership and thus to maintain their anonymity.

Method Five

Likewise, professional facilitators, or gatekeepers, such as accountants, financial advisers, lawyers, real estate agents, and trust and company service providers, can (wittingly or unwittingly) help criminals launder money through real estate. Such services can also provide anonymity to the launderer and add distance between the launderer and his or her financial activity and assets. These facilitators also impart apparent legitimacy to the transaction. Furthermore, launderers can hire multiple professionals throughout the process to further complicate the money trail.

Some examples of the services that professional facilitators offer, and that can be used to further money laundering activity through the use of real estate, include the following:

- establishing and maintaining domestic or foreign legal entity structures
- facilitating the setup and transfer of the ownership of property, including to third parties
- assisting with or conducting transactions on behalf of the criminal
- receiving and transferring funds
- creating financial arrangements
- providing access to financial institutions and other service providers
- offering financial, tax, and legal advice

Method Six

Another laundering method involves using illicit funds to purchase real property, which can be either residential or commercial in nature, for the purpose of conducting criminal activity, such as sex trafficking or the production of illegal narcotics. The revenue generated can be leveraged to purchase additional real estate and to grow the illicit business.

Method Seven

Money can also be laundered through real estate by renting properties to generate rental income. Using this method, the launderer legitimizes his or her ill-gotten gains by providing the tenant with illicit funds to cover the rent payments, either partially or in full. In this way, the launderer uses the tenant to help wash the launderer's dirty funds.

In another version of this scheme, a criminal may purchase a property in the name of a third party and then pretend to rent the property from the third party and pay the rent using illicit funds. This method serves to disguise both the illicit funds and the property's ownership.

And in yet a third iteration of this scheme, criminals can create a fictious rental account and deposit their illicit funds into the account as rent, thereby giving the appearance of legitimate rental income. These illicit funds can be commingled with legitimate rental income in one rental account and thus be integrated into the financial sector.

Method Eight

Another technique to launder money through real estate involves manipulating property values by purchasing and selling real estate at prices above or below its market value. It also includes the collusion of buyers, sellers, and/ or other third parties, such as real estate agents and lawyers, to underestimate or overestimate property values. The difference between the actual price paid and the stated value is settled with undisclosed cash payments. This is analogous to the over- and under-invoicing techniques used in trade-based money laundering.

On the one hand, *undervaluation* involves recording the property value on a contract of sale as less than the actual market price. The difference between the contract price of the property and its actual value is secretly made up using illicit funds. This enables the criminal-purchaser to claim that the contract price paid is consistent with his or her legitimate financial means.

Overvaluation, on the other hand, involves assigning a higher value to the real estate than its actual worth to obtain as large a loan as possible. The larger the loan that can be obtained, the greater the amount of illicit funds that can be laundered in paying off the debt. With this technique, false documentation regarding the true value of the property may be submitted with the loan application. The launderer then repays the loan plus interest with illicit funds.

Method Nine

The resale of real estate in quick succession is another commonly used laundering technique. Selling the property multiple times serves to confuse the audit trail. A related version of this strategy includes what is known as *parking* the property. In this scheme, one buys a property and keeps it for a time before reselling it at a higher value.

Method Ten

Finally, foreign individuals and TCOs buy real estate overseas to hide their wealth from authorities, including tax authorities, in their home country(ies). In such cases, they also use third parties to further conceal the actual ownership of the properties.

GOLDEN VISAS OFFER GOLDEN BENEFITS WITH A GOLDEN PRICE TAG

Many countries, especially those that rely on leisure and tourism for revenue, seek new ways to bring in capital and bolster their economies. Citizenship by investment and residency by investment, often referred to as "golden visas," are national programs designed to attract foreign capital. These programs offer fast-tracked residency or citizenship rights (for example, Cyprus once granted full citizenship in the European Union, a program that has since been abolished as unlawful) in exchange for purchasing real property over a certain amount or for making a significant financial investment in a specific type of business or in a particular low-income area.

A small number of jurisdictions have offered such investment programs for a few decades. The first residency-by-investment program was launched in St. Kitts and Nevis in 1984 and grants investors a fast track to residency for making investments of $250,000.[9] The popularity of these programs has grown in recent years, particularly following the 2008 financial crisis when countries needed additional ways to support their economies. According to Henley & Partners, a firm that helps customers in residence and citizenship planning, more than a hundred countries now have investment migration programs. In fact, high-net-worth individuals have shown an increased interest and demand for these sorts of programs.

Of course, while people may have legitimate reasons for acquiring residency or citizenship certificates (e.g., to study or work in another country), such schemes are also subject to exploitation, which raises concerns about money laundering as well as corruption. The combination of economies that are desperate for capital along with the ease of making significant real estate investments with ill-gotten funds is a recipe for illicit activity. The European Parliament and the OECD, which works to promote economic growth worldwide, have expressed concerns that residency and citizenship programs could assist financial crimes, such as money laundering and tax evasion; could further enable the free movement of criminals and terrorists; and could allow wealthy individuals from Russia, Iran, and Syria to dodge economic sanctions.[10] In fact, the European Parliament urged the EU member states to discontinue such programs since they so quickly and easily allow wealthy foreigners to attain EU citizenship.

Currently, the Chinese are by far the biggest purchasers of both visas and passports, followed by Russians.[11] The two countries already suffer significant capital flight, corruption, and money laundering. Coincidentally, or perhaps not, the majority of the countries currently offering attractive investment migration programs also rank highly as tax havens and secrecy jurisdictions. In 2018 the Tax Justice Network (according to its Financial Secrecy Index) noted that fifty-six high-risk jurisdictions offer passports and residency in exchange for financial payment.[12]

THE REAL IMPACT OF REAL ESTATE MONEY LAUNDERING

Although the true scale of money laundering is difficult to estimate accurately, undoubtedly such criminal financial flows take a socioeconomic toll and have corresponding security implications. In addition to the impacts of money laundering generally, a number of specific and unique consequences are associated with money laundering when using real estate, particularly in cases of foreign investment and overseas buyers.

In recent years, eastern European and Russian investors have held the largest share of high-end residential properties, followed by Middle Eastern, North African, and Chinese purchasers.[13] All of their respective regions of origin have had historically high levels of corruption, according to Transparency International's Corruption Perceptions Index.[14]

More specifically, the extent of the ramifications and the negative impacts on a particular area are most visible in its local housing market. The funneling of illicit funds into the real estate market result in the following damaging effects: distortions in resource allocation and prices (i.e., the availability and affordability of housing, respectively), unfair competition, potentially displaced legitimate activities, negative impacts on direct foreign investment, increased corruption, real estate sector volatility, and widened income gaps.[15]

Inflows of corrupt capital impact property prices not only in the communities where the corrupt funds are directly invested but also in the surrounding communities. The influx of illicit funds raises average real estate prices, making home prices well beyond the reach of many working- and middle-class families. This results in a ripple effect that goes down the property price chain. As housing becomes less and less affordable, residents move out of their communities and into surrounding areas, which in turn drives up the prices of real estate in those nearby communities. This shift also inevitably reduces the availability of affordable housing in those nearby communities and causes a shortage of office space as well. The bubbles in the real estate market that result from rapid inflows of corrupt funds impact both renters and buyers.[16]

Furthermore, given the interest of foreign buyers in high-end properties, developers' priorities shift away from more modestly priced homes toward luxury real estate. Since these foreign-owned homes are typically second, third, and even fourth residences, many of the purchased properties remain vacant after purchase, creating what are known as ghost neighborhoods and ghost communities. The presence of unoccupied houses with foreign owners affects local businesses and community life.

Money laundering through real estate supports a wide range of corrupt and illicit activities. It has been widely reported that drug traffickers dealing in fentanyl had invested millions of dollars in drug proceeds in the Vancouver real estate market, enabling the criminals not only to launder their funds and gain significant interest on them but also to establish a stronghold in the city.[17]

Although money laundering is recognized as a crime risk, not much attention is given to the substantial security implications that money laundering poses. For instance, members of terrorist organizations also make use of laundering techniques that focus on real estate. In particular, members of the Taliban have invested funds in a gated, residential community located outside Afghanistan. Additionally, numerous accounts show how the Taliban and the Haqqani network, an Afghan guerrilla insurgent group that is an offshoot of the Taliban, have used illicit real estate transactions to move money around the world, particularly through Dubai. Significantly, a 2016 FATF report identified major vulnerabilities for terror financing in the high-end real estate sector in the United States that present major national security concerns.[18]

FINCEN TAKES AIM WITH GEOGRAPHIC
TARGETING ORDERS

The United States has historically been a favored destination for laundered funds due to its stable financial system, strong rule of law, and sturdy real estate market. The Panama Papers leak in 2016 spotlighted how US real estate has become a magnet for those who seek to launder illicit funds. Reports uncovered several examples of individuals who had been linked to bribery, corruption, embezzlement, tax evasion, and other financial crimes in their home countries and who, in the name of a shell company or a nominee, purchased residences in large cities throughout the United States.

To address this concern, the FinCEN director issued real estate Geographic Targeting Orders (GTOs) in January 2016. Pursuant to the Bank Secrecy Act, the GTOs impose data collection and reporting requirements for transactions greater than a specified value. The orders applied only to certain title insurance companies and initially required them to identify the natural persons behind companies engaged in all-cash purchases (referring to transactions that do not involve external financing and originally did not apply to wire transfers, a loophole that has since been closed) of luxury residential real estate located in the borough of Manhattan and in Miami-Dade County. Title insurance companies were to report to FinCEN all transactions conducted exclusively in cash and exceeding $3 million in Manhattan or $1 million in Miami-Dade County along with the identification of the beneficial owners behind the transactions.[19] The difference in the purchase price limits between the two areas reflected their real estate market values.

FinCEN reviews, studies, and tracks the data reported in GTOs. In August 2017, FinCEN issued an advisory noting that over 30 percent of high-value, all-cash real estate purchases in New York City and several other major metropolitan locations were conducted by individuals who were previously the subject of a SAR and therefore already suspected of involvement in illicit dealings. FinCEN's finding thus corroborated the value of collecting such information.

Due to the useful information derived from the GTOs, FinCEN has reissued and expanded these orders several times since their initial issuance, even though by statute they are supposed to be temporary measures and effective for up to 180 days. In addition to expanding the number of reporting jurisdictions in the subsequent GTOs, other changes include adding wire transfers as a form of "cash payment" and listing cryptocurrency as a payment method for real estate.

Furthermore, the GTOs have also updated the purchase threshold amount. This threshold previously differed by jurisdiction; now a threshold of $300,000 applies to all title companies in the twelve major metropolitan areas currently subject to reporting. The areas identified in the GTOs include Boston, Chicago, Dallas-Fort Worth, Honolulu, Las Vegas, Los Angeles, Miami, New York City, San Antonio, San Diego, San Francisco, and Seattle.[20] These high-end real estate markets are considered as a particularly high risk for real estate laundering because criminals favor locations with high-value properties.

The GTOs clearly provide useful data to FinCEN, which analyzes this information and uses it to identify money laundering and other financial crime vulnerabilities in the financial industry. However, whether the GTOs will be made permanent remains to be seen. In the meantime, some experts have pointed out that the GTOs, whether permanent or temporary, won't discourage criminals from engaging in the US real estate market. Instead, those who seek to circumvent the orders will simply purchase real estate outside the target areas, take out a loan, or forgo the use of a title insurance company.

Although certainly a step in the right direction, FinCEN's GTOs do not go far enough. FinCEN director Kenneth Blanco also has acknowledged that the United States is increasingly perceived as a haven for money launderers both domestically and abroad, noting that anonymous shell companies pose a key vulnerability. Likewise, in a report published in 2020, the US Treasury Department emphasized the risk that anonymous companies or *strawmen*, who stand in for the actual owner of such companies, can use real estate transactions to purchase assets of high value that remain relatively stable. This risk applies to both domestic and foreign purchases and is especially pronounced in all-cash real estate transactions because information on the source of the funds is not collected nor is the identification of a beneficial owner required. According to the report, "Anonymity in real estate purchases can be abused in the same way as anonymity in financial services."[21]

Besides the exclusive US real estate markets targeted by the GTOs, markets in London, Paris, Toronto, Sydney, Doha, Singapore, and Hong Kong, as well as a handful of other international cities, are also widely reported to have high instances of money laundering through real estate transactions.[22] Governments around the world have started various attempts to stem the purchase of luxury properties with illicit funds; however, unless and until the issue of anonymous ownership is effectively dealt with, such activity will only continue to increase.

In fact, as in many countries, despite the measures taken throughout the EU member states to stem the laundering of illicit funds through real estate, it remains a significant threat in that region. The UK property market in particular has increasingly become a major target of money launderers. In fact, the UK government issued a report in December 2020 that noted its real estate is now deemed a high risk for money laundering, up from a medium risk rating just three years prior. The UK real estate markets considered most at risk are London, Edinburgh, and several other university towns due to the higher value of real estate in these areas.[23]

Besides the United States and the United Kingdom, other countries identified as primary targets of real estate launderers include Canada, Germany, Singapore, and Australia.[24] In Canada, the scenic west coast city of Vancouver is one of the most sought-after, as well as one of the most expensive, real estate markets in the world. Recent government reports commissioned by the province of British Columbia indicate that not only is money laundering in the Vancouver real estate sector a huge problem but also organized criminal gangs are to blame and are increasingly pricing residents out of the market. These gangs include Mexico's Sinaloa Cartel and Iranian and Chinese criminal networks, with the latter having purchased properties in the most fashionable neighborhoods in Vancouver.[25] In Australia, a mysterious Chinese native had bought six houses valued at a total of $37 million yet did not live in any of them. Vacant luxury homes are a common indicator of money laundering through real property.[26]

These countries aren't the only ones where money launderers have targeted the real estate sector, however. Unfortunately, money laundering through property transactions is on the rise in many other countries around the world.[27]

CASE STUDY: GREED, EMBEZZLEMENT, AND REAL ESTATE MONEY LAUNDERING

The 1Malaysia Development Berhad (1MDB) case is one of the biggest financial scandals in history. Originally established to finance infrastructure and promote economic development in Malaysia, 1MDB was an investment fund set up in 2009 with the assistance of Malaysian financier Low Taek Jho (more commonly known as Jho Low) and was owned by the country's Ministry of Finance. Najib Razak, who was at that time the newly appointed prime minister of Malaysia, chaired the fund's advisory board until 2016.

The fund raised billions of dollars in bonds for investment projects and joint ventures. However, Jho Low, Najib Razak, and other high-level officials of the fund, along with their associates, have been accused of embezzling billions of dollars from the fund. According to the US Department of Justice, $4.5 billion was siphoned to offshore bank accounts and shell companies, many of which were ultimately linked to Jho Low. The funds were then laundered through the purchase of US and UK real estate, luxury assets, works of art, and the production of the 2013 movie *The Wolf of Wall Street* by a company cofounded by Riza Aziz, Najib's stepson and a friend of Jho Low's. Malaysian authorities claim that another $4.3 billion or more is still missing. These funds were intended to improve the lives and well-being of the Malaysian people.

Low allegedly attempted to launder the embezzled funds through multiple countries—including the United States, the United Kingdom, and Switzerland—and a network of shell corporations, a strategy that has become the norm in cases of money laundering, corruption, and other financial crimes.[28] The US properties that have since been tied to Jho Low include a Beverly Hills Hotel and two multimillion-dollar condos located in New York City—all purchased through corporate entities. One condo is a luxury four-bedroom penthouse on the seventy-sixth floor of the former Time Warner/Deutsche Bank Center in Manhattan, and the other is a four-bedroom condo in a trendy part of SoHo.

In October 2019, the DOJ reached a combined settlement of its civil forfeiture cases to recover more than $700 million in assets that Jho Low and his family had acquired using the misappropriated funds from 1MDB. The assets subject to the settlement included real estate in Beverly Hills, New York, and London, as well as tens of millions of dollars in business investments. The settlement, which denies Low access to the pilfered funds, is meant to send a signal that the United States will not be a safe haven for the proceeds of corruption.

This strategy, and other money laundering schemes utilizing similar types of methods, relied on the various loopholes and deficiencies in the current legal framework to move large sums of illicit funds through various accounts and across multiple jurisdictions, and to purchase real estate anonymously through corporate entities. This was further enabled by middlemen and other intermediaries, including real estate professionals, lawyers, and title companies, without whom this scheme would not have been possible. That financial crimes are occurring on such a grand scale and in plain sight is a clear indication that the current AML regime simply isn't effective and that real estate professionals and other intermediaries should be subject to comprehensive AML/KYC requirements.

WAYS TO PREVENT MONEY LAUNDERING
THROUGH REAL ESTATE

Money laundering through real estate can be dealt with and prevented in three specific ways: increasing transparency, such as through asset declaration requirements for public officials; regulating the critical gatekeeper professions; and instituting mandatory public registers.

Requiring greater transparency about the salaries of government officials and their ownership interests prior to taking office would make it notably more difficult for them to secretly amass wealth through corrupt practices while serving in their official positions. At the very least, it would allow the public to question their finances. Such public scrutiny would serve as a strong deterrent.[29]

The gatekeeping professions are uniquely positioned to obtain information and to prevent money laundering as well as other financial crimes. Such requirements as money laundering prevention training; mandated customer checks and cross-checks, including identifying beneficial owners and verifying their source of funds; and obligations to file SARs (which are known as suspicious transaction reports in a number of countries outside the United States) would make it much more difficult for illicit actors to engage in money laundering and other schemes.[30]

Last, central property registers should be mandatory. At a minimum, the information should include the location of the property or properties, the full name and date of birth of the beneficial owner(s), and a description of the form of ownership or control exercised. These details should also be kept up to date. At the very least, such information should be available both to financial institutions (so they can share information and better meet AML/KYC obligations, such as due diligence and sanctions screening) and to law enforcement authorities. Such registers would not only provide greater accountability but also make investigations much more efficient and effective by better enabling law enforcement to connect the dots as they conduct investigations.[31]

MITIGATING RISK BY IDENTIFYING SUSPICIOUS ACTIVITY

Mitigating risk and detecting suspicious activity require a familiarity with the normal conduct of business and the ability to identify unusual or suspicious patterns. Suspicious activity generally falls into three categories: customer risk, transaction risk, and geographical risk.[32]

Customer risk relates primarily to the buyer but may include the seller and any other persons involved in the transaction. The ability to identify the real purchaser or ultimate beneficial owner behind the transaction is an essential component of evaluating customer risk. Customer risk also requires specific attention to PEPs as well as sanctions screening.

Transaction risk refers to being able to spot a variety of unusual transactions, such as those that do not appear to make business or commercial sense depending on the facts and circumstances of the particular case. They may include multiple successive transactions, an under- or overvaluation, a mismatch between the buyer and the property, and the use of cash or overly complex loans.

Geographical risk can relate to the property, the buyer, and the source of funding. It includes pinpointing jurisdictions with weak anti–money laundering regimes, such as those that support or fund terrorism or that display a high degree of corruption.

RED FLAGS ASSOCIATED WITH REAL ESTATE MONEY LAUNDERING

As any diligent investigator knows, the trick in detecting money laundering, whether it is done through real estate or some other method, is being able to identify the activity behind the transaction. To help single out real estate transactions that may involve money laundering activity, various organizations, such as the FATF and FinCEN, publish a number of real estate–specific indicators. Many of these red flags include transactions involving the use of intermediaries or nominees, the purchase of real estate in cash or through shell companies or both, and the purchases or sales of real estate involving a significant loss to the client or where the client is otherwise unconcerned about the price. Red flags pertaining to real estate transactions are typically grouped by categories involving the natural person(s), the legal persons (i.e., corporate entities or trusts), the intermediaries, the means of payment, and the nature of the transaction.

Some examples of the more common red flags associated with this type of money laundering include transactions that involve legal entities or legal arrangements domiciled in tax havens or high-risk jurisdictions, that use newly created legal entities, that are begun in one individual's name and completed in another's without a logical explanation, that follow in rapid succession (for example, the purchase and immediate sale of property), and that entail a significant increase or decrease in the price compared with the purchase price.[33]

CONCLUSION

Transparency International has noted that despite international commitments, current rules and practices are inadequate to mitigate the risks and to detect money laundering in the real estate sector.[34] This is certainly the case in the United States. Regulators and law enforcement authorities have warned that money launderers located both at home and abroad target US real estate transactions because they are a relatively effective and anonymous means of cleaning dirty money. But the United States isn't the only country affected. Like money laundering generally, money laundering through the real estate sector has widespread impacts that go beyond those in its immediate area. So while luxury properties in upscale areas where the housing market holds high value are particularly susceptible to such practices, governments across the globe have cause to be concerned, as those jurisdictions experiencing the outflow of illicit funds are prone to greater instability.

Effectively tackling this issue requires a comprehensive approach. In addition to imposing AML/KYC requirements on real estate professionals and other intermediaries, it is important to develop strategies and to build consensus among relevant stakeholders across a range of professions, including those in the legal, real estate, and financial sectors, as well as with law enforcement authorities across jurisdictions. As with other risk management strategies, stakeholders should direct their resources and efforts to the areas of highest risk, including the jurisdictions targeted for real estate laundering and those from which the money is leaving. FIUs and other agencies should continue to identify emerging criminal trends and ML typologies. They should also share this information across jurisdictions and with the private and public sectors, whose collaboration is essential.

Furthermore, asset seizures play an important role in AML since they target criminals economically by disrupting the funding for their operations. Additionally, they ensure that recovered assets benefit the victims of these crimes.[35] However, asset seizures function primarily as a punitive measure and thus far appear to have little effect in the form of deterrence. Therefore, primary efforts should address preventative measures.

Last, international efforts should also focus on sanctioning kleptocrats who move criminal proceeds around the world. Targeted sanctions would prevent criminals from accessing the financial system, thereby making it nearly impossible for them to disguise and transfer illicit funds.

NOTES

1. FATF, "Money Laundering and Terrorist Financing through the Real Estate Sector" (Paris: FATF/OECD, June 29, 2007), https://www.fatf-gafi.org/media/fatf/documents/reports/ML%20and%20TF%20through%20the%20Real%20Estate%20Sector.pdf.

2. FATF, *Money Laundering and Terrorist Financing Vulnerabilities of Legal Professionals* (Paris: FATF/OECD, June 2013), http://www.fatf-gafi.org/media/fatf/documents/reports/ML%20and%20TF%20vulnerabilities%20legal%20professionals.pdf.

3. Maíra Martini, "Doors Wide Open: Corruption and Real Estate in Four Key Markets" (Berlin: Transparency International, 2017), 5, https://images.transparencycdn.org/images/2017_DoorsWideOpen_EN.pdf.

4. Andrew Rice, "Stash Pad," *New York Magazine*, June 27, 2014, https://nymag.com/news/features/foreigners-hiding-money-new-york-real-estate-2014-6/.

5. Martini, "Doors Wide Open."

6. George Hammond, "London Takes Global Top Spot for Luxury Home Sales," *Financial Times*, April 11, 2021, https://www.ft.com/content/350d24f7-5aab-4e80-9ecb-4760b6bc69fe.

7. Olivia Konotey-Ahulu, "London Luxury Homes Are a Prime Location to Hide Dirty Money," Bloomberg Business, December 21, 2020, https://www.bloomberg.com/news/articles/2020-12-21/london-luxury-homes-are-a-prime-location-to-hide-dirty-money#:~:text=The%20U.K.%20property%20market%20is,way%20to%20hide%20dirty%20cash.&text=That's%20probably%20only%20a%20fraction,U.K.%20real%20estate%2C%20it%20added.

8. AUSTRAC, "Strategic Analysis Brief: Money Laundering through Real Estate" (Sydney: AUSTRAC, 2015), 7–11, https://www.austrac.gov.au/sites/default/files/2019-07/sa-brief-real-estate_0.pdf; and Ahmed Taimour, "Money Laundering Schemes in Real Estate," *Corporate Compliance Insights*, February 17, 2016, https://www.corporatecomplianceinsights.com/money-laundering-schemes-in-real-estate/.

9. Anne Machalinksi, "Gold Visas: The Investment Migration Industry Evolves Globally," *Barron's*, August 24, 2020, https://www.barrons.com/articles/golden-visas-the-investment-migration-industry-evolves-globally-01598279613.

10. Cécile Remeur, "Understanding Money Laundering through Real Estate Transactions," Report no. PE 633.154 (Brussels: European Parliamentary Research Service, 2019), 8, https://www.europarl.europa.eu/cmsdata/161094/7%20-%2001%20EPRS_Understanding%20money%20laundering%20through%20real%20estate%20transactions.pdf.

11. Peter Wilson, "Want a Second Passport? Try Buying a House," *New York Times*, May 21, 2019, https://www.nytimes.com/2019/05/21/realestate/visas-residency-passports-property-investment.html.

12. Andres Knobel and Frederik Heitmüller, "Citizenship and Residency by Investment Schemes: Potential to Avoid the Common Reporting Standard for Automatic Exchange of Information" (London: Tax Justice Network, 2018), http://taxjustice.wpengine.com

/wp-content/uploads/2018/03/20180305_Citizenship-and-Residency-by-Investment
-FINAL.pdf.

13. Remeur, "Understanding Money Laundering."
14. Transparency International, "Corruption Perceptions Index, 2019," accessed September
    30, 2020, https://www.transparency.org/en/cpi/2019/results.
15. Remeur, "Understanding Money Laundering."
16. Remeur.
17. Sam Cooper, "Huge B.C. Money-Laundering Investigation Pivots to Drugs and Guns,"
    Vancouver Sun, July 13, 2018, https://vancouversun.com/news/national/huge-b-c-money
    -laundering-investigation-pivots-to-drugs-and-guns; and Sam Cooper, Stewart Bell, and
    Andrew Russell, "Fentanyl: Making a Killing: Secret Police Study Finds Crime Networks
    Could Have Laundered over $1B through Vancouver Homes in 2016," *Global News*,
    November 26, 2018, https://globalnews.ca/news/4658157/fentanyl-vancouver-real
    -estate-billion-money-laundering-police-study/.
18. James Wright, "Dirty Money: Development, Money Laundering, and Real Estate," *War
    Room* (US Army War College), November 16, 2016, https://warroom.armywarcollege
    .edu/articles/money-laundering-in-real-estate/.
19. Stanley Foodman, "New GTO Covers Wire Transfers," *JD Supra*, October 16, 2017,
    https://www.jdsupra.com/legalnews/new-gto-covers-wire-transfers-82572/; and Thom-
    son Reuters, "Five Geographic Targeting Orders (GTO) Best Practices," *Insights*,
    accessed September 30, 2021, https://legal.thomsonreuters.com/en/insights/articles
    /geographic-targeting-orders-best-practices.
20. FinCEN, "FinCEN Reissues Real Estate Geographic Targeting Orders for 12 Metro-
    politan Areas," US Treasury Department, April 29, 2021, https://www.fincen.gov/news
    /news-releases/fincen-reissues-real-estate-geographic-targeting-orders-12-metropolitan
    -areas-3.
21. US Treasury Department, *National Strategy for Combating Terrorist and Other Illicit
    Financing, 2020* (Washington, DC: US Treasury Department, 2020), 18, https://home
    .treasury.gov/system/files/136/National-Strategy-to-Counter-Illicit-Financev2.pdf.
22. Martini, "Doors Wide Open."
23. HM Treasury and Home Office, *National Risk Assessment of Money Laundering and
    Terrorist Financing, 2020* (London: HM Treasury, December 17, 2020), https://www
    .gov.uk/government/publications/national-risk-assessment-of-money-laundering-and
    -terrorist-financing-2020.
24. Cara Tabachnick, "Governments around the World Are Tackling Money Laundering
    in Real Estate," *Mansion Global*, February 18, 2019, https://www.mansionglobal.com
    /articles/governments-around-the-world-are-tackling-money-laundering-in-real-estate
    -121904.
25. Robin Levinson-King, "How Gangs Used Vancouver's Real Estate Market to Laun-
    der $5bn," BBC News Toronto, May 11, 2019, https://www.bbc.com/news/world-us
    -canada-48231558.
26. Edmund Tadros, Angus Grigg, and Neil Chenoweth, "Dirty Money Spotlight on
    Estate Agents," *Financial Review*, November 11, 2019, https://www.afr.com/property
    /residential/dirty-money-spotlight-on-estate-agents-20191107-p538ay.
27. Tabachnick, "Governments around the World."
28. Office of Public Affairs, "United States Reaches Settlement to Recover More than $700
    Million in Assets Allegedly Traceable to Corruption Involving Malaysian Sovereign

Wealth Fund," US Department of Justice, October 30, 2019, https://www.justice.gov /opa/pr/united-states-reaches-settlement-recover-more-700-million-assets-allegedly -traceable.

29. Transparency International, "Three Ways to Stop Money Laundering through Real Estate," September 6, 2019, https://www.transparency.org/en/news/three-ways-to-stop-money -laundering-through-real-estate.
30. Transparency International.
31. Transparency International.
32. Remeur, "Understanding Money Laundering," 2.
33. FATF, "Money Laundering."
34. Martini, "Doors Wide Open."
35. Wright, "Dirty Money."

CHAPTER 5

A DIRTY BUSINESS

Russian Laundromats

Financial crime has always been a threat to the integrity of the financial system. In recent decades, this threat has intensified as criminal schemes have become increasingly sophisticated and global in scope. The latest money laundering schemes that have been identified are known as laundromats. It's an appropriate moniker, as these laundromats are composed of several distinct "washing machines," or entities, that together function similar to a full-scale industrial operation.

More specifically, a *laundromat* describes a vast, secret, and highly complex method of laundering large sums of illicit proceeds. Laundromats are expertly run enterprises that involve powerful figures, multiple banks, and shell companies; span jurisdictions; and utilize various money laundering methods. Multibillion-dollar laundromats have been used to funnel wealth—that is, the proceeds of grand corruption, tax evasion, large-scale fraud, and other crimes—out of Russia and the former Eastern Bloc countries by corrupt politicians, unscrupulous businessmen, and organized criminal syndicates.[1]

Laundromats are enabled by corruption and function through the misuse and exploitation of the international financial network. To operate successfully, laundromats must evade detection from law enforcement and circumvent the regulatory controls of financial institutions that are designed to detect suspicious transactions and to root out nefarious actors. In fact, the laundromats that have lately come to light were uncovered only because of document leaks rather than through policing efforts, regulatory processes, or any internal compliance control mechanisms designed to catch unusual and suspicious activity. That these criminal activities took place on such a large scale, across multiple countries, and using a wide array of banks not only highlights the glaring compliance failures at the various financial institutions involved but also starkly illustrates the inadequacy of AML measures and the striking lack of effective oversight in this area.

COMPLIANCE CHALLENGES
PRESENTED BY LAUNDROMATS

Not surprisingly, laundromats present major compliance challenges for financial institutions because they exploit several areas that are inherently vulnerable to money laundering risks. These risk areas include the involvement of PEPs, nominees, and anonymous shell companies; trade transactions; correspondent banking services; and high-risk jurisdictions. While these factors are all considered to be red flags, which show an increased probability of money laundering or other financial crime, their presence is not necessarily indicative of illegality. It does, however, warrant a heightened review. Furthermore, the more risk factors that are present, the greater the likelihood of illicit activity. A basic knowledge of these risks and how they undermine the financial system is crucial to understanding how laundromats operate and the threats they pose to institutions. The ability to recognize risks and red flags is also a key component of an effective risk mitigation strategy.

Besides their use of legal entities and nominees, or stand-ins, to hide their beneficial owners and to provide anonymity, another defining feature of laundromats is their use of trade-based money laundering. Because TBML takes various forms, all involving the abuse of the legitimate trade system, its activities are very difficult to detect. The particular forms of TBML used in laundromat schemes are commercial in nature and include such activities as transfer pricing and abusive trade mis-invoicing, among other similar methods.

The misuse of correspondent banking services is also typically found in laundromat schemes. According to the FATF, *correspondent banking* is "the provision of banking services by one bank (the 'correspondent bank') to another bank (the 'respondent bank')."[2] It is common for large global banks to act as correspondents for smaller foreign banks. For example, respondent banks use correspondent banks to process transactions originating in foreign countries and to act as the respondent bank's representative abroad. In other words, a correspondent bank acts as an agent on behalf of the respondent bank and provides it with various services, such as international wire transfers, check clearing, and payable-through accounts. (For more on payable-through accounts, see chapter 11.) The correspondent bank can also manage foreign exchange and international investments and facilitate international trade and finance on behalf of the foreign bank.

Correspondent banking thus allows local banks and those with a smaller global footprint to engage in international transactions, for themselves and their customers, in areas where they do not have a physical presence. It serves the important function of enabling respondent banks and their customers to access the global financial system. However, correspondent banking also comes with money laundering risks.

More specifically, correspondent banking relationships are vulnerable to money laundering for two reasons. First, the correspondent bank indirectly services the respondent bank's customers but does not collect customer information on them. Rather, the correspondent bank must rely on the respondent bank's CDD procedures and other anti–money laundering processes, which may not be as stringent or rigorous as those of the correspondent bank or even meet global AML standards. Thus, the primary ML risk derives from the fact that the correspondent bank does not have a direct relationship with the customers of the respondent bank.

The second reason that correspondent banking carries a high money laundering risk has to do with both the large number of transactions that banks undertake daily and the accompanying large amount of money that flows through correspondent accounts. The high volume of activity makes identifying suspicious or illicit activity very difficult.

Another feature of laundromat schemes is that they generally target financial institutions—either local banks or branches or subsidiaries of larger global banks—that operate in high-risk jurisdictions. Those jurisdictions that the FATF identifies as being high risk are considered to have deficient or ineffective AML compliance regimes and/or poor to no enforcement. Consequently, institutions in high-risk jurisdictions frequently have substandard compliance programs as well as poor compliance cultures. As a result, these banks are frequently used as an entry point for illicit funds in laundromat operations.[3]

HOW DO LAUNDROMATS FUNCTION?

Although each laundromat is different, there are notable similarities in the way each system operates. As with all laundering schemes, the process begins with dirty funds. However, laundromats are generally used to wash exorbitantly large sums of dirty money (usually in the range of billions of dollars) that typically originate from Russia or surrounding countries.

To function, a laundromat requires at least five basic components. The first component is a bank that is willing to be complicit (or one with complicit or corruptible employees), has a deficient anti–money laundering compliance program, or is located in a jurisdiction designated as a high risk for money laundering. Typically, the bank has all three of these features. The second component is a large network of shell companies through which to divert funds. Such networks are often highly complex webs of legal entities. The third component entails using proxies or nominees to stand in as the owners and controllers of the shell companies and their bank accounts, while the fourth component involves some sort of elaborate or complex process to cycle or layer the funds to disguise their illicit source while still maintaining control of the funds. And the final component includes connections to high-risk jurisdictions, jurisdictions known to be tax havens, or jurisdictions with strict privacy or secrecy laws. These jurisdictions not only are known for weak AML regimes (including lax or nonexistent KYC processes, transaction monitoring, and suspicious activity reporting) but often also have corrupt judicial and legislative functions.

CASE STUDY: CORRUPTION, LACK OF TRANSPARENCY, AND WEAK INTERNAL CONTROLS MAKE LAUNDROMATS SPIN

Laundromat schemes illustrate the ever-growing complexity of money laundering and shed light not only on the scale of money laundering activity worldwide but also on a major global failure to prevent money laundering despite recent efforts. Four major laundromats, all involving Russian funds and actors, have been identified in the past decade: the Troika Laundromat, the Proxy Platform, the Russian Laundromat, and the Azerbaijani Laundromat. Besides their enormity, these schemes are even more egregious due to the involvement of high-ranking political elites and the witting and unwitting participation of major Western banks, as well as the fact that little is still known about many of the individuals involved.

The Troika Laundromat

The Troika Laundromat operated out of Russia from 2006 to 2013. Its name comes from its connection to Troika Dialog, which was at that time Russia's largest private investment bank and the entity responsible for establishing and operating the laundering scheme.

The primary purpose of the Troika Laundromat was to siphon dirty money out of Russia, although it also functioned as a concealed investment vehicle, slush fund, and tax-evasion scheme.[4] To accomplish this, Troika Dialog established a web of approximately seventy-five offshore shell companies to move billions of dollars through various accounts held at the now-defunct Lithuanian bank Ukio Bankas. In this manner, the two banks jointly facilitated the scheme.

The overall operation relied on the use of TBML strategies whereby illegal payments were made to appear as though they were linked to trade transactions, including the shipments of various goods; however, they were merely ghost shipments supported by fraudulent invoices and falsified contracts created by the shell companies. In fact, no physical goods were involved, and the companies buying and selling them existed only on paper. The banks disguised the illegal payments by linking them to shipments of nonexistent goods to make them appear less suspicious.

Troika Dialog directed the movement of billions of dollars from various sources in Russia and transferred the money among the laundromat's network of numerous shell companies and bank accounts. Thus, it used a series of convoluted transactions to mix legitimate and illegitimate funds, making it virtually impossible to distinguish between them.

Troika hid the ownership of the shell companies it managed by using nominees, who stood in for the people who really owned and controlled the companies. The nominees' names and signatures appear on various documents, such as contracts and loan agreements, but these names belong to otherwise ordinary and even unsuspecting people, including laborers and factory workers. Therefore, it appears that the signatures either were forged or were those of individuals who were paid to stand in as nominees.

As the money left the system, the washed funds passed through various correspondent accounts of major international banks primarily located in western Europe. Documents show the counterparties to the numerous transactions included Citigroup Inc., Raiffeisen, and Deutsche Bank. Among the individuals who received the funds were friends and allies of Russian president Vladimir Putin. Altogether, the value of the transactions among the Troika-managed shell companies has been estimated at $8.8 billion.[5]

The Proxy Platform

The Proxy Platform is another intricate web of anonymous shell companies used to launder billions of dollars in Russia from 2007 to 2011. Numbering in the hundreds, and perhaps even thousands, the shell companies were fronted by *proxies*, or people who act on behalf someone of else. The use of proxies served to hide the identity of the individuals who actually owned or controlled the companies, much like the use of nominees in the case of the Troika Laundromat. In fact, also similar to the Troika nominees, the platform's proxies were simply common people whose names appeared on official documents but who, in most cases, were completely unaware of the existence of the companies.[6] For example, one of the unsuspecting proxies, a Hungarian citizen, was listed as the director of at least 138 companies, all of which were registered in the United Kingdom and involved in the platform.

As in the case of the other laundromats, the network of anonymous companies making up the Proxy Platform held private accounts and engaged in secret deals. Many of the companies involved were set up quickly and dissolved just as fast. Numerous falsified transactions took place between the companies, and the funds were broken up into smaller installments to avoid raising suspicion. The network used multiple companies and agents in the transactions to make them look like regular foreign trade activities. Many of these transactions flowed through cities that have become known as money laundering hubs, such as Auckland, London, Moscow, and Kiev, as well as other cities in former Eastern Bloc countries.

One of the more widely used shell companies at the center of the Proxy Platform is Tormex Limited, a company that was registered in New Zealand in 2007 as an anonymous shell company without any offices, employees, or actual business operations. The beneficial owner of Tormex is still unknown and remains carefully hidden behind convoluted layers of proxies and offshore companies. What is known, however, is that Tormex had a bank account in Latvia, which has one of the least transparent banking systems in the world and consistently ranks low on Transparency International's Corruption Perceptions Index.[7] Through this bank account flowed thousands of transactions from all over the world, mixing and churning the illicit funds before routing them to other offshore entities. This process ensured that the money wouldn't be traced back to its criminal source or its ultimate owners.

Many of the shell companies involved in the platform were registered by GT Group in New Zealand and Midland Consult in London. Both companies were corporate service providers that set up shell companies for criminal organizations, terrorists, and other notorious figures. In fact, an outstanding number of known criminals used GT Group before the New Zealand authorities finally shut it down in 2011.

Like the other laundromats, the Proxy Platform wasn't a singular money laundering event. During its existence, numerous individuals, groups, banks, and companies used the platform to launder illicit funds. Some of these people include members of Asian criminal syndicates and Russians who were linked to the tax fraud exposed by Sergei Magnitsky. Additionally, Wachovia

Bank (now part of Wells Fargo) is also alleged to have used the Proxy Platform when it laundered close to $390 billion for the Sinaloa Cartel.[8]

The Russian Laundromat

The Russian Laundromat, also known as the Global Laundromat and the Moldovan Laundromat, was quite possibly the largest and most complex money laundering scheme known to date. Russian criminals used it in 2010–14 to launder funds originating in Russia that totaled between $20 billion and $80 billion. These illicit funds were most likely derived from fraud, government corruption, and tax evasion, and they constitute money that should have gone to public works and other projects benefiting Russian citizens.

The illicit funds were placed in the laundromat through a series of anonymous shell companies, most of which were incorporated in the United Kingdom. The money was then layered using various transactions conducted through the shell companies at the direction of their disguised company owners. These transactions primarily consisted of fictitious loans made between shell companies that were subsequently made to appear as though they were defaulted on; however, no money ever changed hands. The deals were structured to always include a Moldovan citizen to ensure the use of Moldovan courts. Corrupt judges who were in on the scheme authenticated the debt, which was always guaranteed. To get the money out of the laundromat, a Moldavan judge would order the shell company that guaranteed the debt to repay it into a court-controlled account at a bank in Moldova, thereby cleaning the funds. Some of the money was then spent on luxury items, while the rest was transferred to a bank in Latvia and then passed through more shell companies before being distributed to accounts all over the world. As is almost always the case with laundered funds, much of this money will never be recovered.

Altogether, the funds flowed through 5,140 companies, with accounts at 732 banks, throughout 96 countries.[9] Prominent global banks, including Deutsche Bank, and small, lesser-known banks, including several located in Moldova and Latvia, were either directly involved in the laundering or at one time handled the laundered funds.

Although investigations of the laundromat have been initiated, including in the United Kingdom, Moldova, and Latvia, many have subsequently been put on hold indefinitely. A small number of arrests have been made and some regulatory punishments were issued for the smaller banks involved, but the Russian government's unwillingness to cooperate in the investigations has largely stalled both the recovery efforts and any attempts to hold those responsible for the scheme accountable.[10]

The Azerbaijani Laundromat

Azerbaijan is a small, former Eastern Bloc nation. It is a country rich in oil and natural gas but also one where corruption and human rights abuses are rampant. As a result, it has consistently ranked near the bottom of Transparency International's Corruption Perceptions Index. Taking into account these conditions, the environment in Azerbaijan was conducive to financial crime. Therefore, perhaps it isn't all that surprising that Azerbaijan was at the center of a scandal that came to light in 2017, when Azerbaijan's ruling elite was accused of laundering approximately $2.9 billion, thereby exposing what has come to be known as the Azerbaijani Laundromat.

The Azerbaijani Laundromat operated between 2012 and 2014. It was so effective that much still remains to be discovered about how exactly it functioned, where the illicit funds came from, and where they ultimately ended up. Nonetheless, a significant portion of the dirty money appears to be linked to political figures in Azerbaijan, including the family of the Azerbaijani president and others connected to the government, and it is believed to have come from various forms of corruption, embezzlement, and other financial crimes.

A large portion of the funds has also been tied to several companies, including a mysterious company named Baktelekom, which is believed to be owned by Azerbaijani officials but exists only on paper and is listed as holding a bank account in Azerbaijan. Interestingly, the name "Baktelekom" differs by just one letter from the name of a legitimate company called Baktelecom. It appears as though the shell company's name was purposely chosen to be confused with the name of the lawful company, a tactic commonly employed by those setting up anonymous shell companies for illicit purposes.[11]

Secretive shell companies registered in the United Kingdom also made up the core of this laundromat, further highlighting the need for global AML controls around corporate service providers. The involvement of many PEPs, a common money laundering red flag, is another factor shared with the other laundromat schemes.

AN EXTREME CASE OF COMPLICITY
AND LACK OF OVERSIGHT

It is no coincidence that the Azerbaijani Laundromat came to light the same year as the Danske Bank case, the largest money laundering scandal to date. Copenhagen-based Danske Bank is Denmark's largest bank. At the center of the money laundering scandal is the bank's tiny Estonian branch, which it acquired in 2007. Critically, the Estonian branch did not update its AML program to meet the standards of the rest of the company, making it a target for money laundering activity. Ultimately it led to the laundering of approximately $230 billion as suspicious payments from Russia flowed through the branch to London and other Western financial centers.

According to an internal whistleblower, numerous instances of suspicious activity occurring between 2007 and 2015 were repeatedly ignored, including by the bank's executive board. The suspicious transactions related to an unusually high number of nonresident customers (predominantly from Russia and former Soviet nations) and to foreign shell companies, both of which are common red flags. Egregiously, the bank failed to identify the source of the payments and the purpose of the shell companies. It also didn't obtain adequate information on its customers, some of which were publicly known for prior money laundering activity. For example, subsequent reports showed that some of the bank's customers made payments with suspicious counterparties at other banks, had significant discrepancies between their revenue and account activity, held suspicious properties, and had shared addresses that were unexplainable.[12]

Additionally, as had also happened in smaller banks involved in various other laundromat schemes, several employees at Danske Bank Estonia colluded with criminals to keep the money laundering operation going. Furthermore, employees falsified accounts and financial reports. According to one of the whistleblower reports, the bank knowingly continued to deal with companies that had committed crimes.[13]

Among the links between Danske's Estonian branch and the Azerbaijani Laundromat are the accounts of four UK-registered companies, all with the same ultimate beneficial owner, which was located in Azerbaijan. These accounts made a combined total of over $3 billion worth of unexplainable transactions.[14] The branch also had dozens of customers who appeared to be connected to the Azerbaijani Laundromat, including a large nonresident portfolio linked to the president of Azerbaijan and his family.

Additionally, hundreds of Danske Bank Estonia's customers received payments from the shell companies that formed the core of the Russian Laundromat. It further appears that Danske's Estonian branch laundered the proceeds related to the Russian tax fraud scandal that resulted in the death of Sergei Magnitsky.

Danske Bank has since acknowledged that its money laundering controls in Estonia were insufficient.[15] It ultimately closed its operations in Russia and the Baltic states. Nonetheless, considering the extreme lack of compliance oversight on the part of Danske Bank Estonia and the magnitude of suspicious activity cycling through the branch, it's likely that other connections to illicit activity have yet to be uncovered.

Relatedly, regarding its long-standing relationship with Danske Bank Estonia, the German banking giant Deutsche Bank was hit with fines for numerous compliance failures, including not monitoring activities and not taking appropriate action to prevent the Estonian branch from transferring billions of dollars in suspicious transactions through Deutsche Bank's accounts. Since the late 1990s, Deutsche Bank has been charged with numerous violations for facilitating bank fraud, tax evasion, and money laundering and has incurred multiple fines and penalties from regulators and authorities in both the United States and Europe. Clearly, AML regulations or enforcement or both are insufficient if the world's largest banks can be charged with repeated violations over many years and if they not only continue to engage in the activities that resulted in the violations but also keep making a profit while doing so.

BLOWING THE WHISTLE ON RUSSIAN CORRUPTION AND TAX FRAUD

Present-day discussions of Russian corruption, money laundering, fraud, and shell companies inevitably lead to the Russian whistleblower Sergei Magnitsky. A tax law expert and auditor, Magnitsky exposed a huge tax fraud involving Russian officials, and his subsequent death triggered international media attention. He died at the age of thirty-seven in a Russian pretrial detention facility in November 2009 following eleven months in police custody. Stories conflict about whether his death was the result of intentional murder or extreme negligence.

Magnitsky worked for the Moscow-based law firm Firestone Duncan. In 2007 William Browder, the cofounder of Hermitage Capital Management, hired him to conduct an investigation on behalf of the investment fund and capital management company, which the Russian Interior Ministry had accused of tax evasion and fraud. Magnitsky uncovered the money trail and ultimately found out how Russian oligarchs had siphoned hundreds of millions of dollars in taxes from Hermitage through the use of falsified contracts and sham court judgments.

More specifically, Magnitsky discovered that Russian officials, in collusion with law enforcement officials and a Russian criminal network, embezzled these funds by setting up shell companies based on the stolen identities of three Russian companies that were part of a portfolio held by Hermitage Capital. The group obtained fake judgments against the companies, and then they were able to obtain lucrative tax refunds based on those judgments.[16] They then laundered the illicit proceeds, which represented stolen tax revenue. In fact, it was later found that the shell companies used in the tax fraud scheme were the same ones that laundered over $130 million through the Troika Laundromat. In addition, Tormex Limited, which played a substantial role in the Proxy Platform, was also used to launder a portion of the proceeds from the tax-refund fraud that Magnitsky uncovered.

Magnitsky reported the fraud to Russian authorities and gave testimony against those involved, including police officers, tax officials, and judges. Several weeks later, he was arrested and accused of committing the fraud himself. He was imprisoned for nearly a year awaiting trail when he died. Although the official cause of death was heart failure, there have been widespread allegations that Magnitsky's death was the result of torture.

Just as in the laundromat schemes, not a single Russian official involved in the tax fraud that Magnitsky exposed has been brought to justice. An environment with a weak legal infrastructure, little judicial independence, no political transparency, virtually no public accountability, and no free press will inevitably lead to corruption and other financial crime.[17] That is precisely why Russia has been at the heart of these and several other multibillion-dollar money laundering scandals. Spurred by greed, these corrupt politicians, dishonest businessmen, and criminal organizations have no fear of retribution, knowing they will never be held accountable for their actions. Without any real consequences or deterrents, money laundering, and the underlying crimes that necessitate it, will inevitably persist.

As in the case of Danske Bank, even large, well-reputed international banks—despite having strong internal controls in their Western offices—will continue to be vulnerable in countries that have weak controls, have lax accountability measures, and are known for corruption. Therefore, these major underlying issues must be addressed before effective changes can be made. Since illicit actors will always take advantage of jurisdictions with weak controls to move their wealth into more stable economies for safekeeping, the only solution is to prevent their access to the global financial system.

RED FLAGS ASSOCIATED WITH LAUNDROMAT SCHEMES

As the examples of the various laundromat cases illustrate, these schemes take advantage of four key access points to gain entrance to the financial system:

anonymous shell companies, TBML, correspondent banking, and ineffective AML compliance programs.[18] Red flags associated with any of these four areas, as well as other red flags indicative of money laundering generally, may point to the existence of a laundromat scheme. Various reports published by the FATF, FinCEN, and the Wolfsberg Group, among others, provide useful lists of red flags that can be used to identify activities related to laundromat schemes.

Examples of red flags that are often associated with laundromat-type schemes and may be indicative of money laundering activity generally include the use of extremely complex or layered shell company structures; the involvement of multiple anonymous or opaque companies or companies with nominee owners/directors that are also associated with numerous other companies; the existence of strange or unexplainable trade transactions, unusual documentation relating to such transactions, or product descriptions that don't match the goods supplied; the involvement of PEPs, especially multiple PEPs; and the reports of transactions relating to numerous high-risk jurisdictions, including frequent and high-value transactions.

CONCLUSION

Laundromats expose how easily banks can be exploited to hide and launder the proceeds of crime. Although several countries have strengthened their anti–money laundering laws and regulations over the past several years, criminals have devised schemes of increasing complexity to get around them. Furthermore, enforcement by countries remains inconsistent at best and ineffective at worst. Many cases highlight how the wealthy and politically connected are unlikely to be prosecuted or otherwise brought to justice, particularly in corrupt and developing nations.

Although laundromats use many money laundering methods, the lack of transparency around corporate vehicles is what enables and facilitates laundromat schemes. It also makes it nearly impossible to identify and hold accountable the individuals and groups behind the schemes, and it prevents the pilfered funds from ever being recovered. Hence, laundromats have proven quite effective at disguising and transferring illicit funds; therefore, they will continue to flourish as long as the people behind them are able to remain hidden and are never brought to justice.

As a matter of fact, the laundromats identified in Russia and other former Soviet countries are not the only known laundromats. Similar laundromats have been linked to criminal organizations in Latin America and China.

Furthermore, it is believed that other types of complex laundromats are operating in different parts of the world right now, but anonymity prevents their detection.

Money launderers and other criminals have proved to be resourceful and creative in circumventing laws, ferreting out and exploiting weaknesses in legal and financial systems, and seeking out new routes to launder their proceeds. Accordingly, money laundering schemes are expected to continue to grow in complexity and sophistication, showing that although the individuals involved may not be moral or ethical, they are certainly not stupid. The intricacy of these schemes indicates that the fight against money laundering and other financial crime is likely to become even more challenging.

NOTES

1. Barrow, "Laundromats" (see Introduction, n. 2).
2. FATF, "General Glossary," accessed September 24, 2020, https://www.fatf-gafi.org /glossary/.
3. Barrow, "Laundromats."
4. Paul Radu, "Vast Offshore Network Moved Billions with Help from Major Russian Bank," OCCRP [Organized Crime and Corruption Reporting Project], March 4, 2019, https://www.occrp.org/en/troikalaundromat/vast-offshore-network-moved-billions -with-help-from-major-russian-bank.
5. Radu.
6. Mihai Munteanu, "The Proxy Platform," OCCRP, November 22, 2011, https://www .reportingproject.net/proxy/en/the-proxy-platform.
7. Munteanu; and LETA/TBT Staff, "Latvia Is Not Very Successful with Combatting Corruption," The Baltic Times, January 28, 2020, https://www.baltictimes.com/latvia _not_very_successful_with_combating_corruption_-_transparency_international_ -_latvia/.
8. Mihai Munteanu, "The Proxy Platform: Phantom Account," OCCRP, November 20, 2011, https://www.reportingproject.net/proxy/en/the-phantom-accounts.
9. OCCRP Staff, "The Russian Laundromat Exposed," OCCRP, March 20, 2017, https:// www.occrp.org/en/laundromat/the-russian-laundromat-exposed/.
10. OCCRP Staff.
11. OCCRP Staff, "The Azerbaijani Laundromat," OCCRP, September 4, 2017, https:// www.occrp.org/en/azerbaijanilaundromat/.
12. Gabriella Gricius, "The Danske Bank Scandal Is the Tip of the Iceberg," Foreign Policy, October 8, 2018, https://foreignpolicy.com/2018/10/08/the-danske-bank-scandal-is -the-tip-of-the-iceberg-money-laundering-estonia-denmark-regulation-financial-crime/.
13. Gricius, "Danske Bank Scandal."
14. Kirstin Ridley, "Britain Freezes Bank Account Linked to Azerbaijani Laundromat," Reuters, December 12, 2018, https://www.reuters.com/article/britain-moneylaundering -azerbaijan/britain-freezes-bank-account-linked-to-azerbaijani-laundromat-idUSL 8N1YH5E5.

15. Blythe Logan, "The Case of Danske Bank and Money Laundering," Seven Pillars Institute (SPI) for Global Finance and Ethics, November 12, 2019, https://sevenpillarsinstitute .org/the-case-of-danske-bank-and-money-laundering/.

16. Dick Carozza, "Bill Browder Fights against Corruption in Sergei Magnitsky's Name," *Fraud Conference News*, June 25, 2019, https://www.fraudconferencenews.com/home /2019/6/25/bill-browder-fights-against-corruption-in-sergei-magnitskys-name.

17. Kateryna Boguslavska, "Russia's Money Laundering Risks—What Does the Latest FATF Report Mean in Practice?," Basel Institute on Governance, February 26, 2020, https:// baselgovernance.org/blog/russias-money-laundering-risks-what-does-latest-fatf-report -mean-practice.

18. Jaclyn Jaeger, "Troika Laundromat Reveals the Gaps in AML Compliance," *Compliance Week*, April 1, 2019, https://www.complianceweek.com/aml/troika-laundromat-reveals -the-gaps-in-aml-compliance/26819.article.

CHAPTER 6

OVER THE BORDER
AND THROUGH THE BANK

Money Mules and Cyber Mules

People have been used as couriers to transfer money, drugs, or other contraband across borders for millennia. Drug cartels now commonly use a smuggling technique in which they employ individuals, who are referred to as drug mules, to move hidden narcotics across a border. Similarly, money launderers frequently transfer their illegally acquired funds, whether physically, electronically, or through a courier service, via people who are known as money mules.

There are many variations of money mule schemes, which can often be characterized as a subset of more generic fraud schemes, including scams that attempt to trick people into believing they've won a prize and need to send a payment before they can claim their winnings. In the case of money mule schemes, the scammers aren't done once they get a victim's money. They often subsequently need to have the money moved but aren't willing to take the risk of doing it themselves. That's when the scammers recruit the help of money mules, some witting and others not.

In recent years, money mules have become increasingly common, particularly when it comes to moving funds electronically, and banks are a prime target for money mule activity because they provide direct access to funds. The increased use and accessibility of the internet have caused it to become a major player not just in money mules' schemes but also in the commission of what is now widely known as cyber-related crime, which was virtually unheard of just a few decades ago. As a result of the anonymity and speed of the internet, large-scale cybercrime schemes have become much more prevalent.

WHAT IS THE ROLE OF A MONEY MULE?

Money mules are recruited to move criminal proceeds, usually through various accounts, at the request of or on behalf of a criminal or criminal organization. By doing so, they serve as critical intermediaries for money laundering, breaking the link between the dirty funds and the criminal. In fact, the money mules represent the critical first step in placing illicit funds into the legitimate financial system, although they can also be used in the layering stage.[1] Money mules typically, although not always, receive a small amount of the money being moved as a commission for their efforts. Such individuals may or may not be aware that they are working for a criminal, or that they are dealing with illicit funds, or even that they may be criminally penalized for their activities. In many cases, money mules do not even personally know the criminals behind the money mule schemes.

THE THREE TYPES OF MONEY MULES

Generally, money mules can be categorized into three main groups based on their level of knowledge and complicity. These groups include those individuals who are unknowing or unwitting, those who are witting, and those who are complicit.[2]

Unknowing or unwitting mules do not have any knowledge that they are involved in a criminal undertaking and that they are handling funds of illicit origin, while *witting* mules intentionally ignore warning signs of criminal activity or are willfully blind to the scam in which they are participating. The latter may even receive warnings from bank personnel but continue to open multiple accounts. These individuals generally begin as an unwitting mule.

Complicit mules are aware of their role as a money mule and are aiding and abetting the larger criminal scheme. They might regularly open bank accounts at various institutions with the intention of receiving illicit funds. They may also openly advertise their services as a money mule and actively recruit others.

Whether they are aware of the illegality involved or not, money mules facilitate the laundering of criminally derived proceeds. They do this by enabling the movement of illicit funds and by creating distance between the criminal activity from which the funds were derived and the origin of the funds. The use of money mules as middlemen makes detecting the identity of the criminals behind the criminal scheme difficult.

THE RECRUITMENT OF MONEY MULES

Mule herders or *mule drivers* are criminals who target money mules. The most common ways in which mule herders recruit individuals to work as money mules involve online job websites and classified advertisements, online dating websites, social networking websites, email spam sent directly to an individual's inbox, and darknet forums. Many online scams specifically target unsuspecting individuals who tend to be trusting, gullible, and vulnerable. The most frequently targeted groups are the elderly, recent retirees, individuals with memory loss, teens and college-age young adults, those who are recently divorced or widowed, individuals who are looking for a job or are financially distressed, and recent immigrants and foreign nationals.[3]

Some individuals who are recruited as money mules are knowing and willing participants in the fraudulent scheme, while a small number of others may actively seek out such work despite its illegality. Mule herders typically provide willing participants with specific training on how to establish accounts and may supply them with false documents to enable their transactions.

However, most individuals who are recruited online for mule work are innocent and believe they will be performing legitimate jobs. In fact, money mules are often recruited for online employment under the guise of work-from-home jobs. These types of positions involve transferring funds in various forms and do not require any education or experience. Such job advertisements typically call for "money transfer agents," "payment processors," or similar titles. Such work may be appealing because it doesn't require specific prior knowledge or training, is relatively easy to do, and can be done from home. Although these money mules usually receive some sort of payment for their work, typically in the form of a commission representing a small percentage of the funds they transfer, it's also common for them to never see a paycheck or even to lose their own money.

In fact, money mule scammers specialize in hacking into recruitment websites such as Monster.com and other popular employment search engines. Cybercriminals then gain access to millions of résumés and use them to specifically target people who are currently unemployed or are seeking additional or part-time employment.[4]

Another way criminals target and recruit individuals for mule work is through dating or social networking websites, where the latter are duped into a phony relationship, either romantic or platonic, with the fraudster. In these cases, the criminals work to establish trust with the individuals over time and convince them to use their personal bank account to receive, hold, and eventually transfer money under a host of false pretenses. The targets of this scam may be told to keep a portion of the funds that they receive as a gift or payment for their trouble. In another version of this scam, the fraudsters persuade their victims to give up their own money, leaving them bereft of their savings. The targeted individuals in these cases tend to be the recently divorced or widowed or college students. Generally, these individuals genuinely think that they are helping someone whom they've come to view as a romantic partner or friend.

Other ways in which money mules are recruited include unsolicited email and email spam, as well as on darknet forums. Those recruited through the darknet are, more often than not, complicit participants. In all these cases, the true identity of the solicitor remains anonymous, and the recruited mules never know with whom they are dealing. Therefore, the money mules always run the highest risk of getting caught.

THE EVOLUTION OF CYBER MULES

As noted, the recruitment and use of money mules to move funds is not new. The practice as we know it today appears to have roots in the drug-trafficking trade, whereby individuals are used to smuggle, both domestically and internationally, small amounts of narcotics that were broken up from larger shipments. The same concept applies to present-day money mules. However, rather than crossing borders with money hidden on their body (though it still happens today), money mules are now more commonly used to structure financial transactions and move funds through various accounts electronically.

As one might expect, money mule activity, from the mule's recruitment to the movement of funds, was historically accomplished entirely through real-world interactions. At that time, lower-level members of organized crime groups or petty thieves worked as professional money mules, whose job entailed recruiting other mules (which was done face-to-face rather than online) and physically moving cash from one point to another. Although these types of professional mules still exist, anti–money laundering laws and regulations have made completing their job undetected more difficult.[5]

Instead, with the rise of the internet and the corresponding emergence of online banking systems, criminals have adapted existing methodologies and developed new ones. Now, much of this work is accomplished more quickly, easily, cheaply, and anonymously through electronic means, such as online bank transfers. In fact, money mule activity has proliferated in recent years as a result of advances in online technology. Although mules are still sometimes recruited in person, and some circumstances may call for the physical transport of currency, now mules are more commonly recruited online and move, or assist in the movement of, money through electronic means.

Furthermore, criminals are incorporating modern technology and taking advantage of commercially available malware to complete their illegal activities. In fact, criminals seem to have flocked to the cybercrime industry and have developed various types of malicious software. For example, money mule networks use *crimeware*, a type of malware specifically designed to enable cybercrime, to carry out identity theft and other internet-based crimes. This malware can be spread to victims' computers through email, and it allows criminals to steal their victims' banking information, thus allowing for the transfer of money from victim accounts to mule accounts.

Therefore, the vast majority of money mule activity today is conducted online. According to Europol, more than 90 percent of money mule transactions identified through the European Money Mule Actions are linked to cybercrime. (European Money Mule Actions are similar to the Money Mule Initiative in the United States; both are coordinated law enforcement efforts to disrupt criminal networks that utilize money mules.) Furthermore, the illegal funds are mostly derived from internet-based criminal activities, such as phishing, malware attacks, online auction fraud, e-commerce fraud, business email compromise (BEC) and CEO fraud, romance scams, holiday fraud (booking fraud), and others.[6] Consequently, the traditional money mule has evolved into what could more accurately be termed a "cyber mule."

LARGE-SCALE CYBER HEISTS

Although old-fashioned bank robbery is not quite obsolete, large-scale cyber heists, in which online money mule transactions are then used to launder criminal funds and to conceal the subsequent movement of these funds, are much more common. As compared to physically walking into a bank and drawing a gun while an accomplice waits in the getaway car, cyber heists offer more anonymity and larger proceeds, providing a much more favorable risk-benefit ratio.

To execute a cyber heist successfully, criminals need to take certain steps prior to the attack. They involve recruiting and training money mules and sometimes setting up fraudulent accounts ahead of time (unless the money mules are involved in establishing the accounts after the cyber heist). In fact, such accounts may be opened several months in advance of the heist and simply sit dormant for a time. The existence of preestablished accounts provides credibility with the money mules who will be transferring funds.[7]

The number of money mules involved in any money laundering scheme can vary widely, and this is also the case with cyber heists. Large-scale cyber heists typically engage somewhere upward of ten mules. However, the mysterious Lazarus Group—a cybercrime group with apparent connections to North Korea and about which not much else is known despite its being in existence since about 2009—is connected to a cyberattack against a bank that entailed twelve thousand automatic teller machine (ATM) withdrawals in a two-hour timespan across twenty-eight countries, indicating the work of a large and highly coordinated group of money mules.[8] Since money mules may play a role in multiple stages of the money laundering process, the total number of money mules in a single scheme can vary.

EXAMPLES OF COMMON MONEY MULE SCAMS

There are many different types of money mule schemes. Romance scams, work-from-home schemes, and BEC attacks are some of the most common types. They often utilize *unwitting* money mules to launder ill-gotten funds and, in some cases, to defraud the victim(s).

Romance Scams

Romance scams always involve recruiting unsuspecting victims as money mules. These scams are increasingly on the rise in both the United States and abroad, as are the monetary losses from such scams. One example of a romance scam scenario involves targeting elderly widows. Once the fraudster establishes trust with the victim, the person will ask the widow to send money for a plane ticket to visit her. After the funds are received, the person will claim that the wired funds did not arrive and request yet another transfer. Thereafter, when the fraudster doesn't show as promised, the person will continue defrauding the victim by making other claims and asking for more money. As part of this scheme, the victim may also be persuaded to open bank accounts and/or register an LLC in the victim's name to send or receive funds.

Work-from-Home Schemes

In work-from-home schemes, money mule recruiters, under the guise of a false charity or company, approach their targets (i.e., potential money mules) with a seemingly legitimate work-from-home job offer. This recruitment is typically done through the internet or social media advertisements, emails, or text messages. Once the target accepts the offer of employment, the individual is instructed to move funds through various accounts or to set up a new account. Typically, the money mule's earnings are a percentage of the funds that he or she helps to transfer. The individuals who are targeted for work-from-home schemes may be unwitting as to the illicit nature of their activity, while others may even have a suspicion but do not care.

Business Email Compromise

BEC, also known as *cyber-enabled financial fraud*, is another prevalent type of cybercrime that is frequently utilized in money mule activity. BEC attacks typically target businesses, particularly smaller businesses with less sophisticated cybersecurity controls. However, successful BEC scams have also included government agencies, nonprofit organizations, and other institutions.

A BEC attack primarily involves the use of email fraud, wherein an attacker obtains access to a business email account and imitates the email owner's identity to defraud the company, its employees, its customers, or its third-party partners. To fool the victims, an attacker will establish an email account with an address nearly identical to one on the corporate network.

Although BEC scams can take different forms, in most cases fraudsters target employees with access to company funds and attempt to trick them into wiring transfers to bank accounts that appear to be legitimate, but the account numbers have been altered slightly. The result is that the funds are actually deposited into the accounts of the criminal or criminal group.

BEC scams aren't limited to requests for wire transfers. They may also involve fraudulent requests for checks or for sensitive information, such as personally identifiable information or employee tax records.

HOW MULES MOVE MONEY

The most common way in which mules move money is through electronic means. This is generally done via online bank transfers. First, the mules receive the illicit proceeds, typically into their own personal accounts, and are next instructed to wire these funds into a third party's bank account. In other cases, mules can be recruited to travel to specific locations and withdraw cash from banks or ATMs. Additionally, the mules can be directed to "cash out" the funds they received by purchasing cashier's checks; by converting the funds into virtual currency, prepaid debit cards, or gift cards; or by sending the funds through a money service business. They may even use some combination of these methods.

Money mules may use the bank accounts of other innocent individuals, accessing them either through hacking or through other fraudulent means. Mules may also set up accounts using stolen information or even create phony accounts using falsified documents. Of course, the mules aren't told that the money they are handling is stolen or that the reason for moving it is a lie.

The illegal funds laundered by money mules come from various criminal activities, the most common of which are internet-enabled frauds. They include BEC schemes, online and work-from-home job scams, romance scams, mystery shopper scams, advance fee schemes, reshipping scams, grandparent scams (e.g., grandparents are deceived into believing their grandchildren are being held for ransom), lottery scams, IRS or law enforcement impersonation scams, technical support scams, blackmail attempts, and credit card fraud, among numerous others. Additionally, the illegal money laundered by money mules is also commonly derived from drug trafficking and human trafficking.[9]

Money Mules, Smurfs, Structuring, and Smurfing

Money mules, smurfs, the practice of structuring, and the practice of smurfing all play a critical, though not always a necessary, part in the money laundering process. Although related and seemingly similar, there are important differences between the roles of money mules and smurfs and between the acts of structuring and smurfing.

Money Mules versus Smurfs

Money mules are sometimes also referred to as smurfs; however, there is an important distinction between the two roles. *Smurfs* are individuals who deposit various small cash transactions that all are less than the $10,000 reporting threshold into numerous different financial institutions to avoid detection. Their job is to move money without triggering a bank's reporting obligations. Although money mules can, and sometimes do, make similar numerous small bank deposits, their activities are not limited to breaking up monetary deposits to avoid bank detection. Money mules engage in a far broader range of money movement activity.

Essentially, the job of a smurf is to avoid bank reporting obligations, whereas the job of a money mule is to act as an intermediary.

Structuring versus Smurfing

The BSA imposes certain reporting obligations on financial institutions. For example, it requires financial institutions to report currency transactions (i.e., deposits, withdrawals, exchanges of currency, or other payments or transfers) greater than $10,000 by filing a CTR with FinCEN. Similarly, financial institutions that are subject to BSA requirements must file a SAR in cases where transactions appear to be structured to avoid detection, such as when smaller transactions occur in high frequencies or when transactions otherwise seem to be suspicious. Such reports are not limited to the United States, and many countries have similar requirements in place. Outside of the United States, a suspicious transaction report is the equivalent of a SAR.

Recall that structuring is the act of altering a financial transaction to circumvent reporting requirements, such as the filing of CTRs and SARs. Structuring becomes what is commonly referred to as smurfing when a transaction involving a large sum of money is broken up or structured into a number of transactions that are purposely kept less than the $10,000 reporting threshold to avoid detection. Smurfs are then recruited to make the smaller deposits, typically into several different banks. Therefore, smurfing is the method used to structure the transactions. In other words, smurfing involves using individuals known as runners to perform multiple financial transactions to avoid reporting by a bank or other financial institution.[10] However, it is possible to structure transactions without using smurfs.

While smurfing involves criminally derived proceeds, structuring may involve either legally or illegally sourced funds and is not necessarily done for the purposes of laundering money. Depositing legally earned income into multiple banks to avoid reporting is still considered structuring, however, and structuring the amount and/or frequencies of deposits to avoid scrutiny by a bank is a federal crime.

Example: Structuring versus Smurfing

In an example of structuring versus smurfing, say Person A has $54,000. If Person A deposited the entire sum into a US bank, the bank would have to file a CTR because the amount is greater than $10,000. To avoid the reporting requirement, Person A recruits six people (Individuals 1–6) to make a single deposit of $9,000 each into Banks U, V, W, X, Y, and Z, respectively. With this scheme, a CTR is not triggered because the amount being deposited into each bank is less than the reporting threshold. However, given that Person A structured the deposits and that Individuals 1–6 engaged in smurfing, Person A and Individuals 1–6 have each committed a crime.

CASE STUDY: CYBER MULES, CYBER VILLAINS, AND A $100 MILLION CYBERCRIME SPREE

Known by the online nicknames "aqua" and "aquamo," Russian cybercriminal Maksim Yakubets is the mastermind behind Evil Corp, one of the most sophisticated transnational cybercrime syndicates in the world. Yakubets, along with an associate named Igor Turashev, is alleged to have orchestrated and led a ten-year-long cybercrime spree. They released the most destructive malware packages deployed thus far, primarily targeting the financial services sectors in the United States and the United Kingdom, and it ultimately resulted in the cybertheft of at least $100 million from hundreds of businesses and thousands of consumers in over forty countries.

According to his indictment, Yakubets and others in the international cybercrime network developed and released malware originally known as Bugat (later referred to as Cridex and Dridex as improvements were made to the malware and as functionality was added over time). More specifically, the malware, which was designed to defeat antivirus and other protective programs, was embedded in malicious links or attachments contained within automated emails, and once the recipients clicked on them, the malware infected their computers and stole their banking credentials and other confidential information. Evil Corp was then able to use the compromised login and password information from the malware-infected computers to steal funds from the victims' bank accounts, and a network of money mules moved the money into accounts controlled by Evil Corp.[11]

Yakubets's primary function was to recruit and manage the money mules, who were a central component of the scheme. Serving as either witting or unwitting accomplices, the money mules' job was to help Evil Corp launder the stolen funds and transfer them to members of the conspiracy based in Russia, Ukraine, and other parts of eastern Europe.

Yakubets operated several money mule recruitment websites that were used to recruit individuals via work-at-home job advertisements. People who responded to these ads were instructed to create an account on one of the recruitment websites, to enter their personal and bank account information, and to log in every day to check their messages. To make the scheme seem legitimate, and perhaps to weed out unreliable workers, the mules were assigned busy work, including a variety of menial tasks, for a period before being asked to handle money transfers.[12]

When the recruiter was ready for the money mule to transfer the stolen funds, the recruiter sent an email through the recruitment website with instructions from bogus company managers advising the money mule of an impending funds transfer. These professional-sounding but fraudulent emails said that a client would soon send money to the mule's account, and the mule was instructed to promptly visit the bank, withdraw the incoming payment in cash, and wire the funds (minus the agreed-upon commission) to certain individuals located in eastern Europe. Of course, in each case, the company referred to as "the client" was actually a small business whose payroll accounts the Russian hackers had previously infiltrated.[13] Therefore, in this manner, the network of cybercriminals used the money mules to make thousands of financial transactions that served to move and disguise, and thereby launder, money stolen from innocent individuals and businesses.

In December 2019, the DOJ issued a $5 million reward—the largest reward for a cybercriminal—for information leading to the arrest or conviction of Yakubets. Additionally, the US Treasury Department's Office of Foreign Assets Control (OFAC) subsequently sanctioned Yakubets, Evil Corp, and numerous other associates who helped facilitate activities for Evil Corp.[14]

Yakubets remains on the lam somewhere in Russia. It's highly doubtful that he'll ever be apprehended since Russia is notorious for, among other things, not extraditing its own citizens. It is even more unlikely that Russia will turn him over because Yakubets served as a spy in the successor agency to the KGB.[15] Therefore, unless Yakubets is arrogant enough to fly into the United States—in which case he would be promptly detained and arrested— he'll probably never see the inside of a federal courtroom or US prison cell. In the meantime, whether Yakubets's face on an FBI's "Wanted" poster and the attached $5 million prize will be sufficient incentive for someone to turn him in remain to be seen.[16]

THE EFFECT OF COVID-19 ON MONEY MULE SCHEMES

Criminals, including cybercriminals, are remarkably opportunistic. They capitalize on weaknesses, take advantage of gaps and loopholes, and prey on fear and uncertainty. Consequently, the devastating global COVID-19 pandemic has opened up numerous opportunities for exploitation, particularly regarding cybercrime. The unprecedented numbers of people suddenly working from home (62 percent, according to a Gallup poll), along with scores of children and young people homeschooling online, have created a vast new pool of targets.[17] Additionally, the pandemic and corresponding lockdown have resulted in many people being out of work and desperate for jobs. As a result, not only has online fraud increased significantly, so have money mule recruitment and money mule activity. As noted in chapter 1, since the start of the pandemic, various government agencies—including FinCEN, the FBI, and Europol, among others—have issued advisories to warn people about potential online fraud and money mule scams.

One pandemic-related money mule scheme entailed recruiting money mules to process bogus donations related to COVID-19 relief for various charitable organizations. In addition to romance scams and work-from-home schemes, some of the other more common types of money mule schemes arising in the pandemic that US authorities have detected include imposter scams, where the criminal impersonates a charitable organization, a government official, or an agency such as the IRS to extract money from the victim, and schemes that use money mules to exploit unemployment insurance programs and other pandemic-related benefits.

Moreover, Evil Corp founder Maksim Yakubets and his Moscow-based network of Russian hackers have also tried to exploit the global pandemic. The cyber group has been accused of launching attacks using *ransomware*—a type of malware that blocks access to the computer's system or certain files until a sum of money is paid—that specifically targeted US employees working from home during the pandemic.[18]

BEING A MULE HAS CONSEQUENCES

By transferring funds that are the by-product of a crime, money mules become involved in the furtherance of criminal activity. Whether done wittingly or unwittingly, acting as a money mule is a crime, and the potential consequences are severe. Individuals could be charged as part of a criminal money laundering conspiracy and face a variety of other criminal charges as well. In the United States, potential federal charges include mail fraud, wire fraud, bank fraud, money laundering, transactional money laundering, operating an unlicensed money transmitting business, and aggravated identity theft.[19] A conviction can result in jail time, fines, or community service.

If caught, an individual acting as a mule will likely have a fraud marker put on his or her records. Consequently, that person's current bank account will be frozen or closed, and no further loans or mortgages will be granted. Other consequences may include negative credit ratings and a bar from opening future bank accounts, to name just a few. In some cases, money mules may be personally liable for repaying the losses suffered by victims. However, those individuals who the FBI concludes are merely unwitting, such as the elderly, the lonely, or the confused, generally avoid prosecution.[20]

Additionally, by exposing their own personal information, money mules put themselves at risk for identity theft. Furthermore, mules and their families could face threats from criminals or even be physically attacked if they do not continue to work as a money mule.

With large-scale cyber heists, the money mule is most exposed and therefore most likely to get caught and punished if law enforcement intercepts the heist. In fact, money mules are frequently the scapegoats in such schemes, whereas the real masterminds behind the crime remain hidden and anonymous.

Recognizing the growth of money mule activity, the DOJ and other US state and federal law enforcement agencies, as well as international law enforcement groups, have put in place many initiatives aimed at rooting out money mules in recent years. These campaigns have focused their efforts on a combination of prosecution and public awareness to curb the seemingly endless cycle of money laundering activity.[21] Disseminating relevant information about the dangers, threats, and consequences of money mule activity can help prevent individuals from falling victim to such schemes and keep others from being recruited into criminal activity.

RED FLAGS ASSOCIATED WITH MONEY MULE ACTIVITY

The FBI's Money Laundering, Forfeiture and Bank Fraud Unit published the "Money Mule Awareness Booklet," which provides a list of red flags that may indicate whether someone has been targeted as a money mule.[22] These red flags primarily pertain to unusual or suspicious email communications and offers that seem "too good to be true."

Additionally, FinCEN issued an advisory in July 2019 titled "Advisory on Imposter Scams and Money Mule Schemes Related to Coronavirus Disease 2019 (COVID-19)" that includes a list of financial-specific red flag indicators of money mule schemes. Although FinCEN's list of red flags relates to COVID-19, many of the identified red flags are also relevant in a broader context. These red flags primarily relate to work-from-home schemes, transactions that are inconsistent with the customer's prior transactional history, and unusual activity related to the diversion of funds in quick succession or to unrelated accounts, as well as activity involving foreign jurisdictions.[23] Both documents are accessible online at each of the respective organizations' websites.

CONCLUSION

Cyber-enabled financial crime and related online money mule activity have surged with the ever-increasing use of technology and the rise in telecommunications, including social media. With ongoing advancements, this trend will inevitably continue. The COVID-19 pandemic and the resulting economic downturn, meanwhile, have further exacerbated the rise in cybercrime across the globe. Regardless of the crisis at hand, however, fraudsters will always prey on the uncertainty and fear of the general public and seek to take advantage of gaps in compliance and legal frameworks.

Borders are meaningless when it comes to cybercrime. Individuals and businesses can be victimized regardless of their location, and money can be moved quickly, easily, and anonymously between countries and across the world. If fraudulent schemes are not detected in a timely manner, the funds are nearly impossible to recover. In fact, money mule schemes have become more difficult to detect given the diversification of labor, which has become more specialized, in moving stolen funds. On top of this, data privacy rules have made tracing the flow of money from one bank to another even harder. Further compounding this problem, cybercriminals have proven to be far more technologically adept than those leading the efforts to counter them.

In the meantime, training, education, and raising general awareness of the various cyber schemes are among the best ways to avoid becoming a victim. Going forward, society will need to adapt to the new realities brought on by advancements in technology and to learn how to appropriately balance a sense of trust with the need for increased vigilance and caution.

NOTES

1. BAE Systems and SWIFT, "Follow the Money: Understanding the Money Laundering Techniques That Support Large-Scale Cyber-Heists" (Surrey, UK: BAE Systems and SWIFT, 2020), https://www.swift.com/news-events/news/how-cyber-attackers-cash-out-following-large-scale-heists.
2. FBI, Public Service Announcement, "Money Mules," Alert no. I-111919-PSA, November 19, 2019.
3. US Department of Justice, FBI, Money Laundering, Forfeiture and Bank Fraud Unit, "Money Mule Awareness Booklet, 2019" (Washington, DC: FBI, July 2019), https://www.self-helpfcu.org/docs/default-source/pdfs/money-mule-awareness-booklet-july-2019.pdf?sfvrsn=2.
4. Brian Krebs, "Coronavirus Widens the Money Mule Pool," *Krebs on Security* (blog), March 17, 2020, https://krebsonsecurity.com/2020/03/coronavirus-widens-the-money-mule-pool/.

5. Brian Arrington, "From Smurfs to Mules: 21st Century Money Laundering," *ACAMS Today*, February 28, 2014, https://www.acamstoday.org/from-smurfs-to-mules-21st -century-money-laundering/.

6. Europol, "Money Muling," Public Awareness and Prevention Guides, accessed October 5, 2020, https://www.europol.europa.eu/activities-services/public-awareness-and -prevention-guides/money-muling.

7. BAE Systems and SWIFT, "Follow the Money," 7.

8. BAE Systems and SWIFT, 11.

9. Justice Department, "Money Mule Awareness Booklet."

10. Justice Department.

11. U.S.A. v. Maksim V. Yakubets and Igor Turashev, US District Court for the Western District of Pennsylvania, Indictment, Criminal No. 19.342, November 12, 2019, https:// www.justice.gov/opa/press-release/file/1223586/download.

12. Brian Krebs, "Inside 'Evil Corp,' a $100M Cybercrime Menace," *Krebs on Security* (blog), December 16, 2019, https://krebsonsecurity.com/2019/12/inside-evil-corp-a-100m -cybercrime-menace/.

13. Krebs.

14. US Treasury Department, "Treasury Sanctions Evil Corp, the Russia-Based Cybercriminal Group behind Dridex Malware," press release, December 5, 2019, https://home .treasury.gov/news/press-releases/sm845.

15. Cybereason Intel Team, "Russia and Nation-State Hacking Tactics: A Report from Cybereason Intelligence Group," *Malicious Life* (blog), June 5, 2017, https://www .cybereason.com/blog/blog-russia-nation-state-hacking-the-countrys-dedicated-policy -of-strategic-ambiguity; and John Leyden, "Russia Is Struggling to Keep Its Cybercrime Groups on a Tight Leash," *Register*, June 6, 2017, https://www.theregister.com/2017/06 /06/russia_cyber_militia_analysis/.

16. FBI, "Most Wanted: Maksim Viktorovich Yakubets," accessed October 6, 2020, https:// www.fbi.gov/wanted/cyber/maksim-viktorovich-yakubets.

17. Ellyn Maese and Lydia Saad, "How Has the Pandemic Affected U.S. Work Life?," *Gallup*, March 17, 2021, https://news.gallup.com/poll/339824/pandemic-affected-work -life.aspx.

18. "Russian Hacker Group Evil Corp Targets U.S. Workers at Home," BBC News, June 26, 2020, https://www.bbc.com/news/world-us-canada-53195749.

19. Justice Department, "Money Mule Awareness Booklet."

20. "How Ordinary People Get Duped into Becoming 'Money Mules,'" CBS News, December 27, 2018, https://www.cbsnews.com/news/how-ordinary-people-get-duped-into -becoming-money-mules/.

21. "How Ordinary People Get Duped."

22. Justice Department, "Money Mule Awareness Booklet."

23. FinCen, "Advisory on Imposter Scams and Money Mule Schemes Related to Coronavirus Disease 2019 (COVID-19)," US Treasury Department, FIN-2020-A003, July 7, 2019, https://www.fincen.gov/sites/default/files/advisory/2020-07-07/Advisory_ %20Imposter_and_Money_Mule_COVID_19_508_FINAL.pdf.

CHAPTER 7

THE THRIVING MARKET
OF MODERN-DAY SLAVERY

Human Trafficking and Money Laundering

Illicit trade is a lucrative business, whether it involves commodities or humans. Human trafficking, also referred to as trafficking in persons, is a modern form of the human slave trade, whereby men, women, and children are treated as chattels who can be bought, sold, traded, and discarded. It is both an abhorrent and shameful domestic and global crime as well as a grave violation of human rights. Unfortunately, human trafficking is shockingly prevalent. Although the hidden nature of human trafficking makes obtaining precise data on the number of its victims almost impossible, in 2016 it was estimated that 40.3 million people were in some form of slavery worldwide.[1] Furthermore, trafficking in humans continues to be one of the fastest-growing crimes, affecting nearly every country across the globe.

Like all forms of illicit trade, human trafficking is driven by consumer demand. The United Nations reports that modern slavery's proceeds represent the third most profitable multinational criminal activity, following drug trafficking and counterfeiting of goods. According to the International Labour Organization, human trafficking generates approximately $150 billion per year.[2] Due to the enormity of these proceeds, human trafficking is a common predicate crime to money laundering.

Although the role of financial institutions in human trafficking may not be immediately apparent, banks and other financial institutions are key in the fight against human trafficking, as nearly all traffickers will utilize a financial institution at some point to move funds. Consequently, financial institutions are in a unique position to identify suspicious activity, track the money, and assist law enforcement.

THE ROOTS OF HUMAN TRAFFICKING

As a form of slavery, human trafficking has deep-seated roots. Forced labor and slavery have long been a part of world history. People have been enslaving one another, in some form and with varying degrees of brutality, since the beginning of time. Ancient civilizations are widely known to have had slaves. References to slavery are in the Code of Hammurabi, the Babylonian code of law emblematic of the Mesopotamian civilization, that King Hammurabi enacted during his reign (1792–1750 BC). Various forms of slavery existed in ancient Egypt and included slaves from foreign lands, many of whom lived under punitive conditions. Similarly, slaves played an important role in Greco-Roman society and its economy. According to the Greek philosopher Aristotle, slavery was considered a natural part of life. Pirates, including those from North Africa and the Caribbean, forcibly took not only goods but also human beings, who at that time were viewed as property and generated large profits when sold.

Indentured servitude became popular as part of the economic system in the early modern period in Europe and North America. Like slavery, indentured servitude was a form of unfree labor. But in contrast to slavery, *indentured servitude* was a signed or forced contract between two individuals, whereby one person worked at no pay to fulfill a debt or another legal obligation and usually for a set amount of time. Therefore, this practice differed from slavery in its terms and social status. Nonetheless, its associated working conditions could still be brutal. Although slaves existed in the English colonies throughout the 1600s, many planters chose to employ indentured servants before the 1680s.[3]

Around that time, the African slave trade exploded. From the fifteenth to nineteenth centuries, between 12 million and 15 million men, women, and children were trafficked from Africa to the Western Hemisphere as part of the transatlantic slave trade, representing the largest forced and legally sanctioned migration in human history.[4] Additionally, the nineteenth century also saw the dawn of the "coolie trade," which involved the importation and exploitation of Asian contract laborers (especially the Chinese and Indians) under force or deception for the purposes of slave labor.[5]

Eventually, the ideas that came out of the European Enlightenment started to change the public's perception of slavery. The practice was finally outlawed in the nineteenth century, first in the United Kingdom and then the United States, the world's leading slave-trading powers. However, until that time, their governments both legally sanctioned and tolerated the slave trade. Thus, as history shows, slavery has spanned many cultures, religions, and nationalities, from ancient times to the present day.

In 1948 the United Nations (UN) General Assembly adopted the Universal Declaration of Human Rights. This historic document was the first international agreement to affirm the rights and freedoms of all human beings, and it laid the foundation for future human rights protections. Although not a legally binding document, its provisions have been incorporated into subsequent international treaties and regional human rights instruments, as well as into national constitutions and legal codes.[6] It was not until 2000, however, that the UN officially criminalized human trafficking under the protocols of the United Nations Convention against Transnational Organized Crime.[7]

In the United States, the Trafficking Victims Protection Act of 2000 supplemented existing laws and provided new tools against human trafficking, thereby serving as the first comprehensive federal law to address trafficking in persons.[8] In the years since its passage, Congress has built on this law. Currently, several provisions in the US Code target trafficking in persons, involuntary servitude and slavery, and forced labor. "These provisions are contained in Chapter 77 of Title 18 and are sometimes referred to generally as Chapter 77 offenses."[9]

Yet indentured servitude and other forms of unfree labor, including various forms of human trafficking, persist. In fact, more people are trapped in modern-day slavery today than during any time in history.[10]

WHAT IS MODERN-DAY SLAVERY?

Anyone, regardless of origin, sex, age, or legal status, can be a victim of human trafficking. Likewise, anyone can be a trafficker—from a single individual to a criminal network, terrorist organization, or corrupt government regime.[11]

Human trafficking is a global problem. Any country could serve as the country of origin, transit, or destination—or even a combination of all three—of this crime. However, trafficking mostly occurs from less developed countries, where victims are rendered even more vulnerable, to more developed countries. Although the vast majority of trafficking takes place at the national or regional level, long-distance trafficking has also garnered considerable attention. Europe has been the primary destination for trafficking victims from the widest range of destinations, and Asia is the source of most trafficking victims sent to the widest range of destinations. The Americas, meanwhile, serve as both an origin of and a destination for trafficking victims.[12]

Cities and other areas located near highways and airports are hubs for human traffickers. In the United States, the I-95 corridor from Florida to New York—with quick access to major cities such as Philadelphia and Washington, DC—serves as a popular route for perpetrators to move their victims. In these cities, trafficking at airport hotels and motels is especially prevalent, making it easy to obtain, transport, and harbor victims. Trafficking also commonly takes place in gas stations and rest stops. Many of the victims in these cases are at-risk youth, such as runaways.[13]

Human trafficking is not just an urban problem, however. It occurs in rural areas, small towns, and suburbs. Fake massage parlors where women are forced into sexual service, for example, are common in the United States. They are often found in strip malls, office buildings, and even residential homes, and they frequently go unnoticed.[14] Traffickers also operate online, using popular social media websites such as Facebook and anonymous sites on the dark web to lure victims and advertise their services.[15]

According to FinCEN, *human trafficking* is defined as "a crime that involves exploiting a person for labor, services, or commercial sex."[16] The UN sets out a more comprehensive working definition of human trafficking in the Protocol to Prevent, Suppress and Punish Trafficking in Persons, Especially Women and Children, which constitutes the primary instrument that countries use to tackle the crime of trafficking in persons and serves as the basis for most national laws on human trafficking. According to the trafficking protocol, human trafficking means "the recruitment, transportation, transfer, harbouring or receipt of persons, by means of the threat or use of force or other forms of coercion, of abduction, of fraud, of deception, . . . for the purpose of exploitation."[17] This definition is similar to the one used by FinCEN; however, the definition in the trafficking protocol goes slightly further by including the means of trafficking as an additional element.

As of January 2018, 169 jurisdictions have ratified or acceded to the trafficking protocol, including the United States.[18] The primary purposes of the protocol are to prevent and combat trafficking in persons, to protect and assist victims of trafficking, and to promote cooperation among parties to meet these objectives. The protocol is also intended to provide international consistency on the issue of trafficking in persons for the purposes of legislative and policy development and implementation. Furthermore, it requires that ratifying nations criminalize such practices.

As the definitions cited make clear, the primary objective of human trafficking is to exploit a person for the purposes of acquiring money. Just as profit was the primary driver of the slave trade throughout history, it is also responsible for the continuation of slavery today in the form of human trafficking.

Modern-day slavery, as with slavery in the past, is driven by economics and the laws of supply and demand. Around the world, the demand for cheap labor is high.[19] Further, poverty, social instability, military conflict, corruption, gender bias, and other factors serve to provide a vast supply of vulnerable groups for traffickers to exploit.[20] Globalization, along with the rise of the internet and social media in particular, has greatly enabled traffickers to trade in human lives.

HOW HUMAN TRAFFICKING WORKS

Human trafficking essentially comprises three distinct stages: recruitment or abduction, transportation, and exploitation.

Recruitment or abduction constitutes the first stage of human trafficking and refers to the way in which traffickers obtain their victims. This is accomplished through either deception or force. For example, traffickers commonly procure their victims through kidnapping, false marriages, or fraudulent advertisements offering employment or study abroad. Especially vulnerable to these methods are people from areas that have been affected by economic hardship, armed conflicts, or natural disasters.[21]

The second stage is transportation. This stage occurs after the victims have been obtained. It involves moving victims to locations where they are exploited or sold to other traffickers. They may be transported by any means, including air, sea, and land, to domestic or international destinations.[22]

The final stage of human trafficking is exploitation. During this stage, traffickers make their profit off the victims through many ways: their forced labor, sexual exploitation, and organ removal, as well as their involuntary participation in other crimes or illicit activities.[23]

Human trafficking is highly structured and is therefore considered a type of organized crime. It is typically carried out by a group of individuals and is most frequently the work of numerous smaller criminal networks. The people involved can even include family members or friends of the victim. Thus, in most cases, the traffickers are of the same nationality as their victims.

Furthermore, all human trafficking isn't the same, even among the different types of human trafficking. The various networks of traffickers exhibit different specific and unique typologies, which include the nationality of the parties, the geographical route, and the form of exploitation. For example, traffickers from Southeast Asia typically traffic young Asian women to the West for sex work in massage parlors and nail salons, while both African American and Hispanic women in the United States are more likely to be exploited for commercial sex work in motels.

Likewise, the various trafficking groups also exhibit distinctive typologies in their money laundering schemes. For example, Southeast Asian traffickers are more likely to commingle legitimate and illicit profits from their front businesses, which are frequently the same massage parlors and nail salons. In contrast, other groups of traffickers rely on different methods, such as structuring. Recognizing these differences can help identify trafficking's red flags.

In recent years, human trafficking has become more global in scope. Criminal organizations involved in human trafficking have expanded the geographic range of their activities to reach new markets. As part of their expansion, traffickers have taken on a range of additional criminal activities, and some of these groups have even started to partner and work together. In many cases, traffickers are also involved in multiple criminal pursuits, such as narcotics and weapons trafficking, as well as money laundering.[24] For example, Nigerian and Balkan groups engage in drug trafficking along with human trafficking. Likewise, Latin American drug cartels have also recently started profiting from human trafficking.[25]

Although there isn't "one face" of a human trafficking victim, certain populations are much more vulnerable than others to this crime. The groups of people most affected by human trafficking typically live in poverty; are fleeing violence, natural disasters, or other displacement; or are working on the margins of the formal economy, such as people with irregular employment or migration status. Traffickers also target runaway and homeless youth, children in the foster care system, individuals with a disability, and those who have suffered other types of abuse or exploitation, whether physical, sexual, or mental in nature.

Human trafficking takes place in a broad range of both licit and illicit industries. The sectors of industry that are most frequently implicated are agriculture, construction, garments and textiles (under sweatshop conditions), hospitality, catering and restaurants, domestic work, janitorial services, and entertainment, as well as drug smuggling and distribution and the sex industry. These sectors may also involve a rotation of seasonal laborers, making trafficking more difficult to detect. Human trafficking also affects more mainstream sectors of the economy, including food processing, health care, and contract cleaning. Although human trafficking occurs mainly in the private sector, it has also been documented in public sector employment.[26] Consequently, human trafficking can and does occur in every country, in every economic sector, and along various parts of many industries' supply chains.

TYPES OF HUMAN TRAFFICKING

In line with the definition contained in the UN's trafficking protocol, the FATF identifies three main types of human trafficking:

1. For prostitution or other forms of sexual exploitation
2. For forced labor or slavery
3. For the removal of organs[27]

Sexual exploitation is by far the most commonly identified form of human trafficking, constituting 79 percent of human trafficking cases worldwide, according to the UN Office on Drugs and Crime's *Global Report on Trafficking in Persons*.[28] As a matter of fact, a disproportionate number of women are involved in human trafficking not just as victims but also as traffickers themselves. The latter women may play a larger role in the trafficking ring by luring or recruiting and coaching new victims. This works because oftentimes victims see women as being more trustworthy than men. For example, Ghislaine Maxwell has been accused of working as accused sex trafficker Jeffrey Epstein's accomplice by coaching young girls for sexual abuse.[29] The active participation of women in human trafficking is often seen in cases where former victims become perpetrators as a means of escaping their own victimization.[30]

Victims of sex trafficking are often exploited over an extended period. Offenders are therefore required to meet the victims' basic needs, such as food, accommodations, and transport, so that the former can continue to exploit them. The financial transactions for these expenditures may be conducted either directly by the victim or by the perpetrator or launderer involved in the human-trafficking offense. In identifying money laundering from human-trafficking activity generally, transactions often intentionally appear as regular account activity. Examining the victims' expenses and financial flows may be a more effective way of spotting sex-trafficking victims and of identifying money launderers and the criminal networks responsible for the trafficking.[31]

For example, a common sex-trafficking scheme involves luring women from Southeast Asia to the United States, Canada, or western Europe under the false pretense of offering a better life. However, once the women arrive at their destination, they are forced to work at massage parlors or other front companies, where they are made to perform sexual services to repay their transportation debt and to pay for their accommodations. In many cases, the victims are also forced to hand over their passports, or threats are made against their families to ensure their cooperation. Asian massage parlors, such as the one in Palm Beach County, Florida, where New England Patriots owner Robert Kraft was caught patronizing on video, are notorious for such activity. Although authorities dropped the charges against Kraft (primarily due to the inadmissibility of the video evidence), that particular spa and others in south Florida are still under investigation for sex trafficking.[32]

Human trafficking for the purpose of forced labor or slavery is the second-most common form of human trafficking, representing approximately 18 percent of cases internationally. For example, *debt bondage* (also called peonage), which is the enslavement of people for unpaid debts, falls into the forced labor category regardless of the type of labor being done (whether domestic, construction, or agricultural) and regardless of whether the trafficking victim is an adult or a child.

Of the three forms of human trafficking, this one most likely involves male victims. *Forced labor trafficking* entails work that is performed involuntarily and under the threat of violence, brutality, intimidation, or some sort of penalty. It also concerns situations involving more subtle or seemingly more benign means of exploitation, which nonetheless harm migrants and other individuals and violate their human rights. Such abuses include manipulated debt, retention of identity papers, unsafe work conditions, extremely menial wages, unreasonable restrictions during both work and nonwork hours, or threats of denunciation to immigration authorities. This form of enslavement is easily hidden, particularly in supply chains containing layers of subcontractors, and exists in large part because of the demand for cheaper goods and lower-cost services.[33]

Labor trafficking often begins with some form of initial recruitment of the victim, typically under the pretense of better employment abroad or higher wages. Although forced labor can take many forms, it typically revolves around exploiting another individual's labor for profit. Some common labor-trafficking practices involve forcing victims to work directly for the offender in isolated or rural towns for extremely minimal or no pay, to work legitimate jobs (generally requiring low skills) but taking most or all of their wages and controlling their bank accounts, to undertake gang-related criminal activities, or to engage in shoplifting and pickpocketing in exchange for food and accommodation but no pay.[34]

Human trafficking for the purpose of organ removal represents the minority of human-trafficking cases. Terms such as "organ trafficking," "illegal organ trade," and "transplant tourism" are often used interchangeably with trafficking in persons for the purpose of organ removal, although these practices generally encompass a broader range of illicit activity. The

United States doesn't explicitly recognize human trafficking for organ removal as a separate form of human trafficking in its definition. Nonetheless, organ trafficking is a prohibited practice in the United States.[35]

As is the case with other illicit activity mentioned in this book, because it is conducted in secret, it's nearly impossible to get accurate data about this type of human trafficking. However, the World Health Organization estimates that between 5 and 10 percent of all organ transplants conducted worldwide are conducted illegally.[36] In this form of human trafficking, the victim is exploited over a much shorter time than is the case with other forms of human trafficking but nonetheless suffers significant harm. Simply, once the organ is removed, the trafficker has no further need for the victim.

Kidneys are by far the most common organ trafficked. Victims generally live in extreme poverty and are coerced, deceived, defrauded, or forced into selling an organ. They typically are paid a fraction of what the trafficker, who is usually the member of a criminal organization, receives. Very few victims are informed enough, or have the mental capacity, to give true consent. Following the operation, it is not uncommon for the victim-donor to suffer postoperative complications from the surgery, including infections such as HIV and hepatitis C, or to die.

Human trafficking for organs is a small but extremely lucrative business. A single kidney can net up to $200,000 on the black market. Although trafficking in human organs is illegal in almost every nation, the details of the laws differ, thus making prosecutions very difficult. Cases can implicate the laws of several jurisdictions, depending on the home country of the buyer, the trafficker, and the victim, and on the country in which the operation takes place. For example, in some countries, it is illegal to sell a kidney but not to purchase one. In other countries, it is illegal to buy and sell an organ within the country but not to buy and/or sell an organ abroad.

This form of human trafficking provides the perpetrator—or perpetrators, as this is normally a coordinated effort—with a more significant, albeit one-time, financial gain. Consequently, financial flows offer fewer opportunities to detect organ trafficking. Therefore, it is usually a large payment, one inconsistent with the individual's employment, that would constitute the greatest opportunity for detecting this form of human trafficking. Two additional potential opportunities to detect this type of human trafficking through financial flows include identifying the financing for the infrastructure required to carry out the offense, such as the procurement of medical facilities and equipment, and identifying payments to the various individuals necessary to carry out the offense, such as the surgeons and the brokers.[37] Both of these types of transactions would occur outside the context of ordinary activity.

HUMAN TRAFFICKING VERSUS HUMAN SMUGGLING

Human trafficking and human smuggling are two terms that are often used together but actually refer to quite different activities. To foster a common understanding of human trafficking and human smuggling, and to be able to identify and report transactions that are potentially associated with these practices, it is important to differentiate between them.

Like human trafficking, human smuggling is a serious federal crime punishable by fines and prison time. It is codified in 8 U.S.C. § 1324, which defines *human smuggling* as "acts or attempts to bring unauthorized aliens to or into the United States, transport them within the U.S., harbor unlawful aliens, encourage entry of illegal aliens, or conspire to commit these violations, knowingly or in reckless disregard of illegal status."[38]

Human trafficking and human smuggling differ in four primary ways. First, human trafficking necessarily involves the use of force or coercion and exploitation, whereas human smuggling involves someone choosing to immigrate illegally. Second, human trafficking involves some sort of involuntary or forced act(s), such as forced labor or forced sex, whereas human smuggling is limited to illegal migration or the harboring of undocumented aliens. Third, anyone can be a victim of human trafficking, regardless of origin, sex, age, or legal status, while human smuggling is limited to the involvement of foreign nationals. Last, a person can be trafficked without crossing a border; indeed, individuals can be trafficked within the borders of a country. In contrast, the crime of human smuggling involves illegally crossing a border or transporting or harboring someone who has illegally crossed the border.[39]

Therefore, the main difference between human smuggling and human trafficking is that human smuggling revolves primarily around the movement of unlawful aliens, whereas human trafficking focuses on exploitation. Additionally, human smuggling generates onetime illicit proceeds. In contrast, with the exception of human trafficking for the purposes of organ removal, human trafficking may generate ongoing criminal proceeds.

THE TOUCH POINTS BETWEEN HUMAN TRAFFICKING AND FINANCIAL INSTITUTIONS

Financial institutions can be instrumental in detecting and combating human trafficking and money laundering because FIs provide services that virtually everyone in the modern world, including traffickers and launderers, utilizes at one point or another. With human trafficking, there are four primary touch points between the trafficker and the financial institution. In fact, the trafficker makes contact with the financial institution long before initiating the money laundering process.

The first touch point involves handling payments for the logistics, such as the transportation, food, and lodging associated with trafficking. The second includes moving the money received from customers for sex, labor, or organs, and the third encompasses transferring funds from lower-level traffickers to the larger criminal organization. The final touch point regards using the financial institution to launder the illicit proceeds.[40]

Given the various ways in which human traffickers come into contact with and use financial institutions, the FIs are considered as conduits in the furtherance of human trafficking and money laundering.

Traffickers often open both personal and business accounts to handle the proceeds of their criminal activity. For instance, in the United States, traffickers who operate front companies, such as nail salons, often use business accounts wherein their licit and illicit proceeds are commingled.

In transnational cases, traffickers frequently use financial systems to move the proceeds from human trafficking from one location to another. In these cases, funnel accounts are frequently employed to transfer funds from one geographic location to another. A *funnel account* is either an individual or a business account located in one geographic area that is used to receive cash deposits from a different geographic area, often in a short span of time. The amounts involved are purposely designed to fall below the cash reporting threshold.[41] Funnel accounts further enable traffickers to move proceeds rapidly while maintaining their anonymity.

Third-party payment processors (TPPPs) have also been recognized as a means by which traffickers wire funds both domestically and internationally. This method of moving funds gives the appearance that the TPPP is the originator or beneficiary of the wire transfer and thereby conceals the identity of the true originator or beneficiary. Human traffickers can facilitate payments via TPPPs for the operation of online escort services and illicit online streaming services.[42]

In addition to their other services, banks may underwrite loans or participate in investments that further human trafficking. Besides banks, various types of financial services providers have also been implicated in human trafficking: money services and remittance businesses, credit card companies, cash couriers, dealers in high-value goods, casinos, and others.[43]

Human trafficking happens in the shadows, whereby transactions are conducted covertly, and purchasers seek to remain anonymous. Consequently, most of the associated payments, whether for sex, labor, or organs, are made in cash. As a result, human trafficking generates high volumes of cash.[44]

However, cash is certainly not the sole means of acceptable payment. To a lesser extent, cryptocurrencies are also used. For example, cryptocurrencies are becoming an increasingly common mode of payment for access to online pornography and illicit websites, sectors of the commercial sex industry where human trafficking is frequent.[45] Prepaid cards are also often used because they provide the purchasers anonymity. Additionally, credit cards may also be accepted as a means of payment in cases involving front businesses, such as the massage parlors that are run by criminal organizations.

Based on the various touch points between financial institutions and human traffickers, financial institutions are in a unique position to identify and report suspicious activity related to human trafficking. In addition to CDD reviews, which can uncover such details as criminal histories and financial inconsistencies that can lead to the identification of traffickers, transaction monitoring is a key tool used to ferret out illicit activity. FinCEN recommends that the most effective way to evaluate transactional activity for signs of human trafficking is to review transactions at a relationship level rather than only at the account level. This enables an institution to conduct a more comprehensive analysis of its overall customer relationship, including the customer's behavior and transactional activity. Furthermore, direct interactions by bank personnel with customers make financial institutions especially well suited to spot signs of potential human trafficking, such as when older customers come in with seemingly unrelated or very poorly dressed youths, cannot provide proper documentation, or exhibit other unusual activity. FinCEN has several advisories on its website on how financial institutions can detect and report human trafficking and related activity, along with guidance on SAR filings related to human trafficking.[46]

CASE STUDY: THE DIRTY SECRETS OF JEFFREY EPSTEIN AND DEUTSCHE BANK

A human trafficking case that received considerable media coverage and public attention is the 2019 scandal involving Jeffrey Epstein. Although his case is atypical in many respects (i.e., he was a well-connected multimillionaire and did not represent a typical sex trafficker), it does offer crucial insights into human trafficking, including the sex trafficking of minors in particular. Furthermore, an analysis of Deutsche Bank's customer relationship with Epstein and its extreme AML compliance failures with respect to that relationship, including the risks posed by private banking relationships and bank employee complicity, provides valuable lessons on the critical role of financial institutions in such crimes as human trafficking and the importance of effective AML compliance programs.

Jeffrey Edward Epstein, the mysterious American financier (whose source of wealth still remains unknown), has been the subject of numerous allegations involving procuring sex from minors and sexually exploiting dozens of young girls as early as 2002. Investigations into Epstein were initiated in 2005 after a victim's parent contacted the police and accused Epstein of sexually abusing her fourteen-year-old daughter at his estate in Palm Beach, Florida.

In 2008 Epstein entered into a highly controversial plea deal overseen by Alex Acosta, who at that time was the US attorney in south Florida (and would later become the secretary of labor under President Donald Trump). In fact, former US prosecutor Berit Berger noted in an interview with NPR that nonprosecution agreements, such as Epstein's, are fairly common with the Department of Justice for things such as white-collar crimes but are "almost unheard of" in child sex-trafficking cases.[47] As a result of the deal, despite reportedly overwhelming evidence that he had also sexually abused dozens of minors, Epstein avoided a federal conviction and instead pleaded guilty to two lesser state charges of soliciting prostitution, with one involving a minor.[48] Consequently, Epstein served less than thirteen months in the Palm Beach County jail during which he was allowed extensive time out on work release.

In the meantime, Epstein continued to engage in predatory behavior and was alleged to have sexually abused women and girls as young as fourteen years old. Like other sex traffickers, Epstein preyed on victims who were already vulnerable in one way or another. For example, at least one victim was a runaway, and other victims had suffered past sexual trauma. Epstein lured the girls to his properties under the guise of paying them for a massage. These massages became increasingly sexual in nature, turning into instances of alleged rape in a number of cases.

Epstein used the help of his former longtime girlfriend Ghislaine Maxwell (who has been referred to as Epstein's madam) to groom and get access to the underage girls so that he could sexually abuse them, and in some instances, Maxwell reportedly also participated in the abuse. To maintain a constant supply of victims, Epstein paid some of them to recruit additional girls, thereby creating a vast network of victims for him to sexually exploit. (As noted previously, sex traffickers commonly use victims to groom and recruit additional victims.) Several of Epstein's accusers further claim that multiple famous and powerful men were involved with Epstein's alleged sex ring and that Epstein would "loan" his victims to them. A number of these encounters allegedly took place on an island located in the US Virgin Islands that Epstein owned and named Little Saint James, but locals in the area and others knew it as "Pedophile Island."

Epstein was ultimately arrested again in July 2019 on federal charges for the sex trafficking of minors in both Florida and New York (which along with California and Texas are the states where human trafficking is most prevalent in the country).[49] Epstein's arrest brought under scrutiny many of his high-level connections, including Prince Andrew, President Bill Clinton, and President Donald Trump—all of whom have denied knowing anything about Epstein's crimes. The negative attention following Epstein's arrest also led to Acosta's resignation as labor secretary.[50]

Awaiting trial, Epstein was detained at the twelve-story Metropolitan Correctional Center in lower Manhattan, just blocks from Wall Street. The federal detention facility is as notorious for its overcrowding and squalid conditions as it is for its lineup of high-profile inmates, which have included Mexican drug kingpin Joaquín "El Chapo" Guzmán, Gambino crime family boss John Gotti, World Trade Center bomber Ramzi Yousef, and Ponzi scheme mastermind Bernie Madoff.[51]

When federal authorities raided Epstein's homes, including the ones in Manhattan, Palm Beach, and the US Virgin Islands, they found an extraordinarily large volume of sexually suggestive photographs of nude and partially nude women and girls; numerous sex toys; video recording equipment, including hidden cameras; and notes and messages containing victims' names. They also uncovered a fraudulent passport under a fake name and other evidence suggesting a highly complex criminal enterprise.[52]

Epstein was charged with sex trafficking and conspiracy. Upon conviction, these charges carry a minimum sentence of ten years (which could be raised to a fifteen-year minimum sentence if prosecutors could prove that any of the victims were younger than fourteen years of age) and a maximum sentence of forty-five years. Possible charges of child pornography could further enhance Epstein's sentence by an additional five years.[53]

However, less than one month later, at the age of sixty-six, Epstein mysteriously died in his jail cell. Although the medical examiner officially declared the cause of death to be the result of suicide, the medical examiner's ruling has been widely disputed. Further, there has been significant public skepticism regarding the actual cause of Epstein's death, with some asserting he was murdered to prevent the further exposure and potential criminal proceedings of other powerful individuals.[54]

As for Ghislaine Maxwell, she disappeared for a short time following Epstein's arrest, but the FBI later found her hiding out on a sprawling, 156-acre, secluded, million-dollar New Hampshire estate that was paid for in cash through an LLC structured to hide her identity. Records simply show the buyer of the property was Granite Realty LLC, whose listed manager is a Boston attorney. The real estate transaction was purposely arranged to provide anonymity and was so effectively structured that Maxwell's name was unconnected with the real estate purchase. Neither the prior owner nor the real estate agent who sold the property was aware that Ghislaine Maxwell was the buyer.[55] Maxwell was arrested in July 2020 on multiple charges related to the sexual abuse of young women and girls by Jeffrey Epstein.

In the meantime, Epstein's death may have allowed him to escape potential accountability, but it did not enable Deutsche Bank to evade penalties for several compliance failures resulting from its business dealings with him. A global financial institution headquartered in Frankfurt, Germany, Deutsche Bank also operates in the state of New York and is licensed and supervised by the New York State Department of Financial Services. As such, under the BSA, the bank is required to have an appropriate AML compliance program. In July 2020, Deutsche Bank entered into a consent order following an investigation that found significant compliance failures in connection with its relationship with Jeffrey Epstein. As a result, Deutsche Bank was fined $150 million in penalties, signifying the first enforcement action by a regulator against a financial institution for its dealings with Epstein.[56]

Despite the negative media reports surrounding Jeffrey Epstein—his criminal history, including his prior conviction, and his sex offender status—Deutsche Bank nonetheless welcomed Epstein as a customer. It allowed him to open accounts at its institution and thereafter maintained a profitable customer relationship with Epstein from August 2013 until December 2018.

In fact, documents show that bank personnel handling Epstein's account had knowledge of various red flags associated with him—for example, his prior criminal record in Florida, his numerous out-of-court civil settlements, and other public allegations that should have raised serious concerns for the bank. However, they appeared to disregard these warnings in favor of profits, as at least one of the Deutsche employees who worked on the Epstein account was incentivized for bringing in lucrative clients. Also, evidence documenting a discussion between Deutsche employees specifically noted that Epstein was a potential client who could generate significant revenue for the bank and provide leads to other lucrative clients. Furthermore, two executives at Deutsche Bank, who were in a position to understand the severity of the risk that the client relationship with Epstein presented and had the corresponding authority to act upon this knowledge, critically concluded that the Epstein account did not require further review. They bypassed the bank's own internal controls designed to mitigate such risk and gave their assent to move forward with the business.[57]

Throughout the course of its customer relationship with Epstein, Deutsche Bank failed to adequately monitor his activity and, as a result, processed millions of dollars of suspicious transactions. They included shady payments to individuals who were widely known to be Epstein's coconspirators and remittances for school tuition and hotel expenses, as well as direct payments to numerous unrelated women, assumed to be Epstein's victims—all of which should have raised questions. Yet the bank allowed Epstein to conduct these financial transactions even despite the abundant and publicly available information linking him to serious prior misconduct.[58]

The German bank handled more than forty accounts related to Epstein and individuals and entities associated with him, with hundreds of transactions totaling in the millions of dollars. Among these transactions were payments both for legal settlements and to law firms for the legal expenses of Epstein and his known coconspirators. Also, numerous periodic and unexplainable cash withdrawals totaling over $800,000 occurred within a four-year time frame.[59] These were third-party withdrawals made by one of Epstein's attorneys, who specifically inquired how often he could withdraw cash without triggering an alert that would require the bank to file a CTR, a regulatory filing that may be indicative of the criminal offense of structuring. The attorney later broke up a withdrawal over a two-day period but, when confronted by bank officers, denied any intent to evade reporting requirements and was permitted to continue making the withdrawals.[60]

This case starkly illustrates many compliance failures—most notably, a poor compliance culture that led to complicit bank employees who prioritized profits over compliance requirements.[61] However, Deutsche Bank's regulatory transgressions relating to Epstein are not its only AML-related issues. The institution has been involved in numerous compliance-related breaches and violations over the past twenty years. In the same consent order relating to Jeffrey Epstein, for instance, the bank acknowledged significant compliance failures in its correspondent banking relationships with Danske Bank Estonia and the Federal Bank of the Middle East. Consequently, it's not exactly a stretch to make the analogy that Deutsche Bank, like Epstein, has shown itself to be a serial recidivist.

RED FLAGS ASSOCIATED WITH LAUNDERING THE PROCEEDS OF HUMAN TRAFFICKING

Regulatory agencies and other organizations dedicated to combating financial crime not only have highlighted the risks that human-trafficking networks represent to the financial system but also have worked to convey the importance of detecting illicit financial flows related to human trafficking. Accordingly, the FATF, FinCEN, and others have issued various warnings and advisories, including lists of red flags, related to human-trafficking activity.

Some common red flags are specifically geared to detecting money laundering from human trafficking, while others are more general indicators of money laundering. In most cases, however, identification and detection rely upon better visibility into customer payments.

Red flags are often grouped into categories relating to such details as behavior and financial transactions. For instance, behavioral indicators include customers who exhibit poor dress and hygiene, who act confused, or who are unable to provide basic identification information. Transactional indicators focus on account activity and include accounts that are funded primarily through cash deposits, funds transfers from unrelated individuals, accounts controlled by third parties, and multiple accounts in different names but exhibit common information, such as the same mobile number, address, or employment reference.[62]

CONCLUSION

Human trafficking is a pervasive threat with devastating consequences to which no country in the world is immune. Although convictions in this area are slowly rising as awareness grows, they are still disproportionately low in comparison to the extent of the problem. As in the case of other financial crimes where monetary gain is the primary motive, mandating increased financial transparency across jurisdictions would significantly hinder the ability of criminals to disguise, hide, and transfer illicit funds, thereby removing the profitability from human trafficking and other illegal activities.

AML compliance measures, such as KYC policies and procedures, and other internal controls of financial institutions are critical tools in the fight against this human rights violation. An effective AML approach also entails proper training and education for all employees so they can better understand their role in this process and be equipped with the information and resources necessary to spot red flags.

NOTES

1. International Labour Organization, "Forced Labor, Modern Slavery and Human Trafficking: Facts and Figures," accessed October 12, 2020, https://www.ilo.org/global/topics/forced-labour/lang--en/index.htm.

2. International Labour Organization, *Profits and Poverty: The Economics of Forced Labour* (Geneva: International Labour Office, 2014), https://www.ilo.org/wcmsp5/groups /public/---ed_norm/---declaration/documents/publication/wcms_243391.pdf.

3. "Indentured Servants in the U.S.," *History Detectives Special Investigations*, Oregon Public Broadcasting and Lion Television for PBS, accessed October 16, 2020, https://www.pbs .org/opb/historydetectives/feature/indentured-servants-in-the-us/.

4. Ewelina U. Ochab, "The Transatlantic Slave Trade and the Modern Day Slavery," *Forbes*, March 23, 2019, https://www.forbes.com/sites/ewelinaochab/2019/03/23 /the-transatlantic-slave-trade-and-the-modern-day-slavery/#4561645e2e55.

5. University of Minnesota Immigration History Research Center, "Coolies Trade in the 19th Century," June 16, 2015, https://cla.umn.edu/ihrc/news-events/other/coolie -trade-19th-century.

6. United Nations, "UN Human Rights Law," accessed October 16, 2020, https://www.un .org/ruleoflaw/thematic-areas/international-law-courts-tribunals/human-rights-law/.

7. UNODC, "Convention against Transnational Organized Crime and the Protocols Thereto" (Vienna: UNODC, 2004), https://www.unodc.org/documents/treaties /UNTOC/Publications/TOC%20Convention/TOCebook-e.pdf.

8. US Department of Justice, "Involuntary Servitude, Forced Labor, and Sex Trafficking Statutes Enforced," accessed October 16, 2020, https://www.justice.gov/crt/involuntary -servitude-forced-labor-and-sex-trafficking-statutes-enforced.

9. Justice Department.

10. Ochab, "Transatlantic Slave Trade."

11. FinCEN, "Supplemental Advisory on Identifying and Reporting Human Trafficking and Related Activity," US Treasury Department, FIN-2020-A008, October 15, 2020, https://www.fincen.gov/sites/default/files/advisory/2020-10-15/Advisory%20 Human%20Trafficking%20508%20FINAL_0.pdf.

12. UNODC, "Human Trafficking FAQs," accessed October 17, 2020, https://www.unodc .org/unodc/en/human-trafficking/faqs.html.

13. Alexandra Villarreal, "'Modern Day Slavery': Human Traffickers Haunt Cities with At-Risk Children," NBC News, November 4, 2016, updated February 13, 2017, https:// www.nbcdfw.com/news/national-international/youth-sex-trafficking-casts-a-shadow -over-philadelphia/175293/.

14. National Human Trafficking Hotline, "Fake Massage Businesses," accessed April 26, 2021, https://humantraffickinghotline.org/sex-trafficking-venuesindustries/fake-massage -businesses.

15. Will Neal, "US Court Approves Sex-Trafficking Lawsuits against Facebook," *OCCRP*, April 29, 2020, https://www.occrp.org/en/daily/12224-us-court-approves-sex-trafficking -lawsuits-against-facebook.

16. US Justice Department, "Human Trafficking: Human Trafficking Defined," accessed October 12, 2020, https://www.justice.gov/humantrafficking.

17. United Nations, "Annex II: The Definition of Trafficking in Persons and the Mandate for the Global Report," *Global Report on Trafficking in Persons* (New York: United Nations, 2020), article 3, https://www.unodc.org/documents/data-and-analysis/glotip/Annex _II_-_Definition_and_mandate.pdf.

18. United Nations.

19. Baylee Eby, "The Economics of Human Trafficking," *Institute for Faith, Work and Economics*, April 12, 2016, https://tifwe.org/the-economics-of-human-trafficking/.

20. Ochab, "Transatlantic Slave Trade."

21. FinCEN, "Supplemental Advisory."

22. FinCEN.

23. FinCEN.

24. UNODC, "Human Trafficking FAQs."

25. Shelley, *Dark Commerce.*

26. UNODC, "Human Trafficking FAQs."

27. FATF, *Financial Flows from Human Trafficking* (Paris: FATF, 2018), https://www.fatf-gafi.org/media/fatf/content/images/Human-Trafficking-2018.pdf.

28. UNODC, *Global Report on Trafficking in Persons, 2014* (Vienna: UNODC, 2014), https://www.unodc.org/documents/data-and-analysis/glotip/GLOTIP_2014_full_report.pdf.

29. Kelly McLaughlin, "A Shocking 38% of Sex Trafficking Suspects Are Women—and Many Are Former Victims," *Insider*, August 23, 2019, https://www.insider.com/women-play-a-large-role-in-sex-trafficking-operations-2019-8.

30. UNODC, "Human Trafficking FAQs."

31. FATF, *Financial Flows*, 20–21.

32. Hannah Winston, "Woman Takes Plea in Orchids of Asia Prostitution Case Linked to Robert Kraft," *Palm Beach Post*, February 26, 2020, https://www.palmbeachpost.com/news/20200226/woman-takes-plea-in-orchids-of-asia-prostitution-case-linked-to-robert-kraft.

33. William Lacy Swing, "With Public and Private Sectors at Odds, Traffickers Win. Let's Work Together to Protect Victims," International Organization for Migration (Geneva), July 30, 2018, https://www.iom.int/news/public-and-private-sectors-odds-traffickers-win-lets-work-together-protect-victims.

34. FATF, *Financial Flows.*

35. UNODC, *Trafficking in Persons for the Purpose of Organ Removal: Assessment Toolkit* (Vienna: UNODC, 2015), https://www.unodc.org/documents/human-trafficking/2015/UNODC_Assessment_Toolkit_TIP_for_the_Purpose_of_Organ_Removal.pdf.

36. FATF, *Financial Flows*, 10.

37. FATF, 33.

38. United States Code, Unannotated Title 8 Aliens and Nationality, 8 U.S.C. § 1324.

39. FinCEN, "Supplemental Advisory"; and Human Trafficking and Smuggling Center, "Human Trafficking vs. Human Smuggling: Fact Sheet," June 15, 2016, https://ctip.defense.gov/Portals/12/Documents/HSTC_Human%20Trafficking%20vs.%20Human%20Smuggling%20Fact%20Sheet.pdf?ver=2016-07-14-145555-320.

40. David Murray, "Human Trafficking and Its Intersection with the Financial System," Testimony before the US Senate, Banking Committee, September 3, 2019, https://www.banking.senate.gov/imo/media/doc/Murray%20Testimony%209-3-2019.pdf.

41. FinCEN, "Update on U.S. Currency Restrictions in Mexico: Funnel Accounts and TBML," FIN-2014-A005, US Treasury Department, May 28, 2014, https://www.fincen.gov/resources/advisories/fincen-advisory-fin-2014-a005.

42. FinCEN, "Supplemental Advisory."

43. Matt Friedman, "Fighting Modern Slavery: What the Banking Sector Can Do to Help," *ACAMS Today*, January 9, 2020, https://www.acamstoday.org/fighting-modern-slavery-what-the-banking-sector-can-do-to-help/.

44. FATF, *Financial Flows.*

45. Michelle Lille, "The Connection between Sex Trafficking and Pornography," Human Trafficking Search, April 14, 2014, https://humantraffickingsearch.org/the-connection-between-sex-trafficking-and-pornography/.

46. FinCEN, "Supplemental Advisory"; and FinCEN, "Guidance on Recognizing Activity That May Be Associated with Human Smuggling and Human Trafficking—Financial Red Flags," US Treasury Department, FIN-2014-A008, September 11, 2014, https://www.fincen.gov/sites/default/files/advisory/FIN-2014-A008.pdf.

47. Berit Berger, "Former U.S. Prosecutor Discusses Jeffrey Epstein's 2008 Plea Deal," interview by Steve Inskeep, *Morning Edition*, NPR, July 10, 2019, https://www.npr.org/2019/07/10/740159741/former-u-s-prosecutor-discusses-jeffrey-epsteins-2008-plea-deal.

48. Multiple sources were consulted for the events described in the next two paragraphs, including Jonathan Stempel, "Jeffrey Epstein's Sexual Abuses Began by 1985, Targeted 13-Year-Old, Lawsuit Claims," Reuters, December 3, 2019, https://www.reuters.com/article/us-people-jeffrey-epstein-lawsuit/jeffrey-epsteins-sexual-abuses-began-by-1985-targeted-13-year-old-lawsuit-claims-idUSKBN1Y72K5; Mahita Gajanan, "Here's What to Know about the Sex Trafficking Case against Jeffrey Epstein," *Time*, July 17, 2019, https://time.com/5621911/jeffrey-epstein-sex-trafficking-what-to-know/; Allie Yang, James Hill, and Ali Dukakis, "How Ghislaine Maxwell Went from High Society to Being Accused of Sex Trafficking," ABC News, June 25, 2021, https://abcnews.go.com/US/ghislaine-maxwell-high-society-accused-sex-trafficking/story?id=78474060; Victoria Bekiempis, "Ghislaine Maxwell Trained Underage Girls as Sex Slaves, Documents Allege," *The Guardian*, July 31, 2020, https://www.theguardian.com/us-news/2020/jul/31/ghislaine-maxwell-underage-girls-sex-jeffrey-epstein; and "St. Thomas Residents Paint a Picture of Jeffrey Epstein's Life on 'Pedophile Island,'" CBS News, January 23, 2020, https://www.cbsnews.com/news/jeffrey-epstein-island-residents-share-rumors-surrounding-little-saint-james/.

49. Rebekah Kates Lemke, "7 Things You May Not Know about Human Trafficking, and 3 Ways to Help," Catholic Relief Services, January 5, 2020, https://www.crs.org/stories/stop-human-trafficking.

50. Gajanan, "Here's What to Know."

51. Chris Hondros, "Jeffrey Epstein Jail 'a Gulag' in Lower Manhattan," BBC News, August 12, 2019, https://www.bbc.com/news/world-us-canada-49323320.

52. Pervaiz Shallwani, "Here's What the Feds Found in Jeffrey Epstein's Mansion," *Daily Beast*, July 8, 2019, updated August 19, 2019, https://www.thedailybeast.com/jeffrey-epstein-sex-case-heres-what-the-feds-found-in-his-manhattan-mansion.

53. Matt Clibanoff, "Here's How Much Prison Time Accused Child Sex Trafficker Jeffrey Epstein Is Facing," *Law and Crime*, July 8, 2019, https://lawandcrime.com/high-profile/heres-how-much-prison-time-accused-child-sex-trafficker-jeffrey-epstein-is-facing/.

54. "*60 Minutes* Investigates the Death of Jeffrey Epstein," *60 Minutes*, CBS, produced by Oriana Zill de Granados, January 5, 2020, https://www.cbsnews.com/news/did-jeffrey-epstein-kill-himself-60-minutes-investigates-2020-01-05/.

55. Dan Mangan and Steve Kopack, "Accused Jeffrey Epstein Sex Crimes Accomplice Ghislaine Maxwell Arrested at $1 Million New Hampshire Home," CNBC, July 2, 2020, https://www.cnbc.com/2020/07/02/ghislaine-maxwell-accused-jeffrey-epstein-procurer-caught-in-1-million-home.html.

56. New York State Department of Financial Services, "In the Matter of Deutsche Bank AG, Deutsche Bank AG New York Branch, and Deutsche Bank Trust Company of the

Americas, Consent Order under New York Banking Law §§ 39 and 44," accessed October 14, 2020, https://www.dfs.ny.gov/system/files/documents/2020/07/ea20200706 _deutsche_bank_consent_order.pdf.

57. New York State Department of Financial Services.

58. Matt Egan and Erica Orden, "Deutsche Bank Slammed with $150 Million Fine for Failing to Flag Jeffrey Epstein's Shady Transactions," CNN Business, July 7, 2020, https://edition.cnn.com/2020/07/07/business/jeffrey-epstein-deutsche-bank-fine/index .html.

59. Dan Mangan and Jim Forkin, "Deutsche Bank Hit with $150 Million Penalty for Relationship to Sex Offender Jeffrey Epstein," CNBC, July 7, 2020, https://www.cnbc .com/2020/07/07/jeffrey-epstein-case-deutsche-bank-fined-150-million-penalty-for -relationship.html.

60. Egan and Orden, "Deutsche Bank."

61. New York State Department of Financial Services, "Superintendent Lacewell Announces DFS Imposes $150 Million Penalty on Deutsche Bank in Connection with Bank's Relationship with Jeffrey Epstein and Correspondent Relationships with Danske Estonia and FBME Bank," press release, July 7, 2020, https://www.dfs.ny.gov/reports_and _publications/press_releases/pr202007071.

62. FATF, *Financial Flows.*

CHAPTER 8

INTANGIBLE COINS
AND BLOCKCHAINS

*How Cryptocurrencies Fit
into the Laundering Process*

Enabled by the internet and the anonymity it allows, cybercrime is another profit-driven illicit endeavor that has substantially increased in recent times. Cybercrime, from phishing scams to ransomware attacks, provides a large potential for significant gains in a relatively short period and with a minimal risk of detection. The corresponding proceeds can be laundered just as quickly and easily and with the same low risk. Similar to the ways in which criminals have manipulated, and in some cases even developed, new tools and technologies to financially enrich themselves, they have also devised new methodologies to launder criminal proceeds, including techniques that involve the use of cryptocurrencies.

What is less clear, however, is exactly how big of a threat cryptocurrencies, such as Bitcoin and others, actually pose. Some media headlines suggest, and numerous government agencies and financial regulators have expressed concerns, that cryptocurrencies constitute a major money laundering risk. Notably, Jerome Powell, the chairman of the Board of Governors of the Federal Reserve System, communicated this view when he testified before the House Financial Services Committee: "Cryptocurrencies are great if you're trying to hide money or if you're trying to launder money."[1] European Central Bank president Christine Lagard echoed this perspective when she said that cryptocurrency is to blame for "some funny business and some interesting and totally reprehensible money-laundering activity."[2]

However, although cryptocurrencies can be and are used in furtherance of illegal activity, some disagree over the extent of their role in money laundering. Although law enforcement, including the DOJ, cites cryptocurrencies as both a major money laundering and terrorist-financing threat, the virtual currency community disagrees, noting statistics indicating the opposite. Some studies show that cryptocurrency's use in money laundering and other financial crimes has been extremely low in comparison with cash transactions. According to one noteworthy study, as of 2019, only $829 million in bitcoin has been spent on the dark web, translating into just 0.5 percent of all bitcoin transactions.[3]

Despite the opposing viewpoints on the scope of the threat presented by cryptocurrencies, several high-profile cases, including the headline-grabbing Silk Road case, illustrate how cryptocurrencies have been used to launder illegal profits. These cases not only provide valuable insight into how Bitcoin and other cryptocurrencies can be misused but also suggest how to combat money laundering via this medium. Such analyses are extremely important because, whether the risks posed thus far have been significant or not, the cryptocurrency market is undeniably growing. Valued at $1.03 billion in 2019, the market is expected to increase to $1.40 billion in 2024.[4]

WHAT ARE CRYPTOCURRENCIES AND HOW DO THEY WORK?

Bitcoin was the original blockchain-based cryptocurrency. It was invented in 2008 by the mysterious Satoshi Nakamoto, whose true identity has still not been confirmed. Nakamoto is also the author of the renowned bitcoin white paper, "Bitcoin: A Peer-to-Peer Electronic Cash System," which explains how the peer-to-peer electronic cash system functions and is considered the founding document of Bitcoin and cryptocurrency generally.[5]

Launched in 2009 following the financial crisis, Bitcoin has emerged as an alternative to conventional banking. Although the media often depicts Bitcoin as a tangible golden coin, it is actually an intangible "chain of digital signatures." Despite the emergence of various other new cryptocurrencies, referred to as alternative coins or altcoins, Bitcoin still remains the most popular and most valuable form of cryptocurrency used today. Other common types of cryptocurrency include Bitcoin Cash, Litecoin, Ethereum, Ripple, Zcash, Stellar, and a host of others.

Cryptocurrencies are a type of *virtual currency*, which is a broad term for digital money. In other words, they are a means of payment that exist only in digital, rather than physical, form. Virtual currencies can be broken down into convertible and nonconvertible digital currencies. *Convertible virtual currencies* have an equivalent value in real currency, while *nonconvertible currencies* are specific to a particular virtual domain, such as online gaming, and cannot be exchanged for real currency.[6] Cryptocurrencies, including Bitcoin, are recognized in the United States as a convertible virtual currency, meaning that they may be used as a substitute for an equivalent value in actual currency. So their acceptance as a form of payment is the same as accepting cash. Bitcoin is legal in the United States and most other developed countries, although its legal status varies in many emerging economies.

Unlike *fiat currency*—or real, tangible money, such as metal coins and paper bills—cryptocurrency does not have any physical representation. In that respect, cryptocurrencies function similar to electronic cash in the sense that no physical thing is exchanged, and the entire transaction is conducted online. Therefore, cryptocurrencies are an alternative to the government-issued fiat currency (such as the US dollar, the euro, and other major currencies) used in the present monetary system.

Also, unlike traditional currencies, most cryptocurrencies are decentralized, meaning there is no central administrator, such as a central bank, to issue currency and maintain payment ledgers. Rather, to maintain an accurate system of payments and receipts, cryptocurrencies rely on complex algorithms, an electronic ledger called a blockchain, and a network of peer-to-peer users whereby virtual money is sent directly from one party to another, eliminating the need for a bank or other financial institution.[7]

Blockchain technology is key to the functionality, and part of the appeal, of cryptocurrencies. *Blockchain technology* is used to keep a highly secure online ledger that captures the history of all verified transactions ever conducted on that blockchain. This cryptographic transactional record prevents double-spending and counterfeiting and makes forging transaction histories almost impossible.[8] It also presents issues for anyone looking for anonymity, as it creates a permanent (i.e., immutable) and public transactional record.

Cryptocurrencies are secured by an advanced encryption technique called cryptography, from which the term "cryptocurrency" is derived. *Cryptography* is used to make information and communications safe from third parties seeking to intercept them by converting ordinary plain text into unintelligible text and vice versa. This ensures that only the intended recipients of the information are able to access and process it. Cryptography includes message encryption, digital signatures, data compression, and email compatibility. For example, cryptography is used to securely send passwords when making online purchases.[9]

Cryptocurrencies are created digitally through a process known as mining or crypto-mining, which involves individuals known as miners solving complex mathematical algorithms. Mining requires special computers; a regular laptop is not strong enough to conduct the necessary calculations.

Cryptocurrencies are then stored in a cryptocurrency wallet, which is a digital wallet that exists on a user's computer, in an application (app) on their mobile phone, or in the cloud and is similar to a virtual (i.e., nonphysical) account. Each wallet is assigned a unique ID that functions much like a username and, along with a password, is used to log in to that wallet and access the user's digital assets. Using such wallets, users can send cryptocurrencies to one another, make purchases, or simply manage their cryptocurrency almost in the same manner as they would traditional currencies. The various types of cryptocurrencies can be transferred between people using mobile apps or computers in a way that is similar to sending cash electronically.

Cryptocurrencies can be obtained through marketplaces, sometimes referred to as Bitcoin exchanges, where cryptocurrencies can be bought or sold using traditional currencies. Coinbase is one such leading exchange, and there are several others. Cryptocurrencies can be exchanged person to person, through a cryptocurrency exchange, or through other intermediaries.[10] And just like foreign currency, cryptocurrencies are also subject to exchange rates.

PSEUDONYMITY AND TRANSPARENCY

The unique, chimeric nature of cryptocurrencies means that they provide seeming anonymity *and* transparency. On the one hand, advocates proclaim the levels of anonymity provided by cryptocurrencies and the corresponding privacy protections they afford can be extremely valuable for whistleblowers or activists living under repressive government regimes. On the other hand, opponents point to the numerous scams and other illegal activities associated with cryptocurrencies. The ability to purchase illicit products and services anonymously, they claim, is enabled by the fact that criminals can keep their identities hidden while carrying out cryptocurrency transactions. Regardless of which stance one takes, the dual nature of cryptocurrencies results in a privacy-transparency trade-off that has significant implications in the context of money laundering.

Because cryptocurrency transactions are recorded in a blockchain, or public log or ledger, they can be viewed by anyone, including those who are not parties to the transaction. Also publicly accessible are the transaction ID, or *hash*; the wallet address of both the sender and the recipient; the amount of cryptocurrency involved in the transaction; and the transaction fee. Moreover, all transactions are immutable, which means that they cannot be altered or deleted. This immutability also helps ensure data security, as all transactions related to a given bitcoin address can be reliably traced back to the initial transaction.[11] Therefore, unlike cash, Bitcoin and most cryptocurrencies leave a secure money trail that law enforcement, auditors, regulators, and others can follow.[12] In fact, Bitcoin is considered the most transparent currency in the world.

As a result, cryptocurrencies are generally more pseudonymous than anonymous because they offer only partial, rather than complete, anonymity. In other words, cryptocurrencies are not tied to a recognizable individual but rather to a string of letters and numbers. This string of characters serves as a type of pseudonym.

As with most other cryptocurrencies, the only way to trace Bitcoin transactions is through a Bitcoin address. However, unlike a bank account, identification is not required to obtain a Bitcoin address, nor are any customer checks, such as KYC, performed. Referring to this fact, Ben Weiss, CEO of crypto ATM operator CoinFlip, aptly stated, "You can't buy any large amount of bitcoin without KYC or ID or driver's licenses."[13]

Consequently, cryptocurrency transactions, where transactional information is shared with authorized and involved parties only and is not publicly revealed, are in complete contrast with traditional financial and banking transactions, where account holders must be identified and verified.[14] Furthermore, owners of cryptocurrencies can easily use a different address for each transaction to avoid the transactions from being linked to a single individual.

Therefore, even though a public ledger enables cryptocurrency transactions to be traced, connecting a transaction to a particular individual is difficult unless that individual has previously been identified by a financial institution or has associated himself or herself with a wallet address through other means. Transaction data alone is of limited value in this regard, and the identity of cryptocurrency buyers and sellers remains private. Proponents of cryptocurrencies claim that this perceived anonymity protects the cryptocurrency holder, who may otherwise be an easy target for theft since cryptocurrency transactions are public, allowing anyone to see how much value is being transferred and between which wallet addresses.

Moreover, the different types of cryptocurrencies can vary in their degree of anonymity depending on the public or nonpublic nature of their associated blockchain. For example, although Bitcoin addresses do not have names or specific customer information associated with them, Bitcoin's blockchain is public. Other cryptocurrencies use blockchains that feature varying degrees of privacy, making the transactions far less or not at all transparent. These types of cryptocurrencies, which are referred to as privacy coins or anonymity-enhanced cryptocurrencies, are more difficult to trace. Examples of such cryptocurrency include Dash, Monero, and Zcash, and more are being developed.[15] As a matter of fact, many of these cryptocurrencies were specifically created with the intention of being used in criminal activity.

Therefore, Bitcoin would not be a criminal's best choice of cryptocurrency since the transactions would be traceable. In fact, law enforcement authorities have used forensic analysis of the Bitcoin blockchain to arrest and prosecute several criminals.[16] Nonetheless, Bitcoin continues to be the cryptocurrency that is most often used in illegal activity.

Cryptocurrencies are increasingly used to launder money in the cyberworld in particular. According to his indictment, the alleged creator of the dark-web site AlphaBay, Alexandre Cazes, was found to have over $7 million in at least three different types of cryptocurrency, including Bitcoin, in addition to conventional currency and other valuable assets. And Alexander Vinnik, a Russian computer expert, was accused of having laundered $4 billion through a Russian cryptocurrency exchange where he worked and ultimately was sentenced to serve five years in a French prison for bitcoin laundering.[17]

THE REGULATION, OR LACK THEREOF, OF CRYPTOCURRENCIES

Cryptocurrencies function as pecuniary resources and are used as a medium of exchange and a means of payment. However, as noted previously, unlike traditional currency, or fiat money, the issuance of which is highly centralized and supervised by a nation's central bank, cryptocurrencies are decentralized, meaning that they are not regulated by any government body or financial institution. And unlike bank accounts, cryptocurrency wallets are not insured by the Federal Deposit Insurance Corporation. The value of Bitcoin and other cryptocurrencies are entirely dependent on what investors are willing to pay for it. Although this decentralization means that cryptocurrencies are, at least currently, not subject to government manipulation or interference, no central authority ensures the process is functioning properly or backs its value. Therefore, if a cryptocurrency exchange shuts down, the holders of the cryptocurrency have no chance of recovering the funds.

Despite cryptocurrencies being in existence for well over a decade, the cryptocurrency market is still not regulated, and their legal status is unclear. Financial regulatory bodies in some countries are working to find common standards for cryptocurrencies, particularly given the ease with which cryptocurrencies can be used for criminal purposes, including money laundering.[18] However, for this to happen, many questions must be settled first.

For example, should cryptocurrencies be characterized as money, assets, products, property, or something entirely different? Even in the United States, which has historically been the world's regulatory hub and standard setter, there are notable inconsistencies among federal regulators regarding the classification of cryptocurrencies and disagreements over which authority should oversee cryptocurrency exchanges. Currently, the US Treasury Department views cryptocurrency as a decentralized virtual currency, the Securities and Exchange Commission considers cryptocurrencies as securities, the Commodity Futures Trading Commission classifies them as commodities, and the Internal Revenue Service views them as capital assets. A consensus on these questions will help determine whether cryptocurrencies should be traded freely or whether they will be regulated more tightly. In the meantime, laws governing the crypto industry in the United States vary by state, and federal authorities continue to interpret and regulate them differently.[19]

Significantly, FinCEN does not view cryptocurrencies as legal tender. However, it does consider cryptocurrency exchanges as money services businesses (MSBs). As such, the exchanges are subject to the Bank Secrecy Act and must comply with its AML and CFT protocols, as well as follow the FATF's recommendations on AML compliance and its standards on the regulation of virtual assets.[20]

For example, Coinbase is a digital currency exchange headquartered in San Francisco, California, and is a registered MSB with FinCEN. Therefore, it is subject to the BSA's AML requirements, including the KYC procedures. Thus, even though cryptocurrency users are anonymous on the blockchain, for Coinbase (and several other regulated crypto exchanges) to comply with regulatory requirements, it must identify and verify all its customers. This includes collecting identification information for individuals in connection with one or several Bitcoin addresses.

In fact, in April 2019, FinCEN demonstrated its commitment to the strict regulation of digital currency exchanges by penalizing an individual as an MSB for the first time. California resident Eric Powers was penalized for failing to register as an MSB, failing to have written policies or procedures to ensure compliance with the BSA, and failing to report suspicious transactions and currency transactions. In fact, Mr. Powers was assessed a civil money penalty for failing to file CTRs and SARs, in violation of the BSA, in more than two hundred cryptocurrency transactions from 2012 to 2014.[21]

In Europe, which has one of the highest rates of cryptocurrency transactions and a high proportion of illicit cryptocurrency use, the most important legislative development in this area has been the Fifth AML Directive.[22] Similar to FinCEN's requirements, the directive, which applies to all EU member states, mandates that cryptocurrency exchanges and wallet providers properly identify their clients.[23]

Further complicating the regulation of the crypto industry, however, is that the various types of cryptocurrencies can significantly differ from one another. For instance, some offer more privacy, or anonymity, than others. Additionally, the distributed ledger technology, or blockchain, is still in the early stages. These are just some of the issues that regulators and policymakers at national and international levels need to figure out. They must also address such questions for taxation purposes, as the classification of cryptocurrencies will have different implications. For example, if cryptocurrencies are classified as securities, they will have more onerous rules than if they are classified as currency. The unique nature of cryptocurrencies makes some of these questions very difficult, and the regulatory status of cryptocurrency remains uncertain at this time.[24]

THE MISUSE OF CRYPTOCURRENCIES

The semi-anonymity of cryptocurrency transactions makes them particularly attractive to criminals and others who seek to conceal their activity. According to former secretary of the treasury Steven Mnuchin, cryptocurrencies have enabled "billions of dollars of illicit activity like cybercrime, tax evasion, extortion, ransomware, illicit drugs, and human trafficking," and they even pose a "national security issue."[25]

The use of cryptocurrencies has been particularly high in cybercrime. This is not especially surprising, considering both cryptocurrency transactions and cybercrime are conducted online. In fact, cryptocurrencies have become the default payment method in many cybercrimes, such as ransomware attacks, other online extortion schemes, and criminal-to-criminal payments on the dark web.

Interestingly, ransomware and cryptocurrency are closely linked for a very specific reason that is not readily apparent. Initially, one might guess this connection has to do with the anonymity of crypto payments, but it's actually the transparency associated with cryptocurrency transactions that makes them so attractive. Given that transactions along the blockchain are transparent, a hacker conducting a ransomware attack can simply keep an eye on the blockchain and know the exact moment in which the ransom is paid. The hacker can even automate the return of the victim's files to coincide with receipt of the payment.[26] This method is extremely efficient. However, it also presents a conundrum because the transactional record, which is immutable, permanent, and public, of this transaction's history now exists. For the hacker not to get caught, the person will need to find a way to distance himself or herself from the tainted funds and, consequently, the ransom attack. Although this isn't impossible to do, the blockchain technology makes it difficult because it provides law enforcement with a virtual money trail. The increased regulation of cybercurrencies would make such crimes even more complicated to cover up and thereby also serve as a deterrent to their commission.

Cryptocurrencies have thus become the favored means of remittance in cybercrime. Bitcoin was the primary payment mode used in Silk Road, the first modern darknet marketplace, and has been used in subsequent darknet marketplaces as well, including AlphaBay, which was ten times the size of Silk Road. Cryptocurrencies are also the primary form of payment demanded in ransomware attacks, such as the large-scale CryptoLocker attack that targeted computers running Microsoft Windows in 2013–14.

Around the time that cryptocurrencies emerged, more than 20 percent of crypto transactions were directly attributable to criminal conduct. However, although the level of illicit activity, and cybercrime in particular, has grown substantially, the legitimate use of cryptocurrencies has grown at a much faster rate. By 2019, most Bitcoin transactions were done in connection with legitimate investment and trading activity.[27]

Nonetheless, although the overall percentage of cryptocurrency-related criminal transactions are comparatively low, the amount of cryptocurrency that can be derived from a single illicit transaction is quite high. According to the blockchain security company CipherTrace, cybercriminals netted a total of $4.3 billion in 2019 from crypto-related crime, resulting in a lot of dirty cyber funds in need of laundering.[28]

A recent FATF study that focused on over a hundred reported cases from many jurisdictions in 2017–20 notes several trends in the use of cryptocurrencies for money laundering and terrorist-financing purposes. The study found most illegal activity involving cryptocurrencies entailed various crimes that are considered predicate offenses to money laundering. In addition to these offenses, cryptocurrencies were also used "to evade financial sanctions and to raise funds to support terrorist activity."[29]

Furthermore, of the different types of money laundering–related offenses involved in misusing cryptocurrencies, the most common was illicit trafficking in controlled substances, either where the sales conducted involved direct payments in cryptocurrencies or where cryptocurrencies were used as a layering technique for money laundering. The next most common types of illicit activities involving cryptocurrency misuse included various "frauds, scams, ransomware, and extortion." Moreover, the FATF report notes, professional money laundering networks have started exploiting cryptocurrencies for laundering purposes.[30]

Additionally, it appears that Latin American crime cartels are increasingly turning to cryptocurrencies for the purposes of money laundering. For example, in April 2019, Mexican police arrested a suspected human trafficker who was linked to a prostitution ring that spanned across Latin America and who is alleged to have sexually exploited and blackmailed some two thousand women. However, these crimes did not eventually lead to his arrest. Rather, he was traced through the Bitcoin transactions he used to launder his criminal proceeds. Nonetheless, according to both US and Mexican authorities, the use of Bitcoin in ML activity is rising among drug cartels, such as the Jalisco New Generation Cartel and the Sinaloa Cartel.[31]

As a result of the growth in crime-related cryptocurrency activity, regulatory and other government agencies have started to pay particularly close attention. FinCEN, the Department of Homeland Security, the FBI, and the New York State Department of Financial Services, among others, have assessed numerous fines and penalties in recent years, even as cryptocurrency regulations are still being developed.[32]

THE USE OF CRYPTOCURRENCIES IN MONEY LAUNDERING

In criminal prosecutions involving the use of Bitcoin in illicit activity, originally legal opinions differed about whether cryptocurrencies should be considered money. However, several federal and state courts now hold that bitcoins and other cryptocurrencies technically constitute a form of money. Likewise, the US Treasury Department has also deemed that money laundering while using cryptocurrency services falls under federal money transmission laws. Therefore, clearly both federal and state authorities are consistent in their treatment of cryptocurrencies for the purposes of anti–money laundering prosecutions.[33]

Cryptocurrencies are attractive to criminals because they are easily transmissible across borders and provide a certain degree of anonymity. However, given that cryptocurrency transactions are recorded on the blockchain—a permanent, fixed, and public ledger (i.e., an electronic record book)—these transactions cannot be deleted, reversed, or altered and are visible to the public. While user data, such as the names and identities of purchasers and sellers, is not documented anywhere, the trail and timing of transactions are recorded and therefore traceable. Consequently, using traditional ML techniques and routing bitcoins through multiple wallets and accounts to hide a money trail do not work. With a little time and technical expertise, the path of the transactions can be uncovered. In fact, blockchain analytics firms now specialize in tracking the transactions of money launderers and other criminals. Thus, contrary to popular opinion, cryptocurrency transactions are actually quite transparent. Nonetheless, cryptocurrencies can easily be used to launder illicit criminal funds.

HOW DIRTY BITCOINS ARE LAUNDERED

Bitcoin laundering refers to such processes as moving cryptocurrency from one place to another in a manner that conceals the original source of the funds or otherwise cashing out bitcoins in exchange for fiat currency to distance the bitcoins from their illegal origins. However, although the same concepts that apply to cash laundering apply to bitcoin laundering, including the three stages of the money laundering process, bitcoin laundering is not truly analogous to the laundering of traditional currencies. Bitcoin laundering involves fewer steps. And unless the illegally acquired bitcoins are cashed out into fiat currency and thereby integrated into the legal financial system, the entire laundering process—including placement, layering, and integration—takes place solely within the realm of the cryptocurrency environment.

One way in which cryptocurrencies may be laundered is through cryptocurrency exchanges or trading markets that are unlicensed, unregistered, or otherwise noncompliant with the AML/CFT standards and regulatory requirements that legitimate exchanges follow. The business of exchanges and trading markets is to exchange virtual currency for fiat currency, one form of virtual currency for another, or other types of assets into different currencies and vice versa. Money is laundered through repeated such exchanges. This laundering method typically implicates the placement stage of the money laundering process. In fact, this is the area most vulnerable to bitcoin ML transactions.[34]

Another method of laundering cryptocurrencies is through what are known as mixers or tumblers. For a fee, these online services launder cryptocurrencies by essentially combining a user's cryptocurrency with the cryptocurrencies of various other users so that the cryptocurrencies entered into the mixer come out with a different transaction history. This process increases the anonymity of the transactions, making the cryptocurrency more difficult to trace. These services are typically operated anonymously on the darknet.[35] Although not presently illegal, these types of services have come under recent scrutiny. Furthermore, mixing vast sums of money may implicate structuring laws.

Criminals also employ decentralized and often international peer-to-peer networks where unwitting third parties are used to transfer funds, typically to countries with lax or nonexistent AML regulations. There, the cryptocurrency is converted into fiat currency and spent on expensive and luxury items.

Cryptocurrency ATMs—particularly those with bidirectional functionality, which enables the exchange of cryptocurrency and traditional currency—can also be exploited for money laundering purposes whereby ill-gotten cash is converted to cryptocurrency and vice versa. As of September 2021, the number of Bitcoin ATMs in the United States alone was estimated at twenty-five thousand, and this number is only expected to grow as cryptocurrency use increases.[36] Unlike ordinary ATMs, Bitcoin ATMs provide greater anonymity.

Additionally, the rising use of over-the-counter bitcoin brokers, which facilitate the transfer of millions of dollars in bitcoin across international borders, provides a ready opportunity for money launderers to exploit. Some of these crypto brokers and exchanges have minimal AML compliance controls and KYC processes.

Finally, online gambling services are also commonly used to launder cryptocurrency. This process is very similar to gambling with cash and simply involves betting stolen bitcoins on a few games, then withdrawing the winnings and exchanging them for traditional currency.

These are just a few of the more frequently employed ML strategies used with cryptocurrencies. As with money laundering using traditional currency, criminals have used cryptocurrencies in countless other ways to launder money and will surely come up with new methods and techniques in the future.

The semi-anonymity or pseudonymity of cryptocurrencies and the ability to use them online and to move large sums of money across borders make them very attractive to criminals seeking to launder illicit gains. Furthermore, the emergence of new cryptocurrencies, particularly ones with increased anonymity, provides additional opportunities for launderers to exploit. Finally, while still lacking uniform regulation, the cryptocurrency space remains an ideal environment for money laundering.

THE DARK SIDE OF THE WORLD WIDE WEB AND CRYPTO-LAUNDERING

Cryptocurrencies are most often used illicitly on the dark web, the part of the internet that, unlike the surface web, isn't visible to search engines. In fact, a lot of criminal activity, including money laundering and a host of money laundering predicate crimes, takes place on the dark web. An oft-cited study conducted by London researchers found that of all the live dark-web sites that were studied over a five-week period in 2015, 57 percent hosted illicit material.[37] Therefore, given the significant role of the dark web in illicit activity, it behooves any financial crime and compliance professional to have at least a basic understanding of it and how it's used.

First, however, it's important to differentiate between the dark web and the deep web. While the two terms are often used interchangeably, they actually refer to quite different sets of pages on the World Wide Web. The *deep web*, which is sometimes also called the invisible or hidden web, refers to the parts of the internet that cannot be readily accessed via conventional search engines, such as Google and Yahoo. Much of the content on the deep web consists of information that is private and can potentially be misused. Therefore, it includes information that is behind a paywall or that requires sign-in credentials, such as a username, a password, or some other type of authentication, to access it. This step helps to protect personal information and preserve privacy. As a result, the deep web is a fairly safe place. Some examples of deep web content include personal email accounts, social media accounts, and online banking accounts, as well as membership websites, sites containing medical records and legal documents, other fee-based matter, and data stored on corporate private databases. The deep web is estimated to make up somewhere around 90 percent of the internet, constituting the largest portion of the internet. In fact, only a very small part of the internet, called the clear web, is accessible through a standard web browser.[38]

In contrast, the *dark web*, or the *darknet*, as it is sometimes also called, is a much smaller part of the deep web. Because it is concealed, the actual size of the dark web is not known for certain; however, it is believed to constitute approximately 5 percent of the total internet. In fact, the dark web operates on the principle of total anonymity and thus requires a specific anonymizing browser, known as Tor (short for The Onion Router), to access it. This browser routes web pages through a number of different proxy servers to disguise the user's IP (internet protocol) address so that it cannot be identified and traced. Otherwise, Tor functions similar to a regular browser, and all that is required to access the dark web is simply to install it.[39]

Darren Guccione, a contributing writer for the digital magazine *CSO*, provides a useful depiction of the dark web and what it's like to navigate it in his article "What Is the Dark Web? How to Access It and What You'll Find." According to Guccione, dark-web sites, once a user is able to access them, mostly look and operate similarly to websites on the clear web but with some notable differences. One is the URL naming convention, which uses the domain suffix .onion instead of the common web address endings found on the surface or clear web, such as .com, .org, and .gov. Furthermore, the URLs for dark-web sites are largely unintelligible, consisting of random numbers and letters, and are not indicative of the content on the sites with which they're associated, thus making the URLs difficult to remember. Also, it is not uncommon for some sites to suddenly disappear, as their creators are fraudsters who are always on the move to avoid detection by their victims and law enforcement. Additionally, due to the shifting nature of the dark-web environment, the search engines are slow and repetitive, and often bring up search results that are irrelevant, outdated, or erroneous. Therefore, as one may expect, the dark web is as disorganized as it is seedy, with connections that frequently time out and with marketplaces and sellers that are unreliable at best and outright illegal at worst.[40]

Just about anything one can imagine—legal, illegal, and in between—can be found, bought, and sold on the dark web. This includes stolen information (e.g., Social Security numbers, bank account numbers, hacked Netflix accounts, hijacked webcams), illicit substances (e.g., illegal narcotics, prescription drugs, toxic chemicals), and a vast array of dangerous and appalling items and services (e.g., counterfeit goods, weapons, animal and human body parts, child pornography, endangered species, human trafficking). Although the dark web is most known for illicit and disturbing content, not everything on the dark web is illegal. It also has a legitimate side, however small, where people can join social networks, political chat groups, and chess clubs, for instance. In fact, some believe that with its anonymity and lack of government regulation and interference, the dark web is the only way to obtain and sustain a truly free press.

CASE STUDY: FROM ANCIENT TRADE ROUTE TO ILLICIT ONLINE MARKETPLACE

Named after the ancient system of trade routes connecting Europe and Asia, Silk Road was an illicit online black market and the first modern darknet marketplace. It was launched in February 2011 by twenty-six-year-old Ross Ulbricht, who went by the online moniker Dread Pirate Roberts after the fictional character from the novel and the movie *The Princess Bride*.

Ulbricht, a libertarian and anarchist, wanted to create an anonymous online marketplace where users could buy anything they wanted without government interference, including illegal drugs, which were the site's staple products before it expanded into selling pretty much every other illegal thing that could be sold. Nearly all the transactions were conducted in bitcoins. As the popularity of the darknet marketplace grew, so did its notoriety, and it wasn't long before the Justice Department and the DEA started investigating Silk Road.

Besides the sale of banned substances and contraband, Ulbricht was also alleged to have commissioned several murders. Using bitcoin, he hired hit men to kill his rivals and individuals who interfered with his marketplace. Since Ulbricht paid for the assassinations in bitcoin, the transactions were recorded on the blockchain. However, no bodies were ever found, and it is unclear whether any murders actually took place. As a result, Ulbricht was ultimately not prosecuted for the alleged murder attempts.

Meanwhile, the story just kept getting darker. A federal agent from the Secret Service and another from the DEA, who worked undercover in part of the Silk Road investigation, were found to have provided Ulbricht with information about the investigation in exchange for bribes paid in bitcoin. Fifteen-year DEA special agent Carl Mark Force laundered the bribe payments he received by transferring the bitcoin between traditional and digital banks accounts and then sending $235,000 to an offshore account in Panama. At one point, the agent's Venmo account was frozen due to suspicious activity. He had this account unfrozen by sending Venmo a forged subpoena. Force then paid off his mortgage and a federal loan, and he invested the rest of the money in real estate and businesses.[41]

The other agent, six-year Secret Service special agent Shaun Bridges, a bitcoin expert, laundered his money in part through a shell company. Bridges set up an LLC called Quantum International Investments and opened a bank account in its name in February 2013. He used the Quantum account to accept multiple wire transfers, totaling approximately $820,000 in illicit payments, from a bitcoin exchange in Japan.[42]

Both agents were charged with wire fraud and money laundering and sentenced to lengthy prison terms. Another case was later brought against a third DEA agent who allegedly leaked information about the investigation and tampered with evidence. As if that wasn't enough, during the trail, the presiding judge received death threats after her personal information, including her address and Social Security number, were posted on the dark-web site the Hidden Wiki.

Silk Road was shut down in October 2013. Ulbricht was ultimately convicted of multiple crimes, including money laundering. He was sentenced to two life sentences plus forty years without parole.

Thousands of drug dealers used Silk Road to sell drugs and other illegal products to over 100,000 anonymous buyers, who then laundered hundreds of millions of dollars earned from those illegal sales. The investigation into Ulbricht spawned subsequent investigations into many Silk Road users, most of whom were drug dealers. Although Silk Road was the first cyber supermarket specializing in the sale of illicit and illegal commodities, it was certainly not the last. Numerous online black markets on a much bigger scale than Silk Road have since sprung up. In fact, the same year that the FBI shut down Silk Road, former Silk Road employees launched Silk Road 2.0. In 2014 law enforcement shut down Silk Road 2.0 and arrested its operator. Remarkably, Silk Road 3.0 took its place, only to be taken offline in 2017.[43]

Due to the mystery surrounding the dark web, a lot of people are naturally curious and intrigued about it. As the first major capitalist venture in this realm, a great deal has been written about the Silk Road, and the story of Ulbricht's rise and fall has even been made into a few movies. The 2015 documentary *Deep Web*, which is narrated by Keanu Reeves, chronicles the events and figures surrounding Silk Road, including the arrest and trial of Ross Ulbricht, and other issues related to Bitcoin and the dark web. Likewise, the film *Silk Road*, written and directed by Tiller Russell, dramatizes Ulbricht's online black marketplace.

Similar to Maksim Yakubets, the founder of Evil Corp, Ross Ulbricht is highly intelligent and was technically proficient. Cybercriminals such as Yakubets and Ulbricht, who possess specialized knowledge and expertise, now constitute one of the biggest threats to the financial services industry and to society generally.

RED FLAGS ASSOCIATED WITH CRYPTOCURRENCIES

In September 2020, the FATF released a report titled "Virtual Assets and Red Flag Indicators of Money Laundering and Terrorist Financing." In this report, the FATF outlines an extensive list of red flags and includes real-life case studies to illustrate some of them. Most of these red flags have traditionally been associated with transactions involving more conventional payment means. However, these indicators remain relevant and can therefore be applied to detecting potential illicit activity related to various forms of cryptocurrency. Some of the more prevalent types of red flags associated with using cryptocurrencies include transactions involving the use of multiple cryptocurrencies, despite incurring additional transaction fees; anonymous cryptocurrencies; many unrelated wallets; and IP addresses that differ from a customer's profile.[44]

CONCLUSION

To various extents, criminals have exploited cryptocurrencies and cryptocurrency-related transactions as a means of laundering illicit funds since the emergence of Bitcoin, the first cryptocurrency. This trend will undoubtedly continue as cryptocurrency use becomes more mainstream and as cybercrimes increase and generate more illicit funds. Because large sums of money can be routed in a single crypto-transaction and because cryptocurrencies enable global transfers, many believe that cryptocurrencies will become the value transfer method of choice by transnational criminal organizations and drug cartels, which need to move vast amounts of capital across borders.

What primarily attracts criminals to cryptocurrencies is the anonymity they provide to the user. Although cryptocurrency transactions are transparent and can ultimately be traced, this fact has not stopped illicit actors from using cryptocurrencies in money laundering and a host of other crimes, particularly in cybercrimes. Furthermore, as more anonymous cybercurrencies are developed, their use in money laundering activities will undoubtedly rise.

Governments and businesses need to better understand cryptocurrencies and the technology that enables their anonymity to formulate effective regulations, policies, and other measures. Additionally, an international consensus on cryptocurrency standards and regulations is needed as cryptocurrencies are used across the world.

NOTES

1. Kevin Helms, "Fed Chair: Crypto Has No Intrinsic Value, Not a Store of Value, Great for Money Laundering," *Bitcoin.com News*, July 19, 2018, https://news.bitcoin.com/fed -chair-crypto-no-intrinsic-value-store-of-value-money-laundering/.
2. Carolynn Look, "Lagarde Blasts Bitcoin's Role in Facilitating Money Laundering," Bloomberg, January 13, 2021, https://www.bloomberg.com/news/articles/2021-01 -13/lagarde-blasts-bitcoin-s-role-in-facilitating-money-laundering.
3. "Bitcoin Money Laundering: How Criminals Use Crypto (and How MSBs Can Clean Up Their Act)," *Elliptic* (blog), September 18, 2019, https://www.elliptic.co/our -thinking/bitcoin-money-laundering.
4. "Cryptocurrency Market with Impact of COVID-19 by Offering (Hardware, and Software), Process (Mining and Transaction), Type, Application (Trading, Remittance,

Payment: Peer-to-Peer Payment, Ecommerce, and Retail), and Geography—Global Fore-cast to 2026," *Markets and Markets,* October 2018, https://www.marketsandmarkets.com/Market-Reports/cryptocurrency-market-158061641.html#:~:text=Cryptocurrency%20is%20a%20digital%20currency,generating%20coins%20and%20conducting%20transactions.&text=The%20cryptocurrency%20market%20was%20valued,6.18%25%20during%20the%20forecast%20period.

5. Satoshi Nakamoto, "Bitcoin: A Peer-to-Peer Electronic Cash System," *Bitcoin,* October 31, 2008, https://bitcoin.org/bitcoin.pdf.

6. US Justice Department, *Report of the Attorney General's Cyber Digital Task Force: Crypto-currency: Enforcement Framework* (Washington, DC: Justice Department, 2020), https://www.justice.gov/cryptoreport.

7. Justice Department.

8. Europol, *Internet Organised Crime Threat Assessment (IOCTA), 2020* (Hague: Europol, October 5, 2020), 17, https://www.europol.europa.eu/activities-services/main-reports/internet-organised-crime-threat-assessment-iocta-2020.

9. Zia Sardar, "Cryptography: Why Do We Need It?," *Electronic Design,* April 2, 2020, https://www.electronicdesign.com/technologies/embedded-revolution/article/21127827/cryptography-why-do-we-need-it.

10. Justice Department, *Report of the Attorney General.*

11. "Cryptocurrency Market."

12. Sam Bocetta, "The Role of Cryptocurrencies in the Rise of Ransomware," *Cointelegraph,* Match 25, 2020, https://cointelegraph.com/news/the-role-of-cryptocurrencies-in-the-rise-of-ransomware.

13. Shalini Nagarajan, "Bitcoin Anonymity Is Just a Big Myth—and Using It to Launder Dirty Money Is Stupid, a Crypto ATM Chief Says," *Insider,* June 13, 2021, https://markets.businessinsider.com/news/currencies/bitcoin-anonymous-untraceable-myths-stupid-dirty-money-laundering-crypto-chief-2021-6.

14. Thuat Do, "Crypto and the Privacy-Transparency Tradeoff," *Blocks99,* July 2020, https://blocks99.com/in-depth/crypto-and-the-privacy-transparency-tradeoff/.

15. Jake Frankenfield, "Cryptocurrency," *Investopedia,* May 5, 2020, updated May 25, 2021, https://www.investopedia.com/terms/c/cryptocurrency.asp.

16. Frankenfield.

17. Shelley, *Dark Commerce,* 146; and "Russian Sentenced to French Prison for Bitcoin Laun-dering," AP News, Paris, December 7, 2020, https://apnews.com/article/cryptocurrency-paris-money-laundering-bitcoin-russia-61b5109e954f494b80d51c452b3b18e2.

18. Jennifer S. Freel and Brian L. Howard II, "Do Bitcoin ATMs Make Money Laundering Too Easy? Regulators Try to Keep Up with the Emerging Cryptocurrency Trend," *Vin-son&Elkins Insights* (blog), July 24, 2019, https://www.velaw.com/insights/do-bitcoin-atms-make-money-laundering-too-easy-regulators-try-to-keep-up-with-emerging-cryptocurrency-trend/.

19. Elena Perez, "How the US and Europe Are Regulating Crypto in 2020," *Cointelegraph,* July 12, 2020, https://cointelegraph.com/news/how-the-us-and-europe-are-regulating-crypto-in-2020.

20. Perez; FATF, "Regulation of Virtual Assets," October 19, 2018, https://www.fatf-gafi.org/publications/fatfrecommendations/documents/regulation-virtual-assets.html; and FATF, "Virtual Assets," accessed October 11, 2020, https://www.fatf-gafi.org/publications/virtualassets/documents/virtual-assets.html?hf=10&b=0&s=desc(fatf_releasedate).

21. FinCEN, "FinCEN Penalizes Peer-to-Peer Virtual Currency Exchanger for Violations of Anti–Money Laundering Laws," US Treasury Department, press release, April 18, 2019, https://www.fincen.gov/news/news-releases/fincen-penalizes-peer-peer-virtual -currency-exchanger-violations-anti-money.

22. Yaya J. Fanusie and Tom Robinson, "Bitcoin Laundering: An Analysis of Illicit Flows into Digital Currency Services" (Washington, DC: Elliptic and the Center on Sanctions and Illicit Finance, January 12, 2018), https://cdn2.hubspot.net/hubfs/3883533 /downloads/Bitcoin%20Laundering.pdf.

23. Europol, *Internet Organised Crime.*

24. "Cryptocurrency Market Report and Global Forecast 2024."

25. US Treasury Department, "White House Press Briefing by Treasury Secretary Steven Mnuchin on Regulatory Issues Associated with Cryptocurrency," July 15, 2019, https:// home.treasury.gov/news/press-releases/sm731.

26. Bocetta, "Role of Cryptocurrencies."

27. Europol, *Internet Organised Crime.*

28. Ana Alexandre, "Cyber Criminals Netted $4.3B from Crypto-Related Crime in 2019: Study," *Cointelegraph,* August 12, 2019, https://cointelegraph.com/news/cyber -criminals-netted-43b-from-crypto-related-crime-in-2019-study.

29. FATF, "Virtual Assets and Red Flag Indicators of Money Laundering and Terrorist Financing" (Paris: FATF, September 2020), 4, https://www.fatf-gafi.org/media/fatf /documents/recommendations/Virtual-Assets-Red-Flag-Indicators.pdf.

30. FATF, 4.

31. Diego Oré, "Latin American Crime Cartels Turn to Crypto to Clean Up Their Cash," Reuters, December 8, 2020, https://www.reuters.com/article/mexico-bitcoin/insight -latin-american-crime-cartels-turn-to-crypto-to-clean-up-their-cash-idUSL1N2IJ01D.

32. Adam Barone, "The Future of Cryptocurrency in 2019 and Beyond," *Investopedia,* June 25, 2019, https://www.investopedia.com/articles/forex/091013/future -cryptocurrency.asp.

33. Maeve Allsup and Lydia Beyoud, "Bitcoin Deemed 'Money' under D.C. Financial Services Law (2)," *Bloomberg Law,* July 24, 2020, https://news.bloomberglaw.com/us-law -week/bitcoin-deemed-money-under-d-c-financial-services-law; and Steven Porter, "US Judge Rules That Bitcoin Counts as Money," *Christian Science Monitor,* September 20, 2016, https://www.csmonitor.com/Business/2016/0920/US-judge-rules-that-Bitcoin -counts-as-money.

34. "Bitcoin Money Laundering."

35. Fanusie and Robinson, "Bitcoin Laundering."

36. Sean Dickens, "Bitcoin of America Adds Ethereum Purchases to Its ATMs," Coin Rivert, September 29, 2021, https://coinrivet.com/bitcoin-of-america-adds-ethereum -purchases-to-its-atms/#:~:text=The%20United%20States%20is%20one,high%20of %20approximately%2028k%20machines.

37. Daniel Moore and Thomas Rid, "Cryptopolitik and the Darknet," *Survival: Global Politics and Strategy* 58, no. 1 (February 2016): 7–38, https://doi.org/10.1080/00396338.2016 .1142085.

38. Darren Guccione, "What Is the Dark Web? How to Access It and What You'll Find," *CSO,* July 1, 2021, https://www.csoonline.com/article/3249765/what-is-the-dark-web-how-to -access-it-and-what-youll-find.html; and Ken Colburn, "Curious about the 'Deep Web'? Here's What You Should Know," WTOP News, November 2, 2017, https://wtop.com

/cyber-security/2017/11/curious-deep-web-heres-know/#:~:text=Most%20estimates%20put%20the%20deep,of%20a%20hidden%20web%20address.

39. Guccione.

40. Guccione.

41. Lauren Smiley, "A Federal Agents' Guide to Laundering Silk Road Bitcoin," *Matter*, March 31, 2015, https://medium.com/matter/a-federal-agents-guide-to-laundering-silk-road-bitcoin-65a6e3ecbc3e.

42. Smiley; and Office of Public Affairs, Justice Department, "Former Secret Service Agent Sentenced to 71 Months in Scheme Related to Silk Road Investigation," press release no. 15-1496, December 7, 2015, https://www.justice.gov/opa/pr/former-secret-service-agent-sentenced-71-months-scheme-related-silk-road-investigation.

43. Colin Harper, "The Long and Winding Story of Silk Road, Bitcoin's Earliest Major Application," *Bitcoin Magazine*, October 1, 2020, https://bitcoinmagazine.com/culture/the-long-and-winding-story-of-silk-road-bitcoins-earliest-major-application.

44. FATF, "Virtual Assets and Red Flag Indicators."

CHAPTER 9

A MORE LINEAR MONEY TRAIL

Terrorist Financing

Technological advances and the expansion of travel in the past century have led to serious developments in the use and practice of terrorism, thus making terrorists more mobile and more lethal. Terrorism has become an increasingly global problem, as attacks have grown in scale and the number of their victims has risen. Consequently, the twenty-first century ushered in the war on terrorism after devastating events such as the coordinated attacks on September 11, 2001 (9/11), and the 2013 Boston Marathon bombing, which profoundly changed society.

Terrorists need to raise funds, move money, purchase equipment, and bankroll all aspects of their operations. Inevitably, they do so through both legitimate and illegitimate means and rely on financial institutions to meet their objectives.

As a result, terrorism also threatens the integrity and credibility of financial institutions and the financial system. Furthermore, terrorists often rely on money laundering to conceal their illicit activities and avoid attracting the attention of authorities, and thus they employ many of the same techniques as money launderers. Therefore, terrorist financing and money laundering have long been intimately connected. In many cases, terrorist financing and money laundering also exhibit similar red flags, which financial institutions are uniquely suited to monitor, detect, and report.

CONFLICT, TERRORISM, AND TERRORIST FINANCING

Conflict is the primary driver of terrorist activity. In 2018, 95 percent of terrorist-related deaths occurred in countries enduring violent conflict (e.g., civil war, violent political unrest). This figure rises to 99 percent when including countries with high levels of state-sponsored terrorism (i.e., terrorism that is supported by the government, including the government's backing of nonstate actors engaged in terrorism). Furthermore, terrorism is also correlated with the intensity of conflict. Thus, within countries experiencing conflict, the deadlier the conflict, the more intense the terrorism. In fact, it has been found that terrorist attacks in conflict countries are over three times as lethal, on average, than terrorist attacks in nonconflict countries. Insurgent groups in particular use terrorism as a tactic of war, and since they are rebelling against authority, they are more likely to target the state's infrastructure, police, and military.[1]

Terrorism is a complex and often sensitive topic. Defining it can be controversial largely because terrorism often involves inherently divisive elements, such as polarizing political agendas, cultural and ethnic components, or a particular religious bent, and because of its violence and ferocity. For example, the UN, the EU, the United Kingdom, the United States, and even the League of Arab States' Arab Convention for the Suppression of Terrorism all define terrorism differently. Even within the United States, there are variations in the definition. For instance, the criminal code of the federal government, the Uniting and Strengthening America by Providing Appropriate Tools Required to Intercept and Obstruct Terrorism (USA PATRIOT) Act of 2001, the US Army's *Field Manual No. 3-37.2: Terrorism*, the FBI, and the Department of Defense all define terrorism differently.

Nonetheless, terrorism can still be defined in general terms. Therefore, broadly speaking, *terrorism* refers to the intentional use of violence or threats of violence against civilians or property with the intent to coerce or to intimidate governments or societies in the pursuit of goals that are typically political, religious, or ideological.

At its core, terrorism relies on fear to carry out specific objectives. To garner publicity and attention, as well as generate widespread fear, terrorists engage in increasingly violent, dramatic, and highly visible attacks. These attacks can take various forms, from isolated acts to coordinated efforts. Acts of terrorism can range from the relatively simple, such as the construction of a solitary homemade bomb, to highly sophisticated endeavors.

Terrorist organizations also differ extensively. These groups vary, from large and extremely coordinated organizations that operate akin to governments or businesses to small and decentralized networks, and cover everything in between.

Terrorism also takes different forms. In the early 1980s, Peruvian president Fernando Belaúnde Terry coined the term "narco-terrorism" to describe the attacks against Peru's anti-narcotics police and the use of violence and intimidation to influence government policies. Now the term is used more broadly to include references to terrorist groups that rely on narcotics to finance their operations.[2] Another form of terrorism identified by experts is extreme right-wing terrorism. Also sometimes referred to as far-right or racially and ethnically motivated terrorism, it incorporates elements of hate crime with more organized forms of terrorism.[3]

Terrorist activity also varies widely and may be carried out by a single individual or by organized groups, such as the Islamic State in Iraq and Syria (ISIS), Al-Qaeda, and Boko Haram, which have been listed as the three most dangerous terrorist organizations.[4] Terrorist activities have also been committed by political organizations, nationalistic and religious groups, revolutionaries, extremists, so-called lone wolves, and even state institutions such as armies, intelligence services, and police.

Acts of terrorism have commonly included hijackings, hostage takings, kidnappings, mass shootings, car bombings, and suicide bombings. The locations, and often the victims, are carefully chosen to meet the terrorist's agenda and for purposes of shock value. Busy shopping centers, schools, bus and train stations, airline flights and airports, restaurants, and nightclubs—all have been targets. Other major targets include specific buildings or locations that are considered important economic or political symbols, such as embassies and military bases.

Extreme right-wing groups have demonstrated themselves to be particularly internet savvy and have used the internet for recruitment and radicalization purposes. Such groups and their adherents have also exploited technological platforms to plan, finance, and carry out large-scale terrorist attacks that specifically targeted minorities, such as the 2019 attack on two mosques in Christchurch, New Zealand, among others.[5]

Terrorist financing, as the term implies, is the procurement of funds to support terrorist activity. More specifically, it includes raising, storing, and moving funds, acquired through either licit or illicit means, for the purpose of committing terrorist acts or supporting a terrorist organization. Simply, the goal of terrorist financing is to enable terrorism. While the methods and means of terrorist financing reflect the diversity of terrorist organizations, there is very little difference between terrorists and other criminals in how they use the financial system to fulfill their goals.

SOURCES OF TERRORIST FUNDING AND TECHNIQUES USED TO FUND TERRORISM

Terrorist organizations need money, not only to finance their attacks, including the purchase of weapons and the training of insurgents, but also to sustain the daily operation of their networks. Thus, terrorist groups must generate significant levels of income. Terrorists have demonstrated creativity, adaptability, and opportunism in obtaining funds.

Generally, terrorists obtain funds in two broad ways. One involves raising financial support from governments through state-sponsored terrorism or from donations given directly to the terrorist organization from individuals or entities that support their cause or agenda. The other is through a wide variety of legal and illegal revenue-generating activities. Legitimate funding sources may include legally earned profits from employment, savings, business operations, and charitable organizations.

In fact, charities and nonprofit organizations are particularly susceptible to misuse by terrorists for their funding purposes. These organizations generally have the benefit of public trust, making them a great cover for those who seek to misuse them. Additionally, their activities are generally cash intensive, and the organizations have access to numerous funding sources. Furthermore, many charities and nonprofits either have a global presence or are located in or near conflict zones and other locations that are exposed to terrorist activity.

Terrorist groups misuse charitable and nonprofit organizations to obtain funding in three primary ways. The first involves using fraud to divert funds. For instance, donors are led to believe they are donating money for a certain cause when in fact the charity diverts the money to terrorists. This can take place in parallel with lawful charitable activities and include the involvement of an otherwise legitimate charity. The second way in which terrorists use charities to obtain funds is through the use of a sham organization that poses as a legitimate charity. In this instance, the organization is simply a front for the terror group. And the third manner involves broad exploitation whereby the charity does in fact raise funds for a charitable purpose but actually does so through a terrorist organization.[6]

A number of charities have been accused of having ties to terrorism or have been convicted for using their revenues to fund terrorism. Many of these charities and others with purported ties to terrorist groups appear on OFAC's Specially Designated Nationals and Blocked Persons (SDN) List (which is discussed further in the section about economic sanctions). In fact, multiple individuals connected with terrorist groups who have been identified as SDNs not only had their assets blocked but were also subsequently located and arrested by law enforcement for their role in working or volunteering with such charities. For example, the Holy Land Foundation (HLF), which was originally known as the Occupied Land Fund and had its headquarters in Texas, was at one time the largest Islamic charity in the United States. The HLF's professed mission was the creation of humanitarian programs aimed at helping victims of man-made and natural disasters.

However, in December 2001, the US government designated the HLF a terrorist organization, seized its assets, and shut down its activities. The HLF and five of its founders were ultimately charged and convicted of providing approximately $12.4 million in material support to the militant fundamentalist group Hamas and related offenses.[7]

Illegitimate funding sources are a big revenue generator for terrorist groups and include a variety of criminal activities, such as the drug trade, human trafficking, cybercrime, the smuggling of weapons and other goods, fraud, kidnapping, and extortion. Terrorist organizations may also derive funds from a mix of sources. In fact, terrorist groups are increasingly turning to criminal networks for funding.

ISIS, which at the height of its territorial control in 2015 generated over $6 billion, has been one of the wealthiest terrorist groups in history. It derived its wealth from various legitimate and illegitimate ways, including by operating businesses and collecting taxes and tariffs from the population living on the land under its control. The group also took advantage of and profited from the vast natural resources—namely, oil and gas—existing in the region. Furthermore, ISIS took part in kidnapping and extortion, sold contraband, and looted bank vaults in the Iraqi city of Mosul. Therefore, although ISIS is an anomaly in many respects, an analysis of how the group raises funds offers a prime example of how terrorists often use both legal and illegal sources of funding.[8]

Just as drug trafficking is closely linked with money laundering, it is also closely tied to terrorism and has become one of the primary illegal activities by which terrorists raise funds. In fact, the term "narco-terrorism" refers to terrorism financed by illegal drug proceeds. For example, terrorist groups in Afghanistan generate funds through the sale of heroin in Russia, Europe, and elsewhere. The Taliban, Hezbollah, and other major terrorist groups are involved in the global drug trade, and many other terrorist groups are active at more regional and local levels. The Taliban, for instance, facilitates the largest production of opium in the world to fund their activities, resulting in a devastating impact on the Afghan people.[9] Moreover, the UN Security Council has noted on several occasions the relationship between drugs and terrorism. The DEA and the DOJ have reported similar findings on the relationship between international drug syndicates and terrorist groups.[10]

Terrorist groups are also involved in human trafficking (see chapter 7). Like the illegal drug trade, human trafficking is another profit-intensive crime that can generate significant proceeds. For instance, the trafficking of Yazidi women by ISIS, which sold them as sex slaves, and the trafficking of women and girls by Boko Haram, the militant Islamic group working out of Nigeria, has been widely reported.[11] The East African-based jihadist fundamentalist terrorist group Al-Shabab has been involved in the trafficking of children in Africa for their use as child soldiers, and the Syrian jihadist group Al-Nusra is presently involved in the kidney trade.[12]

Given its lower risk and high profitability, the illicit cigarette trade has also been immensely profitable for terrorist groups, including Hezbollah and Hamas. Even ISIS has benefited from the cigarette trade despite cigarettes being banned under the strict version of Islam that the group espouses.[13]

As these facts demonstrate, terrorists not only use a variety of funding sources but also, with increasing frequency, have been engaging in revenue-generating criminal activities. Therefore, the modern terrorist is a sort of hybrid terrorist-criminal and a money launderer. Given that terrorists often participate in diverse illegal activities in addition to terrorism, perhaps it is no surprise that many terrorists have a criminal history. Consequently, due diligence efforts, including watch list screening, should be able to help financial institutions identify these potential threat actors.

THE MOVEMENT AND LAUNDERING OF TERRORIST FUNDS

Any proceeds that terrorist groups raise must eventually be moved and often-times laundered to evade the attention of law enforcement. To move funds or transfer value, terrorists use the same three main methods that other criminals use. The first method entails utilizing the formal financial system whereby the products and services that banks and other financial institutions offer, such as wire transfers and bank account deposits, serve as vehicles for moving the funds that support terrorist organizations and their acts of terrorism. The second method involves physically moving money, including taking cash across borders, and is accomplished through smuggling and cash couriers, for example. A third method engages the international trade system and involves trade-based money laundering (see chapter 5).

Terrorists and insurgent groups always seek new means to evade law enforcement. Money laundering enables criminals to cover their financial tracks and avoid detection by the authorities and others. Although terrorists use techniques similar to those of other criminals in their attempts to move money, stay anonymous, and hide the identities of their sponsors and others, the specific money laundering method employed is different for each terrorist group. Money movement and laundering methods vary based on several factors, including the size and level of sophistication of the terrorist group, its geographic location, the source and destination of the illicit funds, and the means by which the funds were derived. Just as each terrorist group has its own "business model" for making money, it also has different ways to launder those funds. Hence, it's helpful for compliance personnel, investigators, and others to know the different typologies associated with terrorist groups and other criminal enterprises so the former can better identify and report ML and TF transactions.

The money laundering techniques that terrorist groups commonly exploit include the practice of structuring transactions; the use of corporate entities, such as trusts and anonymous shell companies, and of front companies; the purchase of high-end real estate; and the TBML techniques, among others. Additionally, terrorists, particularly those from the Middle East, also rely on alternative remittance or informal value transfer systems, such as hawala, to launder funds.

HAWALA AND OTHER INFORMAL VALUE TRANSFER SYSTEMS

The word "hawala" means "transfer" or sometimes "trust" in Arabic. *Hawala*, also called hundi in some cultures, is an informal system of transferring money, including from one country to another, that developed before the introduction of Western banking. It is utilized primarily in the Middle East and South Asia, although people in China and Africa also use informal remittance systems similar to hawala. This system is based primarily on trust and the use of an extensive network of personal connections and regional relationships.

Occasionally referred to as an underground banking system, hawala is an alternative remittance system that exists and operates outside of or in parallel with traditional banking. Expatriates and migrant workers find the hawala system a convenient and advantageous method of sending remittances to friends and relatives in their home countries.

Hawala requires at least two hawala dealers, or *hawaladars*, to conduct the transaction. An individual who wants to transfer money to another country contacts a hawala dealer in his or her current country and provides the hawaladar with the funds to be remitted along with a commission and information about the intended recipient of the funds. A password or unique code is exchanged that the intended recipient will have to reveal to confirm that he or she is the intended recipient of the money. The hawala dealer then communicates with a known hawaladar in the country where the intended recipient is located and arranges for that hawaladar to give the same amount of funds to the intended recipient. However, no money is actually moved from country to country because the hawaladar in the recipient's country already has the funds. For example, the hawaladar in the recipient's country may owe a debt to the hawala dealer in the sender's country and simply repays his debt through the transaction.

In this manner, money is transferred through a series of connections and a heavy reliance on trust. In fact, money can be transferred via hawala in just a single day or even a few hours, which is much faster than a transaction can be done through a financial institution, particularly if the sender is an immigrant and doesn't have the required proper identification or Social Security number to engage in banking services.[14]

Because hawala doesn't rely on the formal financial system, there is no government oversight or regulation and no bureaucracy involved. There's also no paperwork as most hawaladars keep very few, if any, records or documentation. Consequently, remittances via a hawala network do not leave a paper trail. It results in a fast, efficient, and reliable way of transferring money; however, the anonymity and the lack of documentation make hawala highly appealing to use in illegal activity, including the transfer of illicit funds. In fact, Al-Qaeda moved much of its money via hawala prior to the 9/11 attacks.[15]

Because hawala is a remittance system, it can be used in any stage of the money laundering cycle. For instance, hawala can provide an effective placement technique. In this regard, when hawaladars receive illicit funds, they can deposit the cash into bank accounts as proceeds from their seemingly legitimate businesses (hawaladars often provide hawala services as part of an otherwise legitimate business they operate, such as a travel agency). Additionally, some of the cash received could be used to pay for legitimate business expenses, thus reducing the need to make bank deposits.[16]

Additionally, since transferring money from one account to another is a main component of the layering stage, hawala transfers can be layered to make following the money even more difficult. Layering can be done by using hawala brokers in several countries and by spreading out the transfers over time. Since hawala transfers aren't generally documented, this activity wouldn't leave any paper trail.[17]

Finally, as part of the integration stage of money laundering, hawala techniques can be used to convert money into other forms, thus providing opportunities for creating the appearance of legitimacy. For example, money can be invested in other assets or reinvested in business ventures and can be sent overseas as part of seemingly legitimate investments abroad as well.[18]

For various reasons, including its large potential for misuse and the difficulties in regulation and enforcement, hawala is illegal in most jurisdictions. Nonetheless, hawala services are still widely advertised in a variety of media, and policing it is difficult because the ads are often in other languages and use purposely covert phrasing, such as the offer of "sweet rupee deals," that isn't necessarily suggestive of hawala remittance services. Businesses that offer hawala also generally have another primary business activity, adding to the difficulty in detecting it.[19]

THE COST OF ACTS OF TERRORISM

In contrast to running their day-to-day operations, terrorists tend to spend very little money to purchase the implements used in their attacks. For example, in 2017, Police Constable Keith Palmer was stabbed in a terrorist attack while guarding the entrance to the United Kingdom's House of Parliament. The assailant used a single kitchen knife to carry out the deadly attack. He had purchased it from a local market along with groceries for the week. Similarly, a terrorist used a single knife in the October 2020 attack at a basilica in the French city of Nice, resulting in the death of three people. The estimated cost to carry out the Boston Marathon bombing in April 2013 was just $500, which represents the total amount the perpetrators needed to construct two home-made pressure cooker bombs from instructions obtained online. The Madrid train bombings that took place on March 11, 2004, cost around $10,000, and the explosions killed 193 people and injured around 2,000. The 9/11 terror attacks cost approximately $500,000 to plan and execute, an incredibly inconsequential amount compared to the astounding damage and death toll that resulted. Consequently, the relatively small sums of money involved in perpetrating terrorist attacks make it difficult for financial institutions and others to detect terrorist-related transactions using traditional AML controls.

THE SIMILARITIES AND DIFFERENCES BETWEEN MONEY LAUNDERING AND TERRORIST FINANCING

Money laundering and terrorist financing are often mentioned together. This makes sense because there are several links between the two, including some notable similarities. Furthermore, the activities often occur together and exhibit common red flags. Therefore, an indicator of one may signal the presence of the other.

Both activities are similar in that they are criminal acts. Relatedly, both money laundering and terrorist financing may be carried out by the same individuals or group of individuals—namely, terrorists and terrorist groups—because, as discussed previously, money acquired illegally to support terrorist activity is often laundered. However, although money laundering always involves proceeds from criminal activities, terrorist financing may be funded with either licit or illicit proceeds.

The motivation or intent behind each activity, meanwhile, drastically differs. On the one hand, money laundering, which is done to disguise criminal proceeds, is ultimately carried out for financial profit and monetary gain. The launderer wants to be able to use the illicit funds without restrictions. Terrorist financing, on the other hand, is motivated by factors that are mainly ideological in nature and is done for purposes of gaining publicity and political power.

Additionally, money laundering occurs after the criminal act, whereas terrorist financing is done to support future criminal acts. Furthermore, the unlawfulness of the funds is different between the two activities. In money laundering, the funds are derived from a criminal source or origin, while in the case of terrorist financing, the ultimate aim and intended use of the funds is criminal in nature.

Another big difference between the two activities is the amount of funds involved. Money laundering becomes necessary when criminals have vast sums of money and need to disguise it. They often structure these large amounts to avoid the reporting requirements of financial institutions. Terrorist financing, however, involves smaller amounts of funds. They are normally below reporting thresholds and are therefore less observable by banks. Given the smaller sums involved in terrorist financing, terrorists may, but don't always need to, launder money.

Money laundering is also most often accomplished via the formal financial system. But terrorist financing tends to favor cash couriers and informal financial systems such as hawala and currency exchange firms.

The detection focus is yet another differentiating factor between money laundering and terrorist financing. With money laundering activity, the focus is on suspicious transactions, such as deposits that are inconsistent with the customer's profile or with the expected account activity for that particular customer based on his or her wealth. With terrorist financing, the focus is on suspicious relationships, such as wire transfers and other money movement between seemingly unrelated parties.

Furthermore, money laundering tends to involve a complex web of transactions, often involving shell or front companies, offshore secrecy havens, and *bearer shares*, which are unregistered equity securities that provide anonymity because the owners' names do not appear on any public register. In contrast, there is no specific financial profile of how terrorists operate.

Terrorist financing involves a much wider variety of transactions that are not easily profiled or categorized.

Finally, the money trails for these activities are distinctly different. Money laundering tends to have a circular money trail whereby the money eventually ends up with the individual who generated it. The opposite occurs in terrorist financing, which involves a linear money trail; that is, the proceeds generated are used to support the terrorist group and its terrorist activities.[20]

ECONOMIC SANCTIONS AND THE OFFICE OF FOREIGN ASSETS CONTROL

Economic sanctions have become the tool of choice for policymakers in responding to major geopolitical challenges, such as terrorism, conflict, and foreign crises. National governments and international bodies have imposed economic sanctions in cases where their interests or security have been endangered or where violations of international laws or norms of behavior have occurred.[21] The purpose of sanctions is to coerce, deter, punish, shame, or change the behavior of the sanctioned party, entity, or government. In some rare cases, the mere hint of sanctions may be enough to encourage parties in conflict to enter into dialogue.[22]

Sanctions have been used strategically to advance a range of foreign policy goals, including counterterrorism, counter narcotics, nonproliferation, democracy and human rights promotion, conflict resolution, and cybersecurity. Although sanctions are a form of intervention, they are generally viewed as a lower-cost and lower-risk course of action falling somewhere in between diplomacy and war. In fact, leaders have occasionally issued sanctions while evaluating more punitive action. For example, the UN Security Council imposed comprehensive sanctions against Iraq just four days after Saddam Hussein's invasion of Kuwait in August 1990 and, several months later, authorized the use of military force.[23]

Sanctions can take various forms, including trade restrictions, travel bans, asset freezes, arms embargoes, and limitations on access to the financial system. Critics of sanctions claim that they are not generally well thought out and are rarely successful in meeting the intended goal. As an example, critics often cite the long-standing, unsuccessful sanctions against Cuba. Sanctions' supporters, meanwhile, assert that they have been increasingly effective. Nonetheless, many experts contend that sanctions, especially targeted sanctions, can be at least partially successful if crafted appropriately.[24]

Each country is free to establish its own sanctions. Among the organizations that make use of sanctions are the UN, the EU, Her Majesty's Treasury Office of the United Kingdom, the Hong Kong Monetary Authority, and the US Treasury Department's Office of Foreign Assets Control. The United States uses economic and financial sanctions to meet its objectives more than any other country.[25]

OFAC administers most of the US economic sanctions programs, although other US government agencies, such as the Department of Commerce's Bureau of Industry and Security, the Department of Labor, and the State Department, have independent prohibitions on transactions with certain individuals or entities beyond those included in OFAC's sanctions listings. OFAC was established in 1950 following China's entry into the Korean War, which spurred President Harry S. Truman to declare a national emergency and to block all Chinese and North Korean assets subject to US jurisdiction. Since then, OFAC's purpose has been to administer and enforce economic and trade sanctions against certain individuals, entities, foreign government agencies, and countries whose interests are opposed to US policy.[26]

OFAC maintains numerous sanctions programs against foreign countries and regimes, traffickers, and those involved in industry-based programs that pose a threat to the United States. These programs can broadly be classified into two main categories—comprehensive and selective or targeted.[27]

Comprehensive programs are generally wide ranging and geographically oriented and are sometimes referred to as embargoes. Such programs prohibit all exports, imports, financing, trade, brokering, facilitation, and commercial activity with the sanctions' target. These sanctions are often imposed on countries or governments that are known to sponsor terrorism, such as Iran and Syria. Other examples of comprehensive sanctions include the long-standing measures against Cuba and North Korea.[28]

Targeted or selective programs focus on specific individuals and entities that have been sanctioned due to their involvement in a broad range of certain activities, such as narcotics trafficking, terrorism, and transnational organized crime. OFAC maintains a list containing the names of more than six thousand targeted individuals, entities (including companies, charities, groups, etc.), and even shipping vessels and aircraft. Collectively known as specially designated nationals (SDNs), they are posted on the SDN List. Osama bin Laden and Saddam Hussein are two individuals who were designated as SDNs (and whose names still appear on the SDN List). The assets of those entered on the SDN List are effectively blocked, meaning that US persons, including US businesses and their foreign branches, are forbidden from transacting with the SDNs. Furthermore, since these individuals and entities may cross borders and move internationally, US persons and businesses are still prohibited from dealing with SDNs regardless of their location.[29] Moreover, according to OFAC's 50 Percent Rule, any entity that is owned by an SDN (defined as a direct or indirect ownership interest of 50 percent or more) is also blocked even if that entity is not listed on the SDN List.[30]

In addition to the SDN list, OFAC maintains a number of other targeted sanctions lists, and its objectives may change from time to time based on foreign policy and national security goals. These lists are available for free and in searchable format on its website. Such list-based sanctions, also referred to as smart sanctions, not only have allowed the US government to more precisely target persons or groups that it views as posing a threat but also have been helpful from a law enforcement perspective.

Although sanctions are traditionally imposed against a specific country, region, group, entity, or individual, the United States has been making increased use of what are known as extraterritorial or secondary sanctions. *Secondary sanctions* are used to discourage non-US parties from doing business with targets of designated sanctions. Therefore, should a non-US company conduct business with the subject of secondary sanctions, OFAC has the power to classify that non-US company as an SDN. Thus, secondary sanctions are often seen as aggressive and invasive, and many countries consider them a violation of their state's sovereignty. In recent years, the US government has applied secondary sanctions most notably to Iran.

Being designated as a sanctions target can have severe consequences, mostly resulting in economic hardship due to the mandated restrictions on trade and commercial activity and the blocked access to the US financial system. It often also leads to reputational damage and the loss of both current and future business. Other repercussions may include additional scrutiny; disadvantages or disqualifications regarding business opportunities, investments, and prospective partners; and even contract breaches, among other hardships.

OFAC's sanctions programs are dynamic and subject to change from time to time based on the government's foreign policy goals and objectives. Therefore, sanctions may be added, amended, or removed, and names may be added to or deleted from the SDN List. However, it is much more common to have a name added to the SDN List rather than for a name to be deleted from it.

Willful violations carry criminal penalties, including fines up to $1 million per violation and possible jail time. However, since US sanctions regulations are generally a strict liability regime, even minor or inadvertent violations result in severe consequences. Civil penalties of a little over $300,000 per violation are applicable for unintentional violations for most sanctions regimes.[31]

CASE STUDY: FINANCING TERRORISM
THROUGH A FAMILY BUSINESS

Kassim Tajideen is a Lebanese businessman who raised millions of dollars in support of Hezbollah, which the United States has long considered a terrorist organization. Tajideen raised these funds primarily through the illegal trade of blood diamonds; then he laundered them through front companies and via trade-based money laundering schemes. His case is a rare example of a complex terrorist-financing enterprise and illustrates how terrorist-financing strategies incorporate money laundering techniques.

Hezbollah is a Shia Islamist political party and militant group that was formed in 1982 to fight Israel's invasion of Beirut. Since its creation, it has become politically powerful in Lebanon and deeply embedded in Lebanese society. It operates its own media and communications channels and provides government-like services, such as collecting garbage and running hospitals and schools, in areas under its control.[32]

Originally from Lebanon, the Tajideen family includes Kassim Tajideen and his two brothers, Ali Tajideen and Husayn Tajideen. The Tajideens also lived in the diamond-rich West African country of Sierra Leone, where they established strong ties with the Lebanese community living there. Having secured citizenship in Lebanon and Sierra Leone, as well as Belgium, enabled Kassim to become a successful diamond trader, whereby he purchased conflict diamonds in Africa and sold them at a discount in Antwerp.[33]

Kassim, along with his brother Husayn, expanded the diamond business into Angola, a hub for moving goods between Africa and Europe. They also set up several other companies that engaged in a variety of businesses dealing in food and household and personal items. The Tajideens used these businesses as front companies to create a veneer of legitimacy while they smuggled conflict diamonds out of troubled African countries and into Europe, thus profiting immensely.[34]

Kassim relocated to Gambia in 1993. There he and his two brothers established Tajco Company LLC and a subsidiary called Gambian Kairaba Supermarket that functioned primarily to disguise the cross-border movement of money and goods and to enable their TBML scheme, which included under-invoicing and documentary fraud. In addition, the funds procured from Tajco Company LLC were reportedly used to purchase and develop properties in Lebanon for Hezbollah's use.[35]

Kassim also operated Soafrimex, an Antwerp-based import-export company that appeared to specialize in providing food commodities to the African continent, but he actually used it to trade blood diamonds and launder money. In 2003 Belgian police raided Kassim's Antwerp offices and arrested Kassim, his wife, and several employees. As a result, Kasim and his wife served short prison sentences on ML charges related to that arrest.[36]

The Tajideens continued to develop their network of companies and branched out into real estate, construction, and illegal logging of timber. As their operations grew, the Tajideens expanded their markets into Latin America and the Caribbean.

As their illicit activity grew, disguising it became increasingly difficult. The Tajideens relied in large part on anonymous corporate entities and front companies to conceal their ownership and transactions. They enlisted the advice and assistance of Mossack Fonseca, the now-defunct Panamanian law firm and service provider infamized by the Panama Papers scandal. Mossack Fonseca helped the Tajideens create the British Virgin Islands company Ovlas Trading S.A. and its subsidiary Ovlas Commodities S.A., which were linked to a Beirut address and specifically set up to hide their ownership. These companies, along with Tajco and others, have since been added to OFAC's SDN List.[37]

Beginning in 2009, the World Federation of Diamond Bourses labeled Kassim as a "rogue diamond trader." That same year Kassim was the first of the Tajideen brothers whom OFAC designated as a "global terrorist" for funding Hezbollah, and it added him and his company to the SDN List.[38] The next year, OFAC also added Husayn Tajideen and Ali Tajideen to its SDN List.

However, the brothers continued to play significant roles in the international network they had built. After they were accused of funding terrorism in 2010, they rebuilt their multibillion-dollar commodity distribution network to purposely conceal Kassim's role, including changing the businesses' names and misrepresenting their ownership to buy food commodities and security equipment. In this manner, Kassim effectively evaded sanctions and illegally conducted business with US companies. This was enabled in large part through Kassim's United Arab Emirates-based Epsilon Trading Fze and International Cross Trade Company, as well as a supply chain of companies registered in the Congo, Gambia, and Angola.[39]

After a multiyear investigation, Kassim Tajideen was arrested on an INTERPOL warrant in Morocco in March 2017 and extradited to the United States. Ultimately, Tajideen pleaded guilty to charges associated with evading US sanctions and money laundering conspiracy. He admitted to conspiring with at least five other people in conducting transactions worth over $50 million with US businesses in violation of US sanctions and to engaging in transactions totaling over $1 billion outside of the United States. He was sentenced to a five-year prison term and ordered to forfeit $50 million.[40]

The Tajideen case demonstrates the practical workings and implications of US economic sanctions, including targeted sanctions against designated individuals and entities, such as terrorists, named on the sanctions lists administered by OFAC. The case also provides a glimpse into just how complex, sophisticated, enterprising, and far-reaching terrorist networks, their financing schemes, and their money laundering techniques can be. Tajideen's network spanned industries and continents, utilized a mixture of legal and illegal enterprises, exploited the international trade system, made use of a vast global conglomerate of companies and banks, and enlisted the help of gatekeepers and others who enabled the scheme. Over the course of twenty-five years, the coordinated enterprise transferred over $1 billion in funds, evaded sanctions, and avoided detection. This case further demonstrates the incredible agility with which criminal networks constantly adjust their tactics to seize new funding opportunities and to skirt restrictions. Finally, the case underscores the numerous connections and nuances between money laundering and terrorist financing.

RED FLAGS ASSOCIATED WITH TERRORIST FINANCING

Red flags associated with terrorist financing are difficult to identify since the amounts of money and the types of transactions involved often appear fairly ordinary and therefore don't tend to raise suspicion. However, understanding the various typologies associated with terrorist groups can be helpful in this regard. The Egmont Group of Financial Intelligence Units has published a useful list based on various typologies identified in case studies.[41] The Federal Financial Institutions Examination Council's *Bank Secrecy Act (BSA)/Anti-Money Laundering (AML) Examination Manual* also includes a comprehensive list of red flags for terrorist financing.[42] Often based on behavior and financial indicators, such red flags include the following: the use of funds by a nonprofit organization that is inconsistent with its established purpose, the involvement of parties (e.g., owner or beneficiary in a transaction) from countries known to support terrorist activities and organizations, and the use of opaque corporate structures (including shell companies, trusts, and foundations), nominees, and third-party accounts to obscure or complicate ownership.

CONCLUSION

Terrorism can be both controversial and difficult to define precisely as it may concern many varying motives, targets, and methods. However, most people agree that it generally involves intentional violence for ideological (e.g., political or religious) purposes.

Much like money launderers, terrorists are constantly adapting the ways in which they exploit the financial system. They have used globalization and technological advances to their benefit in recent times, thus enabling terror attacks that are more violent and kill and injure more people than ever before in history. The associated terrorist groups are becoming increasingly sophisticated. They have shown themselves to be particularly adept at raising the funds and resources necessary to mobilize and train insurgents, finance day-to-day operations, and sustain deadly attacks.

Terrorist organizations raise funds using various methods, both legal and illegal, and use numerous different money laundering techniques to effectively disguise and transfer illicit funds, illustrating the multiple intricate and nuanced connections between money laundering and terrorist financing. Many terrorist groups exhibit their own unique typologies (much like drug cartels and criminal organizations engaged in human trafficking), including in the ways in which they raise funds and move money. A basic understanding of these typologies can help identify suspicious funding flows linked to terrorist activity.

As terrorists have expanded their reach across the globe, terrorism and terrorist financing have taken center stage as international concerns. Economic sanctions, which are designed to influence or punish certain behavior, also often target terrorists, terrorist groups, and states that sponsor terrorism. The efficacy of these sanctions has been debated. Although perhaps good in theory, comprehensive sanctions can have unintended crippling effects on countries, and their impact is most often felt by poor and innocent civilians rather than the targeted governments and officials. For instance, a trade embargo is more likely to affect a subsistence farmer who is unable to sell his crops for export or a factory worker who is unable to receive raw materials. Furthermore, the unilateral use of US secondary sanctions has also been strongly criticized. In the interests of human rights and the prevention of unnecessary harm and destruction, it's crucial to ensure a comprehensive understanding of these measures and their impacts.

NOTES

1. "Conflict Is a Major Driver of Terrorist Activity," *Vision of Humanity*, accessed October 20, 2020, http://visionofhumanity.org/terrorism/conflict-is-a-major-driver-of-terrorist-activity/.
2. Louise I. Shelley, "Illicit Trade and Terrorism," *Perspectives on Terrorism* 14, no. 4 (August 2020): 4.

3. UN Security Council Counter-Terrorism Committee Executive Directorate (CTED), "Member States Concerned by the Growing and Increasingly Transnational Threat of Extreme Right-Wing Terrorism," CTED Trends Alert, April 2020, https://www.un .org/securitycouncil/ctc/sites/www.un.org.securitycouncil.ctc/files/files/documents /2021/Jan/cted_trends_alert_extreme_right-wing_terrorism.pdf.

4. "The Three Most Dangerous Terrorist Organizations," *Investopedia*, March 20, 2020.

5. CTED, "Member States Concerned."

6. FATF, "Terrorist Financing" (Paris: FATF, February 29, 2008), https://www.fatf-gafi .org/media/fatf/documents/reports/FATF%20Terrorist%20Financing%20Typologies %20Report.pdf.

7. United States v. Holy Land Foundation for Relief and Development, United States, District Court (Texas: Northern District, 2008), Homeland Security Digital Library, https://www.hsdl.org/?abstract&did=7740.

8. Colin P. Clarke, "An Overview of Current Trends in Terrorism and Illicit Finance: Lessons from the Islamic State in Iraq and Syria and Other Emerging Threats," Testimony before the US House of Representatives, Financial Services Committee, Subcommittee on Terrorism and Illicit Finance, September 7, 2018 (Santa Monica: RAND Corporation, 2018), https://www.rand.org/pubs/testimonies/CT498.html.

9. FATF, "Terrorist Financing."

10. Shelley, *Dark Commerce.*

11. Shelley; and Salah Hassan Baban, "Sold, Whipped and Raped: A Yazidi Woman Remembers ISIL Captivity," Aljazeera, October 16, 2020, https://www.aljazeera.com/features /2020/10/16/separation-from-my-children-was-more-painful-than.

12. Shelley, *Dark Commerce*; and Shira Rubin, "Desperate Refugees Are Selling Their Own Organs to Survive," *Vocativ*, February 24, 2017, https://www.vocativ.com/404068 /desperate-refugees-organs-black-market/index.html.

13. Shelley, *Dark Commerce*, 166.

14. Patrick M. Jost and Harjit Singh Sandhu, "Hawala: The Hawala Alternative Remittance System and Its Role in Money Laundering" (Vienna, VA: FinCEN and INTERPOL/ FOPAC), 11, accessed October 20, 2020, https://www.treasury.gov/resource-center /terrorist-illicit-finance/Documents/FinCEN-Hawala-rpt.pdf.

15. ACAMS, *Study Guide*, 104–6.

16. ACAMS.

17. ACAMS.

18. ACAMS.

19. Jost and Sandhu, "Hawala Alternative Remittance System."

20. ACAMS, *Study Guide.*

21. Jonathan Masters, "What Are Economic Sanctions?," Backgrounder (Washington, DC: Council on Foreign Relations, August 12, 2019), https://www.cfr.org/backgrounder /what-are-economic-sanctions.

22. United Nations, "UN Sanctions: What They Are, How They Work, and Who Uses Them," United Nations News, May 4, 2016, https://news.un.org/en/story/2016/05 /528382-un-sanctions-what-they-are-how-they-work-and-who-uses-them.

23. Masters, "What Are Economic Sanctions?"

24. Masters.

25. Masters.

26. Office of Foreign Assets Control (OFAC)—Sanctions Programs and Information, "Frequently Asked Questions: Basic Information on OFAC and Sanctions," US Treasury

Department, May 2, 2006, https://home.treasury.gov/policy-issues/financial-sanctions
/faqs/2.

27. OFAC, "Where Is OFAC's Country List? What Countries Do I Need to Worry about
in Terms of U.S. Sanctions?," US Treasury Department, accessed October 21, 2020,
https://home.treasury.gov/policy-issues/financial-sanctions/sanctions-programs-and
-country-information/where-is-ofacs-country-list-what-countries-do-i-need-to-worry
-about-in-terms-of-us-sanctions.

28. OFAC.

29. Masters, "What Are Economic Sanctions?"

30. OFAC, "Where Is OFAC's Country List?"

31. Tahlia Townsend, "The Aggressive Extraterritorial Reach of U.S. Economic Sanctions:
Foreign Company Exposure to OFAC Enforcement," *National Law Review*, April 15,
2020, https://www.natlawreview.com/article/aggressive-extraterritorial-reach-us
-economic-sanctions-foreign-company-exposure-to.

32. Dan Levy, "Hezbollah's Fundraising Activity in Africa: Focus on the Democratic Republic of Congo," Working Papers Series (Hague: International Institute for Counter-
Terrorism, March 2013), https://www.ict.org.il/UserFiles/ICTWPS%20-%20Dan
%20Levy%20-%2012.pdf.

33. William Scott Grob, "Lessons Learned from the Kassim Tajideen Case," *ACAMS Today*,
March 10, 2020, https://www.acamstoday.org/lessons-learned-from-kassim-tajideen
-case/.

34. Grob.

35. Grob.

36. Grob.

37. Grob.

38. Spencer S. Hsu, "Lebanese Businessman Accused of Funding Hezbollah Pleads Guilty to
Money Laundering," *Washington Post*, December 6, 2018, https://www.washingtonpost
.com/local/legal-issues/accused-lebanese-hezbollah-financier-pleads-guilty-in-us-to
-money-laundering-plot/2018/12/06/831b4fdc-f979-11e8-863c-9e2f864d47e7_story
.html; and Counter Extremism Project, "Overview: Kassim Tajideen," accessed October
21, 2020, https://www.counterextremism.com/extremists/kassim-tajideen.

39. Hsu, "Lebanese Businessman Accused."

40. Counter Extremism Project; and United States of America v. Kassim Tajideen and Imad
Hassoun, US District Court for the District of Columbia, Department of Justice, November 3, 2016, https://www. justice.gov/opa/press-release/file/952071/ download.

41. Egmont Group, *FIUs and Terrorist Financing Analysis: A Review by the Egmont Group
of Sanitised Cases Related to Terrorist Financing*, April 18, 2002, https://nav.gov.hu
/data/cms394348/A_terrorizmus_finanszirozasara_utalo_indikatorokrol_keszitett
dokumentum(FIUs_and_Terrorist_Financing_Analysis___A_review_by_the
_Egmont_Group_of_Sanitised_.pdf.

42. Federal Financial Institutions Exam Council (FFIEC), "Appendix F: Money Laundering and Terrorist Financing 'Red Flags,'" *Bank Secrecy Act (BSA)/Anti-Money Laundering (AML) Examination Manual*, vol. 2, February 27, 2015, https://bsaaml.ffiec.gov
/manual/Appendices/07.

CHAPTER 10

HOW WE GOT HERE

A Historical Overview
of Key AML Legislation

Laws and regulations don't develop in a vacuum. Rather, they are influenced by, and reflective of, the events and issues of their time. Therefore, understanding their historical context, along with recognizing the lawmakers' intent and goals behind enacting them, can help us better understand particular pieces of legislation. This is certainly the case with federal anti–money laundering legislation, which not only constitutes the earliest response to money laundering globally but also developed in response to the illegal drug trade that legislatures and law enforcement struggled to address.

Starting in the early 1970s and escalating through the 1980s and into the 1990s, US anti–money laundering legislation developed alongside the war on drugs, which was first declared by President Richard Nixon. In fact, AML laws and regulations are intimately linked with statutes aimed at stemming the flow of illicit cash from drug cartels and from those organized crime groups that also profited enormously from the illicit narcotics trade.

Even today the United States is the largest consumer market for illegal drugs. Furthermore, the US dollar is still the preferred currency in the international drug trade.[1] Since drugs are bought with cash, an abundance of illegal drug proceeds circulates through the US financial system. In fact, tests have shown that roughly 90 percent of the dollar bills in circulation in the United States contain traces of cocaine.[2]

THE BANK SECRECY ACT (1970)

The Bank Secrecy Act, also called the Currency and Foreign Transactions Reporting Act, has long been a significant part of the AML landscape. The

United States took the lead in the battle against money laundering when President Nixon signed the BSA into law in 1970, thus establishing the first piece of money laundering legislation. The law was designed primarily to deter the use of hidden foreign bank accounts and to create a financial audit trail.

The decade preceding the BSA's passage was known for hippies, tie-dye, and bell bottoms, as well as large-scale drug use, including marijuana, heroin, and LSD. By the late 1960s, the illegal cocaine trade had become a significant concern in the United States and a major source of profit for drug cartels. Organized crime groups also profited from illegal narcotics. As a result, US banks started to experience a growing influx of illicit cash. Thus, Congress passed the BSA primarily as a response to the growing cash revenue of criminal syndicates and drug cartels. The law aimed to stop this trend by requiring that banks collect certain information that could be shared with law enforcement. Therefore, the BSA's target was banks, not criminals.

Additionally, unlike what its name might imply, the BSA wasn't intended to preserve or promote bank secrecy. Instead, as denoted by its alternate title, the Currency and Foreign Transactions Reporting Act, it was more of a record-keeping and reporting statute. BSA requirements apply to both individuals (in certain circumstances) and financial institutions (defined broadly under the act). For example, the BSA applies to individuals who physically transport cash over $10,000 into or out of the country, in which case they must file a US customs form.

The types of financial institutions to which the BSA pertains have been expanded over the years to include both banks and nonbank financial institutions, and it encompasses such businesses as money services businesses, casinos, credit unions, insurance companies, and numerous others. Not all provisions of the BSA apply uniformly to all financial institutions, however. Specific record-keeping and reporting requirements for a financial institution differ based on the nature of the services it offers. For instance, the particular BSA obligations of cash-based businesses, such as casinos, will look somewhat different from those of trust companies, which mainly focus on investment and asset management services.

The purpose of BSA requirements is to assist government agencies in the detection and prevention of money laundering. Financial institutions do so primarily by keeping records of certain cash purchases of negotiable instruments and filing currency transaction reports on currency transactions exceeding $10,000 and suspicious activity reports concerning potential money laundering, tax evasion, or other criminal activities. (CTRs and SARs are discussed in further detail in chapter 11.) Many BSA reports focus on cash and monetary instruments, which include cashier's checks, traveler's checks, and money orders. These records and reports serve to create a paper trail and provide valuable evidence to law enforcement and regulatory agencies, which they use to pursue investigations of criminal, tax, and regulatory violations.[3] Furthermore, the BSA also has become a tool to fight terrorist financing.

Immediately following its enactment, however, the BSA got little traction. One reason is because the BSA was challenged as unconstitutional (the USA PATRIOT Act, which amended portions of the BSA, would also be challenged three decades later). Several groups claimed that the BSA violated the Fourth Amendment rights against unwarranted search and seizure and the Fifth Amendment rights of due process. These claims were ultimately rejected in the 1974 case *California Bankers Association v. Shultz*, where the US Supreme Court held that the act did not violate the Constitution.[4] It wasn't until the late 1980s that financial institutions started to comply with the BSA's reporting requirements. They were likely influenced by the indictment in February 1985 of the large and well-respected First National Bank of Boston, which pleaded guilty for failing to report a series of cash transactions totaling more than $1.2 billion. The bank received a fine of $500,000, representing not only the maximum fine that could be imposed for a single felony count under the BSA but also the largest fine to that point that had been imposed on a bank for violating the act.[5]

The BSA has been amended several times. Its amendments have largely focused on expanding the act's scope by broadening and clarifying the definitions of certain terms, strengthening enforcement and penalties, streamlining reporting requirements, and granting greater authority to the Treasury Department. Following its enactment, many other US laws and directives have also focused on suspicious financial activities and deceptive cash transactions. Thus, the main purpose of BSA/AML laws is to help identify the source, volume, and movement of currency and other monetary instruments transported or transmitted into or out of the United States or deposited into US financial institutions. This, in turn, is meant to aid in the investigation of money laundering, tax evasion, terrorism, and other financial criminal activity.

THE ORGANIZED CRIME CONTROL ACT (1970)

In the same year in which President Nixon signed the BSA, he also signed into law the Organized Crime Control Act (referred to more simply as the Crime Control Act), a measure aimed at the Mafia and other crime syndicates. The

Racketeer Influenced and Corrupt Organizations Act (or RICO statute, as it is more commonly known) is contained within Title IX of the Organized Crime and Control Act and makes it a federal crime to conduct or participate, directly or indirectly, in a criminal enterprise. The RICO statute focuses primarily on racketeering and related offenses. Originally used to prosecute the Mafia and others who were actively engaged in organized crime, its subsequent application has been broader.

The RICO statute defines racketeering activity and within its definition lists several predicate crimes that are also considered predicate crimes (including drug trafficking) for money laundering under federal ML legislation (Sections 1956 and 1957). The government successively used RICO charges to bring down some of the most notorious mob bosses and their associates, including John Gotti, Frank LoCascio, and other members of the Gambino crime family, as well as members of the Lucchese family, Bonanno family, and members of the Chicago Outfit, among others.

In response to America's growing drug problem, Nixon also signed into law the Comprehensive Drug Abuse Prevention and Control Act in 1970. This measure replaced over fifty pieces of previous drug legislation and strengthened support for treatment, rehabilitation, and education, as well as regulation and enforcement. The Drug Enforcement Agency was formed three years later. Its mission continues to be the enforcement of the controlled substance laws and regulations of the United States.[6]

THE MONEY LAUNDERING CONTROL ACT (1986)

In 1982 President Ronald Reagan declared illicit drugs a threat to US national security. Huge amounts of cocaine were being shipped into the country, resulting in what was known as the crack epidemic of the 1980s. Drug money, most of it tied to Colombian cocaine traffickers, flowed through major cities throughout the United States and was even credited with powering Miami's economy. *Miami Vice*, the popular television crime series of that time, depicts the cocaine boom of the 1980s.

Furthermore, the failures of savings and loan associations during the 1980s resulted in a financial crisis that led to a rise in white-collar crime. The FBI uncovered many instances of fraud that lay behind those failures. In the ensuing years, various kinds of fraud involving health care, telemarketing, insurance, and stocks became major crime problems. Law enforcement sought new means to combat these crimes, which contributed to the illicit funds circulating through the country's financial system.

Additionally, launderers found new ways to circumvent the BSA. One of the primary means was through structuring cash deposits by dividing up the dirty money and making multiple smaller deposits of less than $10,000 at a number of different banks, thus avoiding the banks' filing of CTRs.

Consequently, in 1986, Congress passed the Money Laundering Control Act. The statute was the next significant development in AML legislation in that it finally made money laundering a federal crime for both individuals and financial institutions, and it outlawed structuring as well. As noted in chapter 1, the act is codified in Title 18 of the US Code and consists of two sections—18 USC § 1956, which is the core MLCA provision that criminalizes active engagement in money laundering, and 18 U.S.C. § 1957, which prohibits the knowing acceptance of tainted funds, including the structuring of transactions to evade CTR filings.

By imposing criminal liability on an institution or an individual who knowingly assists in the laundering of money or who structures transactions to avoid filing a CTR, the MLCA sought to preclude the circumvention of BSA requirements. Additionally, the MLCA introduced civil and criminal forfeiture for BSA violations. It also directed banks to establish and maintain procedures reasonably designed to ensure and monitor compliance with the reporting and record-keeping requirements of the BSA. As a result of the MLCA, financial institution regulatory bodies have developed and implemented BSA/AML compliance program requirements for the institutions they regulate.

THE ANTI-DRUG ABUSE ACT (1986 AND 1988)

The Anti–Drug Abuse Act of 1986 was signed into law by President Ronald Regan and was enacted as part of the war on drugs initiated in the 1970s. The law significantly strengthened the federal government's anti-drug efforts, perhaps most notably by making it easier to seize drug offenders' assets as well as by instituting new mandatory minimum prison terms for the possession of drugs. The 1986 act was amended by the Anti–Drug Abuse Act of 1988, which, among other things, enhanced the penalties for drug offenses, increased the severity of sentences for those involved in the drug trade, restored the use of the federal death penalty, and provided for greater funding to battle the drug epidemic gripping the nation.[7]

The Anti–Drug Abuse Act of 1988 also amended and enhanced the BSA. The act expanded the definition of "financial institution" to include auto dealers and personnel involved in real estate closings and settlements, thus imposing requirements that they also must file reports on large currency transactions. Furthermore, the act requires financial institutions to verify the identity of purchasers of monetary instruments that are greater than $3,000.[8]

THE ANNUNZIO-WYLIE ANTI–MONEY LAUNDERING ACT (1992)

The Annunzio-Wylie Anti–Money Laundering Act of 1992 further amended the BSA and represented a shift in US AML policy. The act was passed partly in response to the Bank of Credit and Commerce International (BCCI) multibillion-dollar fraud that shook the international banking community in 1991. With its multiple layers of entities, holding companies, subsidiaries, affiliates, and nominee relationships, BCCI was structured in such a way that no single government had overall regulatory supervision over it. This lack of oversight enabled the bank's rapid growth, facilitated its illicit activity, and contributed to its eventual demise. At its height, BCCI had more than four hundred branches; operated in over seventy countries, including the United States; and was ranked as the seventh-largest private bank in the world.[9]

All the while, BCCI perpetrated a massive fraud—considered the largest in banking history—that involved pervasive corruption, money laundering, sanctions evasion, and other illegal activity as it exploited the weaknesses in international financial regulations. Among the bank's customers were corrupt politicians, drug traffickers, arms dealers, and terrorists. They included such notorious figures as Saddam Hussein, Panamanian ruler Manuel Noriega, and the Medellín Cartel, among many other criminals, earning BCCI the nickname "Bank of Crooks and Criminals International."[10]

Its criminality was enabled via several techniques, such as purchasing banks through nominees. BCCI also used lawyers, accountants, public relations firms, and politically connected individuals, including American politicians, to hide its activities. In this manner, BCCI also infiltrated the US financial system by secretly purchasing four US banks and opening branches in seven states and the District of Columbia.[11]

The passage of the Annunzio-Wylie Anti–Money Laundering Act turned the focus of AML regulation to financial institutions. Policymakers noted that financial institutions, rather than law enforcement, saw the money launderers first since illicit proceeds are almost always moved through some form of financial institution and that the expertise of financial institutions puts them in a better position to recognize what type of financial activity is or is not suspicious.[12]

The ways in which the act amended the Bank Secrecy Act can be grouped into three primary categories: it significantly increased the penalties for violating money laundering laws, expanded the scope of the BSA, and placed regulatory responsibility under the BSA on financial institutions. Regarding the first category, the Annunzio-Wylie Anti–Money Laundering Act increased the government's ability to punish money launderers. This includes the ability to institute termination proceedings against a financial institution convicted of criminally violating the BSA (e.g., stripping the financial institution of its charter) and to ban individual banking officials from the industry if they are convicted of money laundering.[13]

The second category added certain domestic and foreign crimes within the MLCA's definition of "specified unlawful activity" and expanded the definition of what constitutes a financial transaction. It also instituted verification and record-keeping requirements for wire transfers and criminalized the operation of a money-transmitting business without a license.[14]

The third category included one of the act's most notable changes: it authorizes the US Treasury Department to require financial institutions to file SARs in cases involving a suspected violation of a law or a regulation. The SAR provides a quicker, simplified process and supplants the former criminal referral form—a report that was roughly equivalent to the SAR prior to Annunzio-Wylie.[15] The act further authorized the Treasury Department to issue regulations requiring all financial institutions to maintain "minimum standards" for an internal AML compliance program, standards that essentially mirrored those previously limited to depository institutions under BSA compliance program regulations.

Additionally, the act required the secretary of the treasury to establish the Bank Secrecy Act Advisory Group (BSAAG). Consisting of representatives from federal regulatory and law enforcement agencies, financial institutions, and trade groups whose members are subject to the requirements of the BSA, the BSAAG provides the Treasury Department with advice on the operations of the BSA. The director of FinCEN serves as the chair of the BSAAG and ensures "that relevant issues are placed before the BSAAG for review, analysis, and discussion."[16]

THE MONEY LAUNDERING SUPPRESSION ACT (1994)

The Money Laundering Suppression Act (MLSA) was yet another amendment to the BSA. It's focused on enhancing AML/BSA training, developing AML examination procedures, and improving procedures for referring cases of suspicious activity to appropriate law enforcement agencies.[17] The act also streamlined the CTR exemption process to reduce the filing burden on financial institutions and to concentrate the reporting of transactions to those that are the most relevant and that provide the most value to law enforcement and regulators.[18]

The MLSA further amended the BSA by placing greater scrutiny on money services businesses. As defined by FinCEN, MSBs include the US Postal Service and any individual, whether on a regular basis or not, who deals in currency; cashes checks; issues, sells, or redeems traveler's checks, money orders, or *stored value instruments* (i.e., prepaid cards, such as gift cards, or other instruments, such as phone apps, that carry monetary value stored on the instrument itself rather than being connected to an external account); and serves as a *money transmitter* (i.e., a business entity, such as Venmo, PayPal, or Western Union, that receives and transfers funds on behalf of a customer).[19] The MLSA requires an owner or controlling person of each MSB to register the MSB with the US Treasury Department and that every MSB must maintain a list of those businesses that are authorized to act as agents of the MSB in connection with the financial services it offers. The MLSA also makes operating an unregistered MSB a federal crime and recommends that states adopt uniform laws applicable to MSBs.[20] The cash-intensive nature of the business and one-off transactions that often can't be tracked make MSBs a high risk for money laundering, particularly by drug cartels and terrorist groups.

THE MONEY LAUNDERING AND FINANCIAL CRIMES STRATEGY ACT (1998)

The Money Laundering and Financial Crimes Strategy Act of 1998 required the US Treasury Department, along with banking and government agencies, to develop a national strategy to combat money laundering and related financial crimes. Additionally, the act directed banking agencies to develop AML training for bank examiners. The goal of the legislation was to increase coordination among the various impacted entities—including the public and private sectors, as well as federal, state, and local law enforcement authorities—to impede the growing trend of money laundering in the United States and worldwide.[21]

As part of this effort, the legislation created task forces to identify High Intensity Money Laundering and Related Financial Crime Areas (HIFCAs), or those geographic areas and industry sectors at high risk for money laundering. The HIFCA Task Forces, composed of relevant federal, state, and local enforcement authorities, prosecutors, and financial regulators, concentrated law enforcement efforts in those areas where money laundering was prevalent. HIFCAs may be defined geographically, or they can be created to address money laundering in a particular sector of industry, a financial institution, or group of financial institutions. A HIFCA regional map denoting these high-risk areas is available on FinCEN's website.[22]

THE FOREIGN NARCOTICS KINGPIN
DESIGNATION ACT (1999)

In 1999 President Bill Clinton enacted the Foreign Narcotics Kingpin Designation Act, also known as the Kingpin Act, which targeted the leaders of foreign drug cartels. The intent of the legislation was to deny significant foreign narcotics traffickers, their organizations, and their operatives access to the US financial system and to prohibit all trade and transactions between the traffickers and US companies and individuals. As a result, US financial institutions must screen customers against the names of individuals and entities on the kingpin list, which is updated periodically. First announced in 2000, this list can be found on the OFAC website of the US Treasury Department and is filtered by program, in this case, Foreign Narcotics Kingpin Sanctions Regulations.[23] Some of the groups that have been designated pursuant to the Kingpin Act include the Sinaloa Cartel, which was established in the 1980s; the Mexican criminal syndicate Los Zetas; and the Mexican drug cartel and organized crime syndicate La Familia Michoacana, as well as numerous others.[24]

THE USA PATRIOT ACT (2001)

Terrorism and terrorist attacks heavily impacted the first decade of the twenty-first century as the events of September 11, 2001, forever changed the world. Al-Qaeda, the extremist militant organization founded in Pakistan by Osama bin Laden and several Arabs, was behind the devastating attacks and continued waging terror campaigns around the globe in the years following 2001.[25]

The US government responded to the 9/11 terror attacks by enacting the Uniting and Strengthening America by Providing Appropriate Tools Required to Intercept and Obstruct Terrorism Act, which resulted in significant amendments to the Bank Secrecy Act. In fact, many consider the USA

PATRIOT Act to be the most important piece of AML legislation enacted since the BSA. The USA PATRIOT Act was passed nearly unanimously with the support of members from both sides of the political divide and in near record time.[26] President George W. Bush signed it only forty-five days after the attacks.

The USA PATRIOT Act was designed to strengthen US national security, especially in relation to foreign terrorism. Although it is well known for the sweeping changes it brought to existing BSA requirements, the act is actually far broader in scope. More specifically, the USA PATRIOT Act comprises ten separate titles or sections, each addressing a distinct area. These sections can generally be grouped into three main categories: expanded abilities of law enforcement to conduct surveillance, including domestic and international wire taps; simplified interagency communications designed to enable federal agencies to more effectively use all available resources toward counterterrorism efforts; and enhanced penalties for crimes related to terrorism and a further list of terrorism-related charges.

Due to its wide breadth, the USA PATRIOT Act has generated controversy from the moment it was signed into law. Opponents frequently cite civil liberties concerns, such as the law's infringements on the right to privacy. It has also garnered criticism for being hurried through the Senate with little opportunity to make changes. Some of these issues are explored in Michael Moore's 2004 political documentary, *Fahrenheit 9/11*.

Title III of the USA PATRIOT Act, known as the International Money Laundering Abatement and Anti-Terrorist Financing Act of 2001, is intended to facilitate the prevention, detection, and prosecution of international money laundering and the financing of terrorism. This section amends not only portions of the BSA but also portions of the MLCA. The USA PATRIOT Act and its implementing regulations made the following notable changes:

- increased the number of entities and industries (beyond traditional financial institutions) that are subject to its conditions
- criminalized the financing of terrorism and augmented the existing BSA framework by strengthening customer identification procedures
- prohibited financial institutions from engaging in business with foreign shell banks
- required financial institutions to have due diligence procedures (and enhanced due diligence procedures for foreign correspondent and private banking accounts)
- improved information sharing between financial institutions and the US government by requiring government-institution information sharing and voluntary information sharing among financial institutions

- expanded the anti–money laundering program requirements to all financial institutions
- increased civil and criminal penalties for money laundering
- provided the secretary of the treasury with the authority to impose "special measures" on jurisdictions, institutions, or transactions that are of "primary money laundering concern"
- facilitated records access and required banks to respond to regulatory requests for information within 120 hours
- required federal banking agencies to consider a bank's AML record when reviewing bank mergers, acquisitions, and other applications for business combinations[27]

INTELLIGENCE REFORM AND TERRORISM PREVENTION ACT (2004)

A notable piece of AML legislation passed after the USA PATRIOT Act is the Intelligence Reform and Terrorism Prevention Act, which Congress enacted in 2004. This law further amended the BSA and requires the secretary of the treasury to prescribe regulations mandating that certain financial institutions report cross-border electronic transmittals of funds, particularly in cases where the secretary "determines that such reporting is 'reasonably necessary' to aid in the fight against money laundering and terrorist financing."[28]

FINCEN'S CUSTOMER DUE DILIGENCE RULE (2018)

The US Treasury Department, in its 2015 risk assessment, identified the ease of forming an anonymous shell company in the United States as a key vulnerability to the financial system.[29] The publication of the Panama Papers a year later added a new urgency to address the misuse of corporate entities by criminals, terrorists, and corrupt politicians as a means of hiding illicit activity and laundering illegal proceeds. As part of an attempt to increase corporate transparency through the identification of beneficial owners of legal entities, FinCEN passed the Customer Due Diligence Rule (CDD Rule), whose requirements became mandatory for financial institutions in 2018.

The CDD Rule amended the BSA by clarifying and enhancing CDD requirements for financial institutions, particularly regarding their legal entity customers. More specifically, the CDD Rule compels financial institutions to identify and verify the identity of the natural persons (known as beneficial owners) behind their entity customers at the time they open accounts. A *beneficial owner* is further defined as any individual who owns or controls 25 percent or more of a legal entity. Additionally, financial institutions must implement written policies and procedures to do the following:

1. Identify and verify the identity of customers
2. Identify and verify the identity of the beneficial owners of companies opening accounts
3. Understand the nature and purpose of customer relationships to develop customer risk profiles
4. Conduct ongoing monitoring to identify and report suspicious transactions and, on a risk basis, to maintain and update customer information[30]

PROPOSED FEDERAL LEGISLATION ON CORPORATE TRANSPARENCY

In the decades since the Bank Secrecy Act was passed in 1970, it has seen a number of amendments, most notably by the USA PATRIOT Act in 2001; however, the BSA has not been modernized to account for new threats, developments in technology, new typologies regarding money laundering and terrorist financing, or responses to current data on money laundering and terrorist-financing activity. Perhaps most notably, the BSA does not contain any provisions that address financial transparency.

In the meantime, scandals involving leaked financial documents—such as the Panama Papers, the FinCEN Files, and the Pandora Papers, which constitutes the largest disclosure of confidential data pertaining to the use of secrecy havens to date—have exposed the all-too-common exploitation of corporate structures and how they can be used to gain access to the financial system and conduct illicit transactions globally. On top of this, the United States has experienced an embarrassing and continuous backslide in global rankings on financial secrecy. In fact, the Tax Justice Network has consistently ranked the country as one of the top enablers of financial secrecy.[31] This ranking carries important implications because the US financial system is among the largest and strongest in the world. Therefore, the role of the United States as a leading financial secrecy haven poses a significant risk, not just nationally but also globally.

The United States gained its reputation as a major financial secrecy haven primarily because of the ease with which anonymous shell companies can be formed, particularly in Delaware, Nevada, and Wyoming, and the fact that not a single state collected beneficial ownership information from those seeking to establish a shell company. Once the world leader when it came to the passage of anti–money laundering legislation, the United States simply watched as others took the lead regarding transparency around beneficial ownership. In 2003 the FATF was the first international body to set standards on beneficial ownership.[32] The United Kingdom began imposing beneficial ownership requirements in 2016 and was the first country to implement a beneficial ownership registry. Shortly thereafter other European nations and a host of additional countries followed.

Amid a backdrop of steadily increasing criticism, both domestically and from abroad, including mounting pressure from global watchdogs and others, on January 1, 2021, Congress finally passed the Anti–Money Laundering Act (AMLA) of 2020, a comprehensive new law meant to modernize the existing AML regime. Some of the updates brought by the AMLA include expanded whistleblower rewards and protections, new AML violations and enhanced penalties, increased information sharing among government and private stakeholders, and improved corporate transparency. The AMLA is the most substantial piece of AML legislation since the enactment of the USA PATRIOT Act.

The most notable aspect of the new AMLA is its inclusion of the Corporate Transparency Act (CTA), which focuses on shell companies. Historically, there has been considerable public resistance in the United States toward any government actions that impinge on privacy rights, including laws allowing others to access personal financial information. Consequently, prior iterations of the CTA bounced around Washington for over a decade and underwent multiple revisions after pushback from opponents and challenges from industry groups, mainly on the grounds that the act violates privacy rights and is overly burdensome for small businesses.

The CTA requires certain new and existing small corporations and LLCs to disclose information about their beneficial ownership to FinCEN, with the intent of preventing bad actors from using anonymous shell companies to disguise their illicit activities and evade law enforcement.[33] The CTA directs FinCEN to create and maintain a national federal registry of this corporate beneficial ownership information, a requirement that will finally bring the United States in line with global standards, such as those recommended by the FATF. Similar to other FinCEN databases, the beneficial ownership registry will not be publicly available, and penalties will be imposed for unlawful disclosures of collected information. However, beneficial ownership information will be available, upon written request, to US federal law enforcement agencies and even financial institutions, with the consent of the reporting company, to meet their CDD requirements under the BSA. Prior to the act's passage, beneficial ownership reporting fell almost exclusively on financial institutions. With the CTA, however, this AML compliance burden shifts to the nonfinancial corporations that are its focus.

And finally, the release of the Pandora Papers in October 2021 has spurred US lawmakers to act quickly, resulting in the introduction of the bipartisan legislation known as the Establishing New Authorities for Business Laundering and Enabling Risks to Security (ENABLERS) Act. The bill is intended to seal legal loopholes that are all too often exploited by a variety of intermediaries, such as investment advisers, attorneys involved in financial activity, company service providers (businesses that create companies), accountants, public relations firms, and third-party payment providers, thus allowing criminals to access the US financial system. The proposed law would impose more stringent due diligence requirements on these US-based middlemen in an attempt to prevent the United States from being used as a safe haven for dirty funds.[34]

The bill would also expand Geographic Targeting Orders, making them applicable not only nationwide, instead of just targeting select cities, but also to commercial real estate rather than simply residential real estate. Furthermore, it would create a new national security task force to oversee this initiative.[35]

CONCLUSION

Analyzing the development of AML laws and regulations through the lens of history can provide useful clues and insight for businesses and legal professionals, as well as help ensure compliance with their mandates. This is particularly important in today's high-stakes legal and regulatory environment, where compliance errors can result in significant consequences for organizations and their leadership.

It is noteworthy that efforts to combat money laundering in the United States developed in response to the growing illicit drug trade. AML measures focused on financial institutions because they were identified as the entry point for illicit funds and thereby considered the first line of defense against money laundering. However, criminals quickly adapted and found ways to evade the new restrictions. They turned their efforts to the use of shell companies and other anonymous entities, increased their smuggling activity, and capitalized on technological advances.

Therefore, despite the tougher anti–money laundering laws and increasingly complex compliance obligations, there is little indication that these statutes had any significant effect on halting either the illegal drug trade or the flow of illicit funds. In fact, both researchers and policymakers agree that the war on drugs has been a failure.[36] Similarly, despite all the effort and expense put into anti–money laundering enforcement, between $800 billion and $2 trillion are laundered globally, and less than 1 percent of illegally laundered funds are ever recovered.[37]

The use of anonymous corporate vehicles to disguise and transfer illicit funds has been identified as a major threat to the global financial system and a major obstacle for law enforcement. The creation of beneficial ownership registries and other efforts are finally being put in place to address this issue, but a global response is required for meaningful AML reform to occur.

A review of AML legislation and its overall effectiveness raises noteworthy questions that should be considered. Should money laundering and drug trafficking be targeted in the same legislation? Are anti-money measures equally well suited to address terrorist-financing threats? Should financial institutions continue to bear the burden of countering money laundering and terrorist financing?[38] What other measures can be taken? How can we foster a global approach?

NOTES

1. Matthew S. Morgan, "Money Laundering: The American Law and Its Global Influence," *Law and Business Review of the Americas* 3, no. 3 (1997): article 4, https://scholar.smu.edu/lbra/vol3/iss3/4.
2. Andy G. Rickman, "Currency Contamination and Drug-Sniffing Canines: Should Any Evidentiary Value Be Attached to a Dog's Alert on Cash?," *Kentucky Law Journal* 85, no. 1 (1996): article 7, https://uknowledge.uky.edu/klj/vol85/iss1/7.
3. Herbert A. Biern, Testimony regarding the Bank Secrecy Act and the USA PATRIOT Act, hearing before the US House of Representatives, Committee on International Relations, November 17, 2004, https://www.federalreserve.gov/boarddocs/testimony/2004/20041117/default.htm.
4. California Bankers Assn. v. Shultz, 416 U.S. 21 (1974).
5. John K. Villa, "A Critical View of Bank and the Money Laundering Statutes," *Catholic University Law Review* 37, no. 2 (1988): article 7, https://scholarship.law.edu/lawreview/vol37/iss2/7.
6. US Drug Enforcement Administration (DEA) "Our History," accessed October 23, 2020, https://www.dea.gov/about/history.
7. Deborah J. Vagins and Jesselyn McCurdy, "Cracks in the System: Twenty Years of the Unjust Federal Crack Cocaine Law" (Washington, DC: American Civil Liberties Union, 2006), https://www.aclu.org/sites/default/files/pdfs/drugpolicy/cracksinsystem_2006 1025.pdf; and Darryl K. Brown, "Anti-Drug Abuse Act (1986)," Encyclopedia.com, accessed September 24, 2021, https://www.encyclopedia.com/history/encyclopedias -almanacs-transcripts-and-maps/anti-drug-abuse-act-1986.

8. FinCEN, "History of Anti-Money Laundering Laws" (see chap. 1, n. 11).

9. Steve Lohr, "World-Class Fraud: How B.C.C.I. Pulled It Off—a Special Report; at the End of a Twisted Trail, Piggy Bank for a Favored Few," *New York Times*, April 12, 1991, https://www.nytimes.com/1991/08/12/business/world-class-fraud-bcci-pulled-it-off -special-report-end-twisted-trail-piggy-bank.html?auth=login-email&login=email.

10. John Kerry and Hank Brown, *The BCCI Affair: A Report to the Committee on Foreign Relations of the U.S. Senate*, 102nd Cong., 2nd sess. (Washington, DC: US Senate, Committee on Foreign Relations, December 1992), https://info.publicintelligence.net/The-BCCI -Affair.pdf.

11. Kerry and Brown.

12. Morgan, "Money Laundering."

13. Morgan.

14. Morgan.

15. Morgan.

16. FinCEN, "Bank Secrecy Act Advisory Group; Solicitation of Application for Membership," US Treasury Department, 84 FR 69822, in *Federal Register* 84, 244 (December 19, 2019), https://www.govinfo.gov/content/pkg/FR-2019-12-19/pdf/2019-27358.pdf.

17. Morgan, "Money Laundering."

18. Morgan.

19. FinCEN, "Money Services Business Definition," US Treasury Department, accessed October 26, 2020, https://www.fincen.gov/money-services-business-definition.

20. FinCEN, "History of Anti-Money Laundering."

21. Bradley J-M. Runyon, "Money Laundering: New Legislation and New Regulations, but Is It Enough," *North Carolina Banking Institute Journal* 3, no. 1 (1999): 337, http:// scholarship.law.unc.edu/ncbi/vol3/iss1/16.

22. FinCEN, "History of Anti-Money Laundering;" Runyon, "Money Laundering;" and FinCEN, "HIFCA Regional Map," accessed August 15, 2021, https://www.fincen.gov /hifca-regional-map.

23. OFAC, "Other OFAC Sanctions Lists," US Treasury Department, accessed October 8, 2021, https://home.treasury.gov/policy-issues/financial-sanctions/other-ofac -sanctions-lists.

24. Office of the Press Secretary, "Fact Sheet: Overview of the Foreign Narcotics Kingpin Designation Act," White House, April 15, 2009, https://obamawhitehouse.archives.gov /the-press-office/fact-sheet-overview-foreign-narcotics-kingpin-designation-act.

25. Bruce Riedel, "The Grave New World: Terrorism in the 21st Century" (Washington, DC: Brookings, December 9, 2011), https://www.brookings.edu/articles/the-grave -new-world-terrorism-in-the-21st-century/.

26. US Justice Department, "The USA PATRIOT Act: Preserving Life and Liberty," accessed October 27, 2020, https://www.justice.gov/archive/ll/highlights.htm.

27. FinCEN, "History of Anti-Money Laundering Laws."

28. FinCEN.

29. Congressional Research Service, "Beneficial Ownership Transparency in Corporate Formation, Shell Companies, Real Estate, and Financial Transactions," CRS Report no. R45798 (Washington, DC: Congressional Research Service, July 8, 2019), https://fas .org/sgp/crs/misc/R45798.pdf.

30. FinCEN, "Information on Complying with the Customer Due Diligence (CDD) Final Rule," US Treasury Department, accessed October 27, 2020, https://www.fincen.gov /resources/statutes-and-regulations/cdd-final-rule.

31. "Financial Secrecy Index 2020 Reports Progress on Global Transparency—but Back-sliding from US, Cayman and UK Prompts Call for Sanctions," *Tax Justice Network*, February 18, 2020, https://www.taxjustice.net/2020/02/18/financial-secrecy-index -2020-reports-progress-on-global-transparency-but-backsliding-from-us-cayman-and -uk-prompts-call-for-sanctions/.

32. FATF, "Best Practices on Beneficial Ownership for Legal Persons" (Paris: FATF, Octo-ber 2019), https://www.fatf-gafi.org/publications/methodsandtrends/documents/best -practices-beneficial-ownership-legal-persons.html.

33. Corporate Transparency Act of 2019, H.R. 2513, 116th Congress, October 8, 2019, https://www.congress.gov/congressional-report/116th-congress/house-report/227/1 ?overview=closed.

34. Representative Tom Malinowski and Representative Maria Elvira Salazar, "ENABLERS Act: Confronting the 'Enablers' of International Corruption," Caucus against Foreign Corruption and Kleptocracy, https://malinowski.house.gov/sites/malinowski.house .gov/files/ENABLERS%20Summaries%20Final.pdf, accessed October 8, 2021.

35. Tom Malinowski, "Establishing New Authorities for Business Laundering and Enabling Risks to Security Act," H.R., 177th Cong., 1st sess., October 6, 2021, https://malinowski .house.gov/sites/malinowski.house.gov/files/ENABLERS%20Act%20FOR%20 INTRO_SIGNED.pdf.

36. Betsy Pearl, "Ending the War on Drugs: By the Numbers" (Washington, DC: Center for American Progress, June 27, 2018), https://www.americanprogress.org/issues /criminal-justice/reports/2018/06/27/452819/ending-war-drugs-numbers/#:~:text =Today%2C%20researchers%20and%20policymakers%20alike,not%20a%20criminal %20justice%20issue.

37. UNODC, "Estimating Illicit Financial Flows Resulting from Drug Trafficking and Other Transnational Organized Crimes" (Vienna: UNODC, October 2011), https://www .unodc.org/documents/data-and-analysis/Studies/Illicit_financial_flows_2011_web .pdf.

38. John Pickering, "Money Laundering and Terrorism: A Failed Past and a Bleak Future," The Federalist Society, December 1, 2003, https://fedsoc.org/commentary /publications/money-laundering-and-terrorism-a-failed-past-and-a-bleak-future#:~: text=Money%20laundering%20legislation%20began%20in,the%20traffic%20in%20 illegal%20drugs.&text=Complex%20systems%20of%20front%20companies,legitimize %20high%20dollar%20bank%20deposits.

CHAPTER 11

A SOLID DEFENSE

*AML Compliance Program
Requirements and Standards*

Financial institutions, particularly banks, play a key role in the overall financial system. By serving as intermediaries among diverse parties, they facilitate a wide range of financial transactions. Financial institutions also serve as the entry point for illegal funds into the financial system. Consequently, banks and other financial institutions bear the responsibility for preventing the misuse of the financial system and preserving its integrity.

Although criminal proceeds can be laundered without involving the financial sector, the reality is that hundreds of billions of dollars in illicit funds are laundered through financial institutions every year. In fact, the financial system is one of the primary methods through which criminals launder money. Therefore, it is essential that financial institutions have appropriate controls in place to prevent being used, whether wittingly or unwittingly, in the furtherance of crime. These controls entail the implementation of effective anti–money laundering compliance programs.

The Bank Secrecy Act and USA PATRIOT Act are the two pieces of federal legislation that set forth requirements for AML compliance programs for US financial institutions and US operations of foreign financial institutions. Various national and international organizations also provide guidance and standards to assist institutions in the design, implementation, and ongoing oversight of their AML compliance programs.

The purpose of an AML compliance program is to detect and deter money laundering and terrorist financing. An effective AML compliance program can prevent illicit actors from accessing the financial system and help financial institutions from being used in criminal activity. For example, appropriately designed policies, procedures, and internal controls, such as know your customer and transaction monitoring, are meant to help financial institutions not only identify criminals before they open an account or initiate an illicit transaction but also identify and intercept suspicious activity. Additionally, the various reporting requirements mandated for financial institutions, such as the filing of suspicious activity reports and currency transaction reports, serve to provide law enforcement with valuable information to which they may not otherwise have access. Therefore, AML compliance programs not only serve to protect financial institutions from various risks but also are instrumental in safeguarding the financial system as a whole.

THE ROLE OF FINANCIAL INSTITUTIONS IN COMBATING MONEY LAUNDERING

Financial institutions, such as commercial banks, credit unions, savings and loan associations, and insurance companies carry out all manner of financial transactions. US banks alone handle trillions of dollars in transactions daily. The large volume of business handled every day by financial institutions—particularly banks—exposes them to significant money laundering risks. In fact, banks can be used in every stage of the money laundering cycle.

Banks and other financial institutions provide the infrastructure for moving money and therefore have been and continue to be an important mechanism for transferring and disposing of criminal funds. Furthermore, the bank-customer relationship affords a direct point of contact between the financial institution and the criminal, who may frequently use it to deposit, hold, invest, withdraw, or transfer illicit funds.

Numerous media reports and enforcement actions have shown how banks, either knowingly or unknowingly, have been used to launder billions of dollars in illegal profits and further illustrate that their failure to implement and maintain a compliance program can result in potentially severe consequences, including for well-reputed and long-standing global banks. The period following the 2008 financial crisis in particular, when banking standards declined as banks struggled to survive, witnessed the movement of vast sums of illicit funds. Multimillion-dollar and, in some cases, multibillion-dollar penalties were levied on some of the largest financial institutions—including Citibank, Deutsche Bank, HSBC, and Wachovia—for moving billions of dollars in drug money, further illustrating the critical role financial institutions play in facilitating financial crime.[1]

The imposition of fines and penalties against financial institutions for AML violations isn't limited to periods of financial crisis, such as that in 2008. Banks, both large and small, global and domestic, have continued to be hit with heavy fines for compliance failures. Although AML enforcement has been increasing, 2019 in particular was a stand-out year, as global enforcers from fourteen different countries levied more than $8 billion in AML fines and penalized twelve of the world's top fifty banks.[2] And in an increasing number of cases, multiple regulators have imposed fines against a single institution. The Dutch-based lender Rabobank is just one such example. In 2018 and 2019, respectively, both US and Dutch regulators fined Rabobank for having poor AML controls that allowed high-risk customers to move hundreds of millions of dollars through the financial system.[3]

Banks are not the only type of financial institution that criminals misuse. Wire transfer businesses have also moved illicit funds, including profits from drug and human trafficking. Western Union in particular has been implicated in several money laundering cases. In 2001 sex traffickers used its services to move funds into eastern Europe. In 2010 in an action by the state of Arizona, Western Union paid a $94 million fine and was placed under compliance monitorship for moving illicit funds that came from cross-border narcotics trafficking for drug cartels. In testimony against Western Union, the former state attorney general of Arizona said the company was "by far the largest provider of illicit money-movement services."[4] Then again in 2017, Western Union was levied a $586 million fine in the United States for not preventing criminals from using its platform to move illegal proceeds from illegal gambling, fraud, and drug and human trafficking. Authorities said Western Union employees knowingly "allowed or aided and abetted" the criminals in processing their illicit proceeds. However, rather than terminating these employees, Western Union permitted them to continue working for the company and even awarded them bonuses. Authorities specifically pointed to Western Union's "flawed corporate culture" and insufficient or poorly enforced policies as enabling these crimes. Western Union admitted to these criminal violations and its willful failure to maintain an effective anti–money laundering program.[5]

Although financial institutions implicated in money laundering may not have a direct role in the production of illegal funds, their laundering of those funds is nonetheless a crime. If illegal proceeds are easily processed through a financial institution—as happens in cases where an institution has ineffective or lax compliance controls, for instance—the institution may be considered actively complicit with the illegal activity. Even though money laundering may not affect customers directly, it enables criminal activity to continue, and that could result in harm to clients. Therefore, under federal law—namely, the Money Laundering Control Act—financial institutions can be held criminally liable for knowingly assisting in the laundering of illegal funds.

Additionally, financial institutions are subject to AML laws and regulations that require them to implement compliance programs containing effective internal controls—such as tailored, risk-based policies and procedures, monitoring, and oversight—that are designed to combat money laundering and terrorist financing. Policymakers and others view banks and other financial institutions as uniquely situated to detect and identify suspicious transactions and illicit activity within their organizations and thus consider them as the first line of defense against money laundering and other financial crime.

AREAS OF MONEY LAUNDERING CONCERN FOR BANKS AND OTHER DEPOSITORY FINANCIAL INSTITUTIONS

Banks and other depository institutions offer a wide variety of accounts, financial products, banking arrangements, and services that present diverse levels of money laundering risk. As a result, these institutions can be exploited in many ways to move illicit proceeds. Although it isn't possible to cover them all here, some of the more notable areas of particular money laundering concern that the Financial Action Task Force and other groups have identified include electronic funds transfers, correspondent banking, payable-through accounts, concentration accounts, private banking relationships, and bank complicity.

Electronic funds transfers refer to any movement of money that is initiated by electronic means, such as through a computer, mobile phone app, automated teller machine, or automated clearinghouse transaction. Electronic funds transfers and wires are used to move money quickly from one bank account to another, within a single country, or between countries. Millions of such transactions are used to transfer trillions of dollars daily. Therefore, electronic funds transfer systems enable money launderers to rapidly move money between accounts and across the world.

Illicit transfers are easily disguised among the millions of legitimate transfers. They may be initiated through unauthorized debits and may involve the use of stolen credit cards. Illicit fund transfers are often used in the layering stage of the money laundering cycle, where the goal is to move money around and make it difficult for law enforcement and investigators to trace the funds' source. Criminals can use a number of methods to avoid detection, such as varying the amount of money sent and limiting the sums to small amounts (significantly under the CTR reporting threshold) so they do not draw attention.[6]

Recall from chapter 5 that *correspondent banking* occurs when a correspondent bank, which is usually a large international bank, provides banking services to a respondent bank that is located in a different part of the world. This relationship is considered a high risk for money laundering due to the indirect relationship between the correspondent bank and the customers of the respondent bank and because of the large volume of money that flows through correspondent accounts. These factors present significant difficulties for customer verification and for identifying suspicious transactions, making correspondent banking vulnerable to money laundering.[7] Criminals have manipulated correspondent banking relationships in sophisticated laundromat schemes.

Payable-through accounts are a type of correspondent banking account through which the respondent bank's customers can directly control funds at the correspondent bank. As such, the respondent bank's customers are permitted to conduct transactions—for instance, make wire transfers, deposits, and withdrawals, and have other check writing privileges—through the respondent bank's correspondent account. This differs from a traditional correspondent banking relationship in which the correspondent bank executes transactions on behalf of its customers. Payable-through accounts present money laundering risks because the banks providing the accounts may not have access to information about the third parties who are accessing the account, or they may not subject the end customers to the same level of scrutiny that they would for their own customers.[8]

Concentration accounts are deposit accounts that financial institutions use to aggregate funds from several locations into one central account and to facilitate the processing and settlement of internal bank transactions, usually on the same day. This service allows for the simple and efficient movement of cash, but its ability to quickly move funds can also facilitate money laundering. The risk of money laundering also arises in the case where the customer identification information is separated from the transaction. In this case, the audit trail will be lost, and the account can be misused or improperly administered.[9]

Private banking is a highly lucrative and extremely competitive global industry. It is typically aimed at exclusive clientele, referred to as high-net-worth individuals, whose assets are valued at $1 million or more. For these clients, *private banking* provides a wide range of personalized financial services and products, including wealth management, portfolio management, investing, insurance, and tax, trust, and estate planning. These services and products are not only highly customized for each client but usually also confidential. Private banking is often a separate, semiautonomous division within certain banks. Because relationship managers are generally compensated based on the assets under their management, frequently they face fierce competition among private bankers for wealthy clients and are under intense pressure. This can lead to particular money laundering risks such as engaging clients who are politically exposed persons and may be corrupt, enabling the formation of anonymous accounts and companies in secretive jurisdictions or other high-risk areas, failing to conduct necessary enhanced due diligence on prospective clients, and avoiding other compliance protocols and requirements to acquire and maintain a lucrative customer relationship. The risks associated with private banking relationships are highlighted in the Jeffrey Epstein case (covered in chapter 7), where the lure of lucrative client relationships and the potential profitability for the banks outweighed their associated money laundering and financial crime risks.

Bank complicity is another significant AML compliance concern for financial institutions. *Bank complicity*, which comes in varying degrees and is perhaps more often associated with insider fraud, also occurs when bank employees facilitate money laundering. Oftentimes, money laundering activities perpetrated by bank employees or insiders will remain undetected for extended periods because many institutions simply don't monitor these kinds of risks. However, the early identification and detection of any employees engaging in complicit acts is crucial to avoiding and mitigating potentially serious impacts on the financial institution. Therefore, financial institutions and other businesses need to maintain not only KYC programs but also know your employee programs.

Bank complicity was a major issue in many high-profile money laundering cases in recent years. They include the Danske Bank scandal, where numerous suspicious transactions involving nonresident customers were ignored, resulting in the largest money laundering scandal to date, and the Deutsche Bank settlement after Jeffrey Epstein's relationship manager and other bank employees were found to have purposely disregarded red flags. Bank complicity was also either a known or suspected issue in the Russian Laundromat schemes that moved illicit proceeds out of Russia.

THE SUPERVISORY ROLE OF GOVERNMENT AGENCIES IN AML COMPLIANCE EFFORTS

Several government agencies play a critical role in promulgating BSA regulations, developing examination guidance, ensuring compliance with the BSA, and enforcing its provisions. These agencies include the Financial Crimes Enforcement Network and the five federal banking agencies known collectively as the Federal Financial Institutions Examination Council: the Board of Governors of the Federal Reserve System (more commonly known as the Federal Reserve Board), the Federal Deposit Insurance Corporation, the National Credit Union Administration, the Office of the Comptroller of the Currency, and the Consumer Financial Protection Bureau. Although each agency is tasked with its own specific responsibilities and functions independently, they all oversee BSA/AML compliance for the banking organizations they supervise, including those banking entities operating in the United States and their foreign branches. This oversight entails ensuring that banks take appropriate steps to combat money laundering and terrorist financing, and to minimize associated risks.[10]

More specifically, the federal banking agencies require that each bank under their supervision must establish and maintain an AML compliance program in accordance with the BSA and the USA PATRIOT Act and must include policies, procedures, and processes to identify and report suspicious transactions to law enforcement. (*Note:* An AML compliance program that is designed in accordance with the requirements laid out in Section 352 of the USA PATRIOT Act and that satisfies BSA regulatory requirements is known more formally as a BSA/AML compliance program. However, the more general term, "AML compliance program," is used throughout this book.)

As part of their supervisory process, the federal banking agencies conduct examinations to evaluate a bank's AML compliance program and its compliance with regulatory requirements. Jointly developed by federal and state banking agencies in collaboration with FinCEN, the FFIEC's *Bank Secrecy Act (BSA)/Anti-Money Laundering (AML) Examination Manual* provides guidance to examiners for conducting BSA/AML and Office of Foreign Assets Control examinations. The manual includes an overview of the BSA/AML requirements and guidance on regulatory expectations and industry best practices; therefore, it is a valuable resource for any AML compliance practitioner. The FFIEC updates the manual from time to time, and it can be accessed online for free on the FFIEC's website.

The US Treasury Department partners with the federal banking agencies to oversee compliance with the AML requirements in banking organizations. The department also administers the foreign sanctions program through OFAC. Although OFAC's requirements are separate and distinct from those of the BSA, both OFAC and the BSA have a common national security interest. For this reason, compliance with OFAC sanctions is connected with BSA compliance obligations. Therefore, supervisory examinations focused on BSA compliance also include the examination of a financial institution's compliance with OFAC sanctions.

CONSEQUENCES OF NONCOMPLIANCE
WITH AML PROGRAM REQUIREMENTS

The consequences for AML compliance failures vary depending on the particular issue and the circumstances involved. They can be severe, ranging from regulatory fines and penalties to civil suits, reputational risk, and lost business for the financial institutions.

When a federal agency identifies deficiencies in an institution's AML compliance program or other BSA-related violations, it may take a variety of enforcement measures, including the issuance of formal or informal enforcement actions or cease and desist orders, among other supervisory actions. Similar to FinCEN, the federal banking agencies may also bring civil money penalty actions for violating the BSA.[11]

The Department of Justice administers prosecutions for money laundering or for criminal violations of the BSA. It can bring cases against individuals or banks, and penalties can be severe. Criminal actions may result in criminal fines, imprisonment, and forfeiture actions. Additionally, banks can lose their charters, and bank employees can be removed and barred from banking (as long as the violation was not inadvertent or unintentional).[12]

Criminal violations for money laundering are treated separately from criminal violations of the BSA. (Criminal money laundering is addressed in the two sections of the MLCA, 18 U.S.C. § 1956 and § 1957.) Criminal penalties for willful violations of the BSA are covered under 31 U.S.C. § 5322, and criminal penalties for structuring transactions to evade BSA reporting requirements are covered under 31 U.S.C. § 5324(d). Under these provisions, individuals, including bank employees, who willfully violate the BSA face criminal fines of up to $250,000 or five years in prison or both. The fine and prison term are doubled in cases where the individual also violates other US laws or participates in other criminal activity. Banks that violate the BSA face criminal penalties of up to $1 million or twice the value of the transaction, whichever is greater.[13] Additionally, a civil monetary penalty may be imposed for any BSA violation, notwithstanding that a criminal penalty is imposed for the same violation.[14]

Although the amount of AML fines and penalties and the number of AML enforcement actions fluctuate somewhat from year to year, the clear trend since 2015 has gone steadily upward, and this is expected to continue. Multimillion-dollar fines are common and can range in the hundreds of millions of dollars to the billions.[15] For example, ING and US Bancorp were fined $900 million and $613 million, respectively, for AML failures, while Australia's Westpac Banking Corporation, Goldman Sachs, and UBS all paid fines in the billion-dollar range.[16] Furthermore, although US and UK regulators are typically the most active (and have transparent legal and regulatory systems), penalties have been handed out by multiple jurisdictions across a number of continents, including North America, Europe, Asia, and Australia. In fact, it's increasingly common for a single institution to be penalized by multiple regulators for actions arising out of the same incident(s). Such was the case with Bank Hapoalim, Israel's largest bank, which US prosecutors, the DOJ, the Federal Reserve, and the New York State Department of Financial Services fined more than $900 million for tax evasion and money laundering relating to the FIFA scandal.[17] (This case reflects a growing tendency for authorities to combine AML prosecutions with other enforcement actions, such as tax evasion and bribery.) Moreover, besides fines and monetary penalties, regulators can also restrict an institution from engaging in a certain line of business or from taking on new clients.

Recent years have brought increased and more complex compliance obligations and greater scrutiny upon financial institutions. Not only has the wave of investigations and enforcement actions ushered in record-setting fines and penalties for institutions but also individuals have increasingly been held personally liable, with the intent that it would serve as a strong deterrent. As a result of the heightened emphasis on AML compliance, organizations have significantly had to increase compliance staff and spending. Studies show that AML compliance teams grew tenfold in just the five years between 2012 and 2017.[18] Taking into account the continued growth of AML enforcement since 2017 and extrapolating this figure, one can easily estimate that this number has grown.

STANDARD-SETTING ORGANIZATIONS AND AML GUIDELINES, DIRECTIVES, AND RECOMMENDATIONS

Several national and international organizations have been established to assist in efforts targeted at combatting money laundering and terrorist financing. These groups play various roles, from setting standards and guidelines to assisting with policy development and implementation, as well as fostering the exchange of information. This section discusses a few of the key players that have been instrumental in the field. Also covered are some of the main international measures and recommendations that have been developed to assist both governments and the private sector in implementing anti–money laundering and counter-financing of terrorism policies, procedures, and legislation.

The World Bank Group and the
International Monetary Fund (1944)

The World Bank Group and the International Monetary Fund (IMF) were founded at the Bretton Woods Conference in New Hampshire in 1944 with complimentary missions and are now headquartered in Washington, DC. The World Bank Group works with developing countries to reduce poverty and increase shared prosperity, while the IMF serves to stabilize the international monetary system and acts as a monitor of the world's currencies.[19]

Both organizations actively support the FATF's efforts in the battle against money laundering, and since 2001 they have required countries that receive their assistance (e.g., financial and structural programs) to maintain effective money laundering controls. In addition to their collaboration with the FATF, both organizations work closely with the Basel Committee on Banking Supervision, the Organization for Economic Cooperation and Development, and others on various anti–money laundering efforts. The World Bank and IMF have published numerous reference materials and, starting in 2002, jointly developed the *Reference Guide to Anti-Money Laundering and Combating the Financing of Terrorism*, which provides a primer on AML/CFT, the basic requirements for an effective AML/CFT framework, and the role of the World Bank and IMF in these endeavors.[20]

The Basel Committee on Banking Supervision (1974)

The Basel Committee on Banking Supervision consists of banking supervisory authorities responsible for banking regulation. Established by the central bank governors of the Group of Ten countries in 1974, the committee is based in Basel, Switzerland, and has forty-five members from twenty-eight jurisdictions. The committee provides a forum for ongoing cooperation on banking supervisory issues, with the objective of promoting the understanding of these issues and improving the quality of banking supervision globally.

The Vienna Convention (1988)

The United Nations Convention against Illicit Traffic in Narcotic Drugs and Psychotropic Substances was adopted in December 1988 in Vienna and is referred to more simply as the Vienna Convention. It was the first international tool for fighting organized crime, particularly drug abuse and illicit narcotics trafficking, and addresses the issue of criminal proceeds derived from laundering drug money.[21]

Although the Vienna Convention itself does not criminalize money laundering, it does require that signatory jurisdictions establish money laundering as a criminal offense and provide for the forfeiture of property acquired from such offense. While the convention remains an international benchmark in identifying measures to counter money laundering, compliance with its mandates has not been widely adopted, and a significant number of countries have failed to implement laws criminalizing the laundering of drug proceeds.[22]

The FATF (1989)

The Financial Action Task Force on Money Laundering is the leading global ML and TF watchdog and an international standard-setting organization. It was established by the Group of Seven industrialized nations (known as the G-7) at its annual economic summit in Paris in 1989, and its secretariat is based at the OECD in Paris. The FATF currently has thirty-nine members, with representation from most major international financial centers. The US Treasury Department serves as the lead authority for the United States in the FATF delegation.

The FATF was formed in response to growing concerns over money laundering, and its creation has accelerated the pace of international activity in the field of AML. Since its formation, the FATF has contributed to major changes in the ways that financial institutions and other organizations conduct business, and it has fostered significant developments in AML/CFT laws and other governmental operations around the world.

First developed in 1990 and since revised multiple times, the FATF has issued Forty Recommendations, a detailed listing of standards to address and control money laundering and terrorist financing that its member countries are expected to adopt. (These measures offer nonlegal guidance, and the FATF does not have the power to impose fines or penalties.) The FATF has also provided various interpretive notes to clarify the recommendations and to offer additional guidance for applying them. More than two hundred jurisdictions have committed to implementing the FATF's recommendations.

Designed to provide a complete set of countermeasures against money laundering and terrorist financing, the Forty Recommendations are widely recognized as international standards, including by the IMF and the World Bank. The recommendations address broad topics that cover the following categories: the assessment of risks and the application of a risk-based approach, the criminal offense of money laundering and confiscation, the financing of terrorism and proliferation of weapons of mass destruction, the preventative measures (such as customer due diligence and suspicious activity reporting), the measures for transparency and identifying the beneficial ownership of legal persons and arrangements (such as corporate entities and trusts), the powers and responsibilities of competent authorities and other institutional measures (including regulatory supervision and law enforcement), and the need for international cooperation (including mutual legal assistance and extradition).

Following the 9/11 attacks, the FATF also adopted Nine Special Recommendations of Terrorist Financing. These recommendations act in tandem with the Forty Recommendations as a framework to aid in the detection, prevention, and eradication of terrorism funding.

Since 2000, the FATF also issues a "blacklist," known more formally as the list of Non-Cooperative Countries or Territories. The FATF updates the list regularly and includes countries that it judges to be noncooperative in the global fight against money laundering and terrorist financing. It also urges its members and other jurisdictions to apply EDD protocols to transactions with countries identified on this list.

The Strasbourg Convention (1990)

The Council of Europe is an international organization that was founded in 1949 to promote democracy and law and order in Europe and to advance human rights. In 1990 the council adopted the Convention on Laundering, Search, Seizure, and Confiscation of the Proceeds from Crime, which is also known as the Strasbourg Convention. Its aim is to facilitate international cooperation and mutual assistance among foreign jurisdictions in the investigation of crime, including tracking down, seizing, and confiscating its illegal proceeds.

The Strasbourg Convention encourages its members to harmonize legislation and adopt common practices. Like the Vienna Convention, the Strasbourg Convention requires each party to adopt legislation that criminalizes money laundering; however, unlike the Vienna Convention, it does not limit the underlying predicate offense to drug trafficking. Thus, the Strasbourg Convention covers proceeds from all types of criminal acts while noting particular offenses that are known to generate large profits, such as drug offenses, arms dealing, terrorist offenses, and trafficking in children and young women.[23]

FinCEN (1990)

Established in 1990, the Financial Crimes Enforcement Network is a bureau of the US Treasury Department. FinCEN is the delegated administrator of the BSA and, as such, is instrumental in the oversight and regulation of AML compliance programs for US financial institutions. FinCEN fulfills its mission "to safeguard the financial system from illicit use" through several activities.[24] It issues regulations and interpretive guidance (e.g., the CDD Rule and FAQs), supports federal banking agencies in their BSA examinations of banks within their jurisdictions, and even pursues civil enforcement actions.

Its other major responsibilities include assisting law enforcement in investigations and fostering international cooperation with other financial intelligence units that have been formed in many countries to obtain and process financial disclosure information and support anti–money laundering efforts. FinCEN also serves as the repository for various BSA reports, including SARs, CTRs, and others. FinCEN obtains valuable information from these reports that may be shared with law enforcement and that FinCEN mines for data to identify and communicate trends and patterns in financial crime. Consequently, FinCEN's self-described motto, which embodies its primary activities, is "Follow the money."

Its work has also been portrayed on the big screen. The 2016 action-thriller film *The Accountant* centers on a fictious FinCEN investigation in which the main character, played by Ben Affleck, is a forensic accountant and math savant whose job involves "un-cooking the books" of dangerous criminal and terrorist organizations that have been embezzled.[25]

The Egmont Group (1995)

The Egmont Group of Financial Intelligence Units is an international organization that was founded in 1995 at the Egmont Palace in Brussels; now it is permanently headquartered in Toronto. It started as an informal group of 24 FIUs and currently comprises a unified network of 167 FIUs. FinCEN serves as the US FIU in the Egmont Group.

FIUs are central national agencies that serve as intermediaries between private entities, which are subject to AML/CFT obligations, and law enforcement agencies. These units receive, analyze, and transmit to the competent authorities the disclosures of financial information concerning suspected proceeds of crime and potential criminal activity that have been identified and filed by the private sector.

The group's goal is to provide a forum for FIUs from around the world and to facilitate the secure exchange of expertise and financial intelligence to combat money laundering and terrorist financing. It strives to foster cooperation among the FIUs and promotes the implementation of domestic programs in this field.[26]

The Wolfsberg Group (2000)

The Wolfsberg Group, created in 2000 and based in Geneva, Switzerland, is an association of thirteen global banks. Its aim is to develop frameworks and guidance for managing financial crime risks, particularly with respect to KYC, AML, and CFT policies.[27]

One of the group's primary initiatives has been the drafting of anti–money laundering guidelines for private banking. This work resulted in the *Wolfsberg Anti–Money Laundering Principles for Private Banking*, which was first published in 2000 and revised in 2002 and 2012. The group has also published other documents to provide financial institutions with an industry view toward effectively managing financial crime risk. Many of these publications are considered financial industry standards for AML, KYC, and CFT measures.

The EU's AML Directives

To fight against money laundering and terrorist financing, the European Union adopted comprehensive legislation in the form of AML directives. Unlike the voluntary guidelines and standards of the Basel Committee, the Egmont Group, the Wolfsberg Group, and the FATF, the EU's directives carry legal weight for member states. They require that EU member states achieve specified results, usually by a certain date. The EU adopted the First AML Directive (AMLD1) in 1990 and has revised and enhanced it in the form of subsequent AML directives.

AMLD1 was aimed at preventing the misuse of the financial system for purposes of money laundering; therefore, its scope was limited to financial institutions. As with most AML legislation passed in the 1990s, AMLD1 was also confined to proceeds from drug trafficking. AMLD1 also provided the initial framework for the second and third directives. It introduced requirements for applying CDD, including identifying and verifying the identity of clients, monitoring their transactions, and reporting suspicious activity.

The Second AML Directive (AMLD2) was passed in 2001 and required stricter AML controls than its predecessor. It also expanded the scope of AMLD1 beyond drug crimes, thus covering all serious crimes, including corruption and fraud. It further established a reporting framework and brought investment firms and money exchangers within AML coverage, as well as introduced the power to freeze assets arising from criminal activity.

Based on the FATF's revised Forty Recommendations, the Third AML Directive (AMLD3) came into force in 2005, following not only the 9/11 terror attacks but also the Madrid bombings in 2004 and the 2005 Islamist suicide attacks in London. AMLD3 focused on preventing the use of the financial system for money laundering and terrorist financing and included the funding of terrorism as a main focus. The EU also expanded the directive's application to encompass certain nonfinancial sectors, including lawyers, notaries, accountants, estate agents, providers of gambling services, trust and company service providers, and dealers of high-value goods when payments are made in cash exceeding €15,000. It also introduced additional EDD requirements for situations posing a higher risk of money laundering and terrorist financing. These stipulations include identifying PEPs and identifying and verifying beneficial owners of legal entity customers.

The EU adopted the Fourth AML Directive in 2015, nearly a full decade following the adoption of AMLD3. AMLD4 resolved the ambiguities in AMLD3, focused on a risk-based approach, and took into account the comprehensive FATF standards update of 2012. It extended the scope of impacted persons to include traders of luxury goods and reduced the applicable cash transaction amount from €15,000 to €10,000. It also introduced new requirements: the establishment of a central register containing identification details of ultimate beneficial owners of legal entity customers and the obligation to report suspicions of ML or TF activity to authorities and to screen domestic PEPs. Further, AMLD4 expanded the EDD requirements to include such situations as dealing with banks outside of the EU and with entities located in high-risk non-EU countries.

The Fifth AML Directive came into effect in 2018, not long after the revelations of the Panama Papers scandal of 2016. AMLD5 introduced new requirements for cryptocurrencies and prepaid card transaction limits to restrict their anonymity. To further enhance transparency, it mandated that beneficial ownership information collected in UBO registers be publicly accessible, clarified the powers of FIUs in EU members states to broaden their access to information, and expanded the criteria for assessing financial flows from high-risk non-European countries.

The EU's Sixth AML Directive (AMLD6), which was adopted just a few months after AMLD5 in 2018 and came into force in June 2021, focused on money laundering offenses. More specifically, AMLD6 provided uniformity among EU member states by defining money laundering and detailing the types of criminal predicate activity that give rise to potential ML offenses, such as participating in an organized criminal group, terrorism, human trafficking, sexual exploitation, illicit trafficking in narcotics, and corruption. AMLD6 also expanded criminal liability to legal persons, including companies and partnerships, who fail to prevent illegal activity and increased the maximum imprisonment for offenses.

THE FIVE PILLARS OF AN AML COMPLIANCE PROGRAM

Because of their significance in the functioning of the financial system, banks are considered the front line of AML efforts. Thus, banks and other financial institutions are required to establish and maintain effective AML compliance programs that are reasonably designed to detect and deter money laundering and terrorist financing. For example, an effective AML program helps financial institutions identify suspicious transactions indicative of efforts to launder illicit proceeds and, in turn, prevent those funds from ever entering the US financial system.[28] An effective AML program not only satisfies regulators but can also boost an organization's profits by reducing major business risks.

Although every bank is required to have a comprehensive AML program that complies with BSA requirements (referred to more specifically as a BSA/AML compliance program), each institution's program should be commensurate with its risk profile for money laundering, terrorist financing, and other illicit financial activity. Therefore, every financial institution will have a unique AML compliance program that is tailored to its specific risks and takes into account the size of the institution, the locations of its operations, the products and services it offers, the customer base, and so on. Thus, a local community bank's AML compliance program will differ from the program of a large multinational bank with branches all over the word. Similarly, a money services business, a private trust company, a casino, and a broker dealer will all have very different AML compliance programs. In fact, regulators don't want to see a "canned" compliance program, meaning a generic or template compliance program that isn't customized to fit the particular institution. Nor do they want to see "paper" compliance programs, where the program exists only on paper and isn't followed in practice. In addition to tailoring the AML compliance program to fit the institution, banks must also communicate it to their employees, conduct training for relevant personnel, and ensure its adherence.

To appropriately tailor an AML compliance program, a financial institution must identify the specific risks it faces. This is done primarily through conducting an AML risk assessment. Although a risk assessment is not a legal requirement, a well-developed analysis helps a financial institution not only to identify risks but also to develop appropriate internal controls, such as policies, procedures, and processes to mitigate those risks. It also enables the institution to identify any existing gaps in its internal controls so that it can make any necessary changes or adjustments.[29] Ultimately, this process helps ensure the efficacy of an institution's AML compliance program.

It is generally recommended that an institution perform risk assessments every twelve to eighteen months, although it may need to be done sooner or more frequently if the institution's risk profile changes in some way— for example, if the institution offers a new product or service, opens a new branch in a foreign country, or undergoes a merger or acquisition. Additionally, risk assessments should be documented in writing and communicated with appropriate staff across the organization, including the management and the board of directors.

Section 352 of the USA PATRIOT Act sets forth the requirement that financial institutions establish AML programs. It further grants to the US Treasury Department the authority to set minimum standards for such programs. The current *minimum* standards for AML programs consist of the following components, commonly referred to as pillars:

1. AML internal controls
2. Designated AML compliance officer
3. Ongoing employee AML training
4. Independent AML testing (also referred to as an independent audit function)

These programs must be documented in writing, approved by the institution's board of directors, and noted in the board's minutes. Acting through senior management, the board of directors is ultimately responsible for ensuring that the bank maintains a comprehensive AML compliance program in accordance with BSA regulatory requirements. The board also plays a critical role in fostering an organizational culture that makes compliance a priority. Part of this role includes holding senior management accountable for implementing the bank's internal controls.

Additionally, financial institutions must now have appropriate risk-based procedures for conducting ongoing CDD. Sometimes referred to as the fifth pillar, this requirement is the result of FinCEN's passage of the CDD Rule in May 2018. Although banks were required to conduct customer due diligence prior to the effective date of the CDD Rule, the process was greatly inconsistent. Therefore, the rule essentially served to formalize the CDD process and added a requirement to identify the beneficial owners of a bank's legal entity customers.

AML Internal Controls

An organization's internal controls consist of written policies, procedures, and processes that address its unique AML risks and therefore make up its overall AML compliance program. Internal controls should be proportionate with the bank's size, complexity, and organizational structure to adequately address money laundering and terrorist-financing risks. As part of its internal controls, an institution should include a description of the risks it faces and how it addresses those risks. Among other things and at a minimum, its policies and procedures should include KYC account opening and onboarding processes, including a customer identification program that enables the bank to form a reasonable belief that it knows the true identity of its customers; ongoing CDD and EDD procedures; suspicious activity monitoring and reporting; a description of its training program, the frequency of the training, the topics covered, and the employees being trained; and the regulations and requirements that the institution must meet.

Designated AML Compliance Officer

Every financial institution must have a qualified individual (or individuals) who possesses the requisite skills, training, and experience to serve as its AML compliance officer. Appointed by the board of directors, this person bears responsibility for coordinating and monitoring daily AML compliance activities and manages all aspects of the AML compliance program. This work includes supervising the institution's compliance with applicable BSA regulatory requirements, designing and developing AML processes and procedures, and ensuring AML training and education are provided to relevant staff. Therefore, the designated AML compliance officer must have the appropriate authority, independence, and access to resources to adequately administer the AML compliance program for the institution.

Furthermore, the AML officer should provide regular reports to the board of directors and senior management regarding the status of the overall AML compliance program and the institution's compliance with the BSA. The reports should include any other pertinent BSA-related information, such as notifications of SAR filings, so the management can make informed and timely decisions.

Ongoing Employee AML Training

Financial institutions are required to provide AML training for senior management, the board of directors, and appropriate personnel, including those individuals whose duties and responsibilities require knowledge of or involve some aspect of AML compliance. Therefore, the training requirement is not limited solely to compliance staff or employees who work directly on AML-related matters.

Although the regulation doesn't specify which departments should receive training or how often, ideally all employees should receive some sort of basic AML training shortly upon being hired and periodically thereafter. Furthermore, AML training should be tailored to each individual's specific responsibilities, meaning that some employees will need to receive enhanced, additional, or more frequent training that covers aspects relevant to their duties. The content of the training should be kept up to date, and the timing or frequency of training should be adjusted to address relevant changes in systems, policies, procedures, or applicable regulations.

The training program should ensure that employees understand their role in AML compliance, including applicable AML policies and procedures and appropriate tailored examples, for each operational area. The board of directors and senior management should receive sufficient foundational training, incorporating developments in the BSA and supervisory guidance, to provide adequate oversight of the AML program.

Training programs should also be documented and include such information as the dates of the training, the attendance records, and the topics covered. Any failures by required personnel to take AML training in a timely manner should be addressed.

Independent AML Testing

Independent testing is also sometimes referred to as an independent audit function. Its purpose is to evaluate the bank's compliance with applicable BSA requirements. This testing may be conducted by the internal audit department within the organization, outside auditors, consultants, or other qualified independent parties as long as the parties conducting the testing are not responsible for the oversight, monitoring, or daily activities of the AML compliance program.

Although neither the timing nor the frequency of the testing is specified in applicable regulations, testing should be conducted commensurate with the organization's risk profile and management strategy and/or when the institution's risk profile, compliance staff, or internal processes and procedures change significantly. As noted previously, testing is generally done every twelve to eighteen months; however, more frequent testing of certain areas may be appropriate in cases where deficiencies or higher risks have been identified.

The results and findings of the independent testing should be documented and include such details as the scope of the testing, the relevant documents reviewed, and any supporting work papers. This report should reach a conclusion about the overall adequacy of the institution's AML compliance program and make any recommendations that address the audit's findings. Furthermore, testing results should be communicated to the board of directors.

Risk-Based Procedures for Ongoing Customer Due Diligence

As of May 2018, each financial institution must have risk-based procedures in place for conducting ongoing CDD. This requirement, covered in FinCEN's CDD Rule, is essentially the fifth pillar of an AML compliance program. It seeks to ensure that banks and other financial institutions "understand the nature and purpose of customer relationships." This includes understanding who their customers are and in what types of transactions they would normally engage. Furthermore, institutions must conduct "ongoing monitoring to identify and report suspicious transactions and, on a risk basis, to maintain and update customer information," including beneficial ownership information for legal entity customers.[30] The aim of this requirement is to promote more consistency among banks' widely divergent CDD practices.

The CDD Rule does not require institutions to collect any particular customer information other than what is necessary to develop a customer risk profile. Thus, institutions should make a risk basis determination about what information is needed to adequately understand a particular customer relationship and to identify potentially suspicious activity.

THE IMPORTANCE OF BSA REPORTING

Pursuant to the BSA, financial institutions are required to assist US government agencies in detecting and preventing money laundering. An important aspect of this requirement is the filing of BSA reports, with the two most common being CTRs and SARs. BSA reports provide critical information, such as leads and missing data, to law enforcement and may help authorities connect the dots in investigations. FinCEN also analyzes information contained in BSA reports and uses it to identify trends.

The Role of Currency Transaction Reports

CTRs are reports that financial institutions must file for all currency transactions—withdrawals, deposits, transfers, currency exchanges, or payments—greater than $10,000, a threshold amount that has not changed since 1970. *Currency* refers to coins, paper money, official foreign bank notes, Federal Reserve notes, US notes, and US silver certificates. Multiple transactions by or on behalf of the same individual totaling more than $10,000 in a single business day must be aggregated and treated as one transaction for reporting purposes. The monetary reporting threshold is the only trigger for filing a CTR; no other suspicious activity needs to be involved (although the filer can mark the suspicious transaction checkbox on the form if suspicious activity is also present). Most bank software will automatically generate a CTR. Therefore, a bank may file numerous CTRs daily, depending on the size and volume of its transaction activity. In 2019 alone, filers submitted 16,087,182 CTRs.[31]

Consistent with BSA requirements, other businesses that qualify as financial institutions under the BSA, such as casinos, MSBs, and mutual funds must also file CTRs. Mobile payment businesses, such as Venmo and PayPal, are also required to file CTRs. However, three categories of "exempt persons" do not trigger the filing of a CTR when conducting currency transactions over $10,000: US banks, government agencies, and public corporations. All of these organizations routinely engage in high-value transactions and are already subject to government scrutiny and other filing requirements. Therefore, subjecting these institutions to filing requirements would be overly burdensome and provide little value.

Banks do not have to tell a customer about the $10,000 reporting threshold unless asked. Upon learning about a CTR, a customer cannot lower the amount of the transaction to avoid the CTR, as doing so would constitute the federal offense of structuring, which is punishable against both the customer and the bank employee. Therefore, bank staff must deny any such requests. Furthermore, if a customer chooses to discontinue the transaction, the bank employee is required to file a SAR. Additionally, routine transactions just less than the $10,000 threshold may also attract scrutiny and trigger the filing of a SAR.[32]

Before the development of the CTR, responsibility fell upon individual bank tellers to make judgment calls and inform authorities about suspicious transactions. Although this wasn't efficient, it was deemed necessary to protect customers' financial privacy and to protect financial institutions from liability. This changed in 1986 with the passage of the Money Laundering Control Act, which made allowances for reporting transactions of $10,000 or more and set forth that financial institutions will not be held liable for releasing suspicious transaction information to FinCEN.

Although CTRs may be burdensome and having a CTR on file increases an individual's chances of being audited by the IRS, it is not illegal to transfer $10,000 or more, nor are CTRs intended to prevent people from handling large amounts of cash. Rather, CTRs are used to identify illicit proceeds, spot tax evasion, and enforce tax compliance. Therefore, even though CTRs are filed electronically with FinCEN, they may be shared with the IRS and other government agencies.

Similarly, trades and businesses must use BSA Form 8300 to report any cash payment greater than $10,000 in a transaction. Roughly equivalent to a CTR, it is used to trace cash movement in the retail sector of the economy. This generally includes businesses that receive large cash payments—such as cannabis businesses, art dealers, boat and car dealerships, and antique merchants, among others—and are therefore highly susceptible to being used in furtherance of money laundering.

THE IMPORTANCE OF SUSPICIOUS ACTIVITY REPORTS

The BSA requires that financial institutions report suspicious or potentially suspicious activity attempted or conducted through the institutions in a SAR, which is filed electronically with FinCEN. FinCEN and federal banking agencies use SARs to identify and analyze trends and patterns associated with financial criminal activity. Additionally, SARs provide information regarding financial transactions that is not otherwise publicly available and is therefore highly valuable to law enforcement in criminal investigations. For example, while looking for potential leads in a DEA investigation of a specific individual, special agents may check the FinCEN database containing SARs, CTRs, and other BSA reports for additional information, such as the existence of bank accounts, the names of associates, the geographic locations where the suspect has previously transacted, or the person's aliases.

Thus, the content of a SAR narrative and the quality of SAR data are extremely important. It is crucial that banks and other financial institutions file SARs that are complete and timely. A financial institution has thirty days from the date the suspicious activity is initially detected to file a SAR. This deadline allows the institution time to investigate the incident and gather the necessary information to include in the report. This time frame is extended to sixty days in cases where a suspect cannot be identified. If the suspicious activity continues, the institution must file SARs every ninety days, unless it decides to terminate the relationship with the customer. The failure to file these SARs exposes the financial institution to fines and penalties.

The following circumstances trigger the filing of a SAR:

- insider abuse involving any amount (i.e., no monetary minimum requirement)
- violations aggregating to $5,000 or more in cases where a suspect can be identified
- violations aggregating to $25,000 or more regardless of a potential suspect (i.e., the bank has no substantial basis for identifying a possible suspect)
- transactions aggregating to $5,000 or more that involve potential money laundering or violations of the Bank Secrecy Act

Institutions may also file a voluntary SAR in cases when the suspicious transaction is believed to be relevant to a potential violation of a law or regulation. The types of activity typically reported in SARs include cash transaction structuring, money laundering, check fraud and kiting, computer intrusion, wire transfer fraud, mortgage and consumer loan fraud, embezzlement, self-dealing, identity theft, and terrorist financing.

SARs are strictly confidential. Unlike a CTR, federal law prohibits financial institutions from revealing the existence of a SAR, particularly to the subject of the SAR or anyone involved in any activity that prompted the SAR filing. Therefore, when investigating the suspicious activity that led to the SAR, financial institutions should keep any communications limited to those absolutely necessary.

The reason for the confidentiality requirement is to encourage financial institutions to freely file SARs without fear of a lawsuit or other retaliation. Furthermore, a SAR is not an indictment, nor does it provide conclusive evidence of criminal activity. Bank personnel should investigate the circumstances that led to a SAR to mitigate any other potential risks to the institution and to provide the information required to complete the SAR form. Otherwise, bank personnel are not expected to do the job of trained criminal investigators or criminal prosecutors.

Congress enacted the safe harbor provision of the BSA to shield financial institutions, their officers, and their employees from civil liability for reporting known or suspected criminal offenses or suspicious activity through the filing of a SAR. However, to receive this protection, the filing must be done with a "good faith" belief that a possible violation of the law occurred.

According to the FinCEN Files, US financial institutions submitted more than two million SARs in 2019, with the vast majority filed by large global banks.[33] This makes sense as they are more likely to encounter suspicious activity than smaller banks with fewer branches and fewer customers.

FINCEN FILES LEAK (2020)

In an unprecedented action, a former FinCEN employee leaked more than two thousand SARs to a reporter, and they were subsequently published as a collection of investigative stories that became known as the FinCEN Files. The leaked SARs reference over $2 trillion in financial transactions and reveal how the top global banks—notably, JPMorgan, HSBC, Standard Chartered Bank, Deutsche Bank, and Bank of New York Mellon—profited from criminality. Moreover, the banks continued to move enormous sums of illicit cash in violation of federal laws and regulations, even after having been fined by US authorities for prior AML failures, and in blatant disregard of warnings that they'd face criminal prosecutions.[34]

Included in the reports are detailed accounts of the roles various banks played in connection with the 1Malaysia Development Berhad scandal, the Paul Manafort case, and the looting of the Venezuelan government, as well as their links to corrupt politicians, their connections with criminal activities in Russia and Ukraine, and their involvement in many other suspicious transactions. The FinCEN Files make a strong claim that financial institutions not only have failed in their roles as the first line of defense against money laundering and other serious financial crimes but also operate in a system that has no significant consequences and does not result in the requisite deterrence.[35]

One of the more egregious cases revealed in the FinCEN Files shows how Deutsche Bank transferred over $750 million, which was allegedly looted from a Ukrainian bank, and subsequently directed it to Ukrainian billionaire Ihor Kolomoisky's business interests in the United States. The reports further show that much of this money was funneled through shell companies incorporated in Delaware and the British Virgin Islands.[36]

A Fenergo report examining global AML regulatory fines and penalties and enforcement trends found that a staggering total of $10.1 billion in AML-related fines was issued in just the fifteen months between October 2018 and December 2019. However, of the banks fined, the fines amounted to a mere 1 percent of their average net income.[37] Therefore, as the FinCEN Files illustrate, either the AML regulations aren't sufficient to detect and prevent money laundering and other illegal activity or the fines imposed for AML violations aren't sufficiently punitive to produce a deterrent effect given the potential profits to be gained.

KEY REASONS FOR AML FAILURES

The majority of the fines imposed by US regulators on financial institutions are related to sanctions violations and failures to apply CFT controls, such as when a bank transfers funds to an OFAC-sanctioned country. Regardless of the financial institution's size, AML violations that lead to enforcement actions generally result from a deficiency in one or more of the five pillars of its AML compliance program. A pillar violation signals that the institution's AML compliance program has a serious defect. Besides regulatory fines and penalties, flaws in any of the AML compliance program pillars can also lead to criminal sanctions in cases of willful conduct, such as efforts to conceal deficiencies from authorities or to obstruct access to information. AML pillar deficiencies and violations have been noted in multiple major enforcement actions over the past decade, including those involving Wachovia Bank, HSBC, US Bancorp, Rabobank, JPMorgan Chase, Citigroup/Banamex, and others.

A common violation reflecting flaws in the internal controls pillar involves an institution's failure to monitor and report suspicious activity, including the timely filing of SARs and CTRs. Numerous banks, including Wells Fargo, HSBC, Capital One, and others, have been penalized for failing to file multiple (usually thousands of) SARs and/or CTRs. Another example of a common pillar violation involves defects in AML staffing needs and resources, which fall under the second pillar requiring the designation of an AML compliance officer with access to adequate resources. Both US Bancorp and Rabobank allocated minimal resources to their respective compliance programs and suffered serious consequences as a result.

Violations that lead to enforcement actions generally include ongoing, recurring, and systemic issues. Often they also stem from a culture that does not promote compliance, including cases where senior management ignores problems and fails to adequately fund or provide resources for compliance programs. Other major reasons contributing to compliance violations include weaknesses in customer due diligence and monitoring. Financial institutions with a history of AML deficiencies are at risk of greater penalties for not correcting these flaws.

DOJ AND OFAC GUIDANCE ON CORPORATE COMPLIANCE PROGRAMS

Financial institutions and other organizations can also look to the DOJ's guidance published in the document "Evaluation of Corporate Compliance Programs," which is updated periodically. Although it is intended to assist prosecutors in making charging decisions and focuses on overall corporate compliance programs rather than AML compliance programs specifically, the document nonetheless reveals crucial insight into what the government considers an effective corporate compliance program. This guidance, which is meant to correspond with international standards, complements BSA/AML compliance expectations by stressing the need for continuously updated, appropriately tailored, and risk-based compliance programs. It centers on three important considerations:

1. Is the corporation's compliance program well designed?
2. Is the program being applied earnestly and in good faith? That is, is it adequately resourced and empowered to function effectively?
3. Does the corporation's compliance program work in practice?[38]

Similarly, OFAC has developed a document titled "A Framework for OFAC Compliance Commitments," which provides useful guidance for organizations regarding the design and implementation of a sanctions compliance program. According to OFAC, a sanctions compliance program should incorporate the following five minimum components: management commitment, risk assessment, internal controls, testing and auditing, and training. This framework also comports with BSA/AML compliance program requirements.[39]

Although not required by law, OFAC "strongly encourages" organizations subject to its jurisdiction to employ its recommendations. Notably, OFAC has made clear that the existence of a sanctions compliance program, designed in accordance with its framework, can potentially mitigate civil monetary penalties in cases of a sanctions violation.

PREVENTING AML COMPLIANCE FAILURES

In short, the best defense is a strong offense. A comprehensive AML compliance program designed in accordance with BSA/AML obligations, and that further incorporates guidance from both the DOJ and OFAC, will serve as the best defense to any potential violation.

More specifically, institutions must continuously assess and update their money laundering countermeasures, including their policies, procedures, and processes. They should not only account for changes in laws and regulations but also respond to changes in potential risks as the organizations grow, expand into new jurisdictions, take on new types of customers, and offer new products and services. Additionally, any identified issues and deficiencies should be remedied in a timely manner. Furthermore, financial institutions must ensure that growth does not outpace their AML compliance infrastructure.

Financial institutions, which are notoriously conservative and much slower than nonfinancial businesses to embrace new technologies, must adopt technological solutions, including digitization and automation, to effectively handle large quantities of data. In fact, FinCEN and other banking regulators across the globe strongly advise streamlining processes to increase efficiency.[40] In cases where budgets are tight, financial institutions should strategically allocate resources using a risk-based approach.

Although more work needs to be done, the direction of AML legislation in the United States and abroad, and the increased enforcement of AML by regulators across the globe, strongly suggests that AML regulations are coming more in line with international FATF standards. Therefore, financial institutions, including smaller community banks and local credit unions, should keep apprised of global developments and revisit their policies frequently. Organizations are extremely unlikely to be penalized for implementing stricter compliance controls than are required, but they will almost certainly be punished for not doing enough and for not meeting their obligations in a timely manner.

Finally, the boards of directors of financial institutions must be kept well informed of the status of their respective institutions' AML compliance programs, including any gaps and plans to close them. They also need to keep abreast of the current and emerging trends that are likely to impact their particular institutions.

CONCLUSION

Financial institutions provide a conduit through which money, including laundered funds, flows. Illicit funds are most identifiable when first introduced into the financial system. Because of this, banks and other financial institutions are the focus of anti–money laundering initiatives. Given their centrality in the financial system, financial institutions must apply appropriate measures to prevent money laundering and counter terrorist financing.

The BSA and the USA PATRIOT Act are the two main sources of federal AML legislation. Together, they provide minimum requirements for the design, implementation, and ongoing management of AML compliance programs in the United States. A risk-based AML compliance program that is properly designed, effectively implemented, and appropriately managed is meant to safeguard the financial institution, and consequently the financial system, from criminals seeking to use it to disguise and transfer illicit funds. Since banks are ultimately businesses, and therefore cannot regulate themselves, it is up to governments to regulate money laundering. As a result, a group of federal banking agencies has been tasked with oversight of AML compliance at financial institutions.

Financial institutions respond to high-profile enforcement actions by enhancing compliance resources, often at great cost. Yet the largest global banks still seem to be the repeat offenders. Although AML-related fines and penalties continue to increase, they pale in comparison to what financial institutions seek to gain by continuing to permit and enable illicit transactions, bringing into question the long-debated efficacy of enforcement actions. At the macroeconomic level, if left unchecked, money laundering, including a bank's complicity in it, can adversely affect international capital flows and exchange rates, ultimately eroding the stability of a nation's financial institutions and impacting the global financial system.

NOTES

1. Shelley, *Dark Commerce*.
2. Todd S. Fishman and Eugene Ingoglia, "Active U.S. Enforcement of Anti–Money Laundering Rules Continues Unabated," *New York Law Journal*, June 3, 2020, https://www

.law.com/newyorklawjournal/2020/06/03/active-u-s-enforcement-of-anti-money-laundering-rules-continues-unabated/.

3. Karen Freifeld, "Rabobank Agrees to Pay $368 Million over Processing Illicit Funds," *Reuters*, February 7, 2018, https://www.reuters.com/article/us-rabobank-fraud-usa/rabobank-agrees-to-pay-368-million-over-processing-illicit-funds-idUSKBN1FR2U4; and Irene Madongo, "Rabobank Fined over Poor Anti–Money Laundering Controls, KYC, Beneficial Ownership," *KYC360 News*, Risk Screen, February 15, 2019, https://www.riskscreen.com/kyc360/news/rabobank-fined-over-poor-anti-money-laundering-controls-kyc-beneficial-ownership/#:~:text=Dutch%20lender%20Rabobank%20has%20been,CDD)%20and%20beneficial%20ownership%20issues.&text=%E2%80%9CSince%20then%20we%20have%20made,which%20includes%20anti%2Dmoney%20laundering.

4. Shelley, *Dark Commerce*, 145.

5. Shelley, 145; and Lauren Debter, "Western Union Slammed for Aiding Crooks, Agrees to Pay $586 Million," *Forbes*, January 19, 2017, https://www.forbes.com/sites/laurengensler/2017/01/19/western-union-anti-money-laundering-consumer-fraud-violations/?sh=4e353ef87238.

6. ACAMS, *Study Guide.*

7. Wolfsberg Group, "Wolfsberg Frequently Asked Questions ('FAQs') on Correspondent Banking," 2014, https://www.wolfsberg-principles.com/sites/default/files/wb/pdfs/faqs/18.%20Wolfsberg-Correspondent-Banking-FAQ-2014.pdf.

8. Wolfsberg Group.

9. Julia Kagan, "Concentration Account," July 15, 2020, updated January 2, 2021, *Investopedia*, https://www.investopedia.com/terms/c/concentration-account.asp#:~:text=A%20concentration%20account%20is%20a,often%20with%20same%2Dday%20settlement.

10. FFIEC, "Introduction," *BSA/AML Examination Manual*, https://bsaaml.ffiec.gov/docs/manual/01_Introduction/01.pdf.

11. FFIEC.

12. Biern, testimony (see chap. 10, n. 3).

13. FFIEC, *BSA/AML Examination Manual.*

14. 31 U.S.C. § 5321(d), Criminal Penalty Not Exclusive of Civil Penalty.

15. Brian Monroe, "Fincrime Briefing: AML Fines in 2019 Breach $8 Billion, Treasury Official Pleads Guilty to Leaking, 2020 Crypto Compliance Outlook, and More," Association of Certified Financial Crime Specialists, January 14, 2020, https://www.acfcs.org/fincrime-briefing-aml-fines-in-2019-breach-8-billion-treasury-official-pleads-guilty-to-leaking-2020-crypto-compliance-outlook-and-more/.

16. Toby Sterling and Bart H. Meijer, "Dutch Bank ING Fined $900 Million for Failing to Spot Money Laundering," *Reuters*, September 4, 2018, https://www.reuters.com/article/us-ing-groep-settlement-money-laundering/dutch-bank-ing-fined-900-million-for-failing-to-spot-money-laundering-idUSKCN1LK0PE; and Pete Schroeder, "U.S. Bancorp to Pay $613 Million for Money-Laundering Violations," *Reuters*, February 15, 2018, https://www.reuters.com/article/us-usa-usbancorp/u-s-bancorp-to-pay-613-million-for-money-laundering-violations-idUSKCN1FZ1YJ.

17. "Five Biggest AML Fines on Banks," Medici, November 29, 2020, https://medium.com/@gomedici/five-biggest-aml-fines-on-banks-18145f93ede8.

18. "The 2021 Guide to Customer Due Diligence," GetID, April 21, 2021, https://getid.ee/guide-to-customer-due-diligence/.

19. World Bank and the International Monetary Fund (IMF), "Who We Are," accessed October 30, 2020, https://www.worldbank.org/en/about/history/the-world-bank-group-and-the-imf.

20. ACAMS, *Study Guide,* 161–63.

21. United Nations, "United Nations Convention against Illicit Trafficking in Narcotic Drugs and Psychotropic Substances" (Vienna: United Nations, 1988), https://www.unodc.org/pdf/convention_1988_en.pdf.

22. William R. Schroeder, "Money Laundering: A Global Threat and the International Community's Response," *FBI Law Enforcement Bulletin* 70, no. 5 (May 2001), https://www.ncjrs.gov/App/Publications/abstract.aspx?ID=188586.

23. Schroeder.

24. FinCEN, "Mission," US Treasury Department, accessed October 29, 2020, https://www.fincen.gov/about/mission.

25. "The Accountant (2016 Film)," *Wikipedia,* last edited November 14, 2020, https://en.wikipedia.org/wiki/The_Accountant_(2016_film).

26. Egmont Group, "About," accessed October 29, 2020, https://egmontgroup.org/en/content/about#:~:text=%EF%82%A7%20The%20Egmont%20Group%20is,financing%20(ML%2FTF).

27. Wolfsberg Group, "About," 2018, https://www.wolfsberg-principles.com/.

28. D'Antuono, "Combating Money Laundering" (see chap. 1, n. 26).

29. FFIEC, *BSA/AML Examination Manual.*

30. FinCEN, "FinCEN Guidance: Frequently Asked Questions Regarding Customer Due Diligence (CDD) Requirements for Covered Financial Institutions," US Treasury Department, FIN-2020-G002, August 3, 2020, https://www.fincen.gov/sites/default/files/2020-08/FinCEN_Guidance_CDD_508_FINAL.pdf; and FinCEN, "Information on Complying" (see chap. 10, n. 30).

31. FinCEN, "Notice: Agency Information Collection Activities; Proposed Renewal; Comment Request," May 14, 2020, in *Federal Register,* 85 FR 29022, May 14, 2020, pp. 29022–30, https://www.federalregister.gov/documents/2020/05/14/2020-10310/agency-information-collection-activities-proposed-renewal-comment-request-renewal-without-change-of#:~:text=Breakdown%20of%20the%202019%20CTR,CTRs%20filed%20during%20the%20year.

32. Adam Hayes, "Currency Transaction Report (CTR)," *Investopedia,* May 29, 2020, https://www.investopedia.com/terms/c/ctr.asp.

33. Fergus Shiel and Ben Hallman, "FinCEN Files: Suspicious Activity Reports, Explained," *International Consortium of Investigative Journalists (ICIJ),* September 20, 2020, https://www.icij.org/investigations/fincen-files/suspicious-activity-reports-explained/.

34. ICIJ, "FinCEN Files: Global Banks Defy U.S. Crackdowns by Serving Oligarchs, Criminals and Terrorists," *ICIJ,* September 20, 2020, https://www.icij.org/investigations/fincen-files/global-banks-defy-u-s-crackdowns-by-serving-oligarchs-criminals-and-terrorists/.

35. ICIJ.

36. Michael Sallah and Tanya Kozyreva, "Money Laundering: With Deutsche Bank's Help, an Oligarch's Buying Spree Trails Ruin across the US Heartland," *ICIJ,* September 22,

2020, https://www.icij.org/investigations/fincen-files/with-deutsche-banks-help-an
-oligarchs-buying-spree-trails-ruin-across-the-us-heartland/.

37. Laura Glynn, Rachel Woolley, and Graham Barrow, "Another Fine Mess: A Global
Research Report on Financial Institution Fines and Enforcement Actions: The Regulatory Environment at the End of a Pivotal Decade (October 2018–December 2019)"
(New York: Fenergo), 6, accessed November 2, 2020, https://www.fenergo.com/assets
/files/industry-knowledge/Reports/AML%20Fines%20Global%20Report_FINAL
_23.04.2020.pdf.

38. US Justice Department, Criminal Division, "Evaluation of Corporate Compliance
Programs" (Washington, DC: Justice Department, updated June 2020), https://www
.justice.gov/criminal-fraud/page/file/937501/download.

39. OFAC, "A Framework for OFAC Compliance Commitments" (Washington, DC: OFAC,
2020), https://home.treasury.gov/system/files/126/framework_ofac_cc.pdf.

40. Board of Governors of the Federal Reserve System, Federal Deposit Insurance Corporation, Financial Crimes Enforcement Network, National Credit Union Administration,
and Office of the Comptroller of the Currency, "Joint Statement on Innovative Efforts to
Combat Money Laundering and Terrorist Financing," December 3, 2018, https://www
.federalreserve.gov/newsevents/pressreleases/files/bcreg20181203a1.pdf.

CHAPTER 12

FINAL THOUGHTS

Reflections and Recommendations

Money laundering combines elements of the legal and illegal economies. Starting with ill-gotten funds generated from criminal activity, launderers frequently utilize legitimate financial institutions and employ the services of recognized professionals to hide illegal transactions among legal ones and mix licit and illicit funds.

It is expected that at some point, most illicit funds will pass through the financial system. Therefore, AML laws and regulations impose strict requirements on financial institutions that are intended to prevent criminals from gaining access to the financial system. Once the funds have made their way into a financial institution, however, they are difficult to detect and easily transferred. Dirty money can be moved between banks, through various accounts, in the form of different financial instruments, to and from legal arrangements, and in multiple currencies. Thus, no financial institution can ensure that all the money flowing through it is legally derived. Consequently, financial institutions bear a huge burden as the front line of defense and face an uphill battle against money laundering, terrorist financing, and other financial crime.

By its nature, money laundering involves stealth and secrecy, making detection difficult for financial institutions and hindering law enforcement efforts. The greatest obstacle to combating money laundering includes insufficient transparency concerning corporate structures and legal arrangements that are used to shield the beneficial owner and thereby enable the anonymous movement of illicit funds. Another stumbling block is a lack of regulation for the gatekeeper professions, which serve as middlemen in illicit schemes by enabling the formation of anonymous entities, permitting nontransparent transactions, failing to properly vet clients, and providing advice on the circumvention of laws and regulations. Individuals in these professions may be witting, unwitting, or simply indifferent participants in the illegality.

Despite the AML efforts of the past few decades, which predominantly focused on financial institutions, money laundering continues to be a global problem with no signs of decreasing. In fact, the success rate of money laundering controls, at only about 0.1 percent, has been deemed "almost completely ineffective."[1]

Furthermore, the successful prosecution of money laundering is also extremely low, even in the United States, which appears to have the highest conviction rate for money laundering prosecutions in the world. Therefore, the returns to the launderer are relatively large compared to the risks.[2]

GATEKEEPERS OR GATE-CRASHERS?

A class of diverse professionals who act as intermediaries between financial institutions and their clients, conduct financial dealings for or on behalf of their clients, or serve as financial liaisons are referred to as the gatekeeper professions.[3] Gatekeepers include lawyers, real estate agents, trust fund managers, sales representatives, tax advisers, company and trust formation agents, brokers, and other middlemen. These individuals generally possess an advanced education and have specialized expertise in their respective fields. Many cater toward wealthy customers, whom they assist in using money to their best advantage. Oftentimes, the nature of their work presents many opportunities and incentives (both legal, such as high commissions, and illegal, such as bribes) to help clients circumvent, and even break, the law.

These professional intermediaries engage in a variety of transactions that enable their clients to move large sums of money. Such transactions mainly include the buying and selling of real estate; the management of clients' money, securities, or other assets; and the creation, operation, or management of legal entities and arrangements such as companies and trusts.[4] For example, lawyers, company service providers, and other middlemen have the ability to advise on and establish anonymous companies that can be used to open bank accounts, to transfer illicit proceeds, to purchase and sell real estate and other assets anonymously, or to simply safeguard corrupt funds. Real estate professionals may facilitate all-cash deals to transfer wealth or assist with purchasing investment properties. Investors and other advisers enable criminals to hide wealth in investments and maximize their illicit gains through returns gained on these investments. And tax planners can help launderers compound the value of their laundered gains by avoiding the payment of taxes on illegally earned proceeds.

Additionally, criminals can use the services of intermediaries in all phases of the money laundering cycle, from the initial placement of dirty funds into the legitimate financial system to their integration into the economy as clean funds. Thus, gatekeepers allow illegitimate funds to enter the financial system through the backdoor and thereafter to navigate through it undetected. As a result, gatekeepers should also play a role in safeguarding the financial system and do their part in preventing financial crime, or otherwise they should be held accountable when they abuse or misuse their function.

Although helping clients save and invest their earnings certainly isn't illegal or even unethical, the FATF, the US Treasury Department, and others have long identified these associated professions as being at risk for facilitating (whether wittingly or not) the laundering of illicit and criminal funds. In fact, it was a California-based lawyer who willingly helped Obiang establish anonymous shell companies along with multiple other corporate vehicles to disguise Obiang's identity and evade AML controls. Lawyers in the United States are not required to follow the FATF's guidelines, and the attorney who assisted Obiang wasn't sanctioned even though his client went to prison and was made to forfeit tens of millions of dollars of illicit gains.[5] Given such cases, the FATF specifically calls for imposing transparency measures, such as due diligence on clients and the filing of SARs, upon the gatekeeper professions.

Gatekeepers operate in a client-facing role, a position that enables them to readily access and collect client information. Thus, they should not find AML obligations, such as a requirement to obtain KYC documentation on clients, overly burdensome. Moreover, given their critical role as middlemen and their ability to gather critical client identification, gatekeepers should have to adhere to AML regulations, including KYC requirements; yet, depending on the specific profession, they are currently subject to minimal, if any, AML rules. Additionally, no uniform legislation governing these professions currently exists. Thus, the responsibility for detecting and preventing money laundering is placed almost exclusively on banks.

Furthermore, a host of individuals, organizations, and networks make a living and specialize in assisting criminals and organized crime groups to launder the proceeds of their criminal activities and to evade sanctions. These professional money launderers operate under many different business models and, for a fee, will provide a range of services.[6] For example, the US Treasury Department designated Altaf Khanani's network as a money laundering organization (Khanani MLO) because it laundered illicit funds for organized crime groups, drug trafficking organizations, and a number of designated terrorist groups. OFAC has similarly targeted the Khanani MLO for engaging in third-party money laundering, including the transfer of funds to financial institutions on behalf of drug traffickers.[7] Although commission rates for money laundering services vary and exact figures are hard to come by, criminals are clearly willing to pay for such services.[8] In fact, some experts have pointed out that the increased complexity of AML standards has made criminals more reliant upon the services of the gatekeeper professions to get around the tougher controls.[9] Therefore, these middlemen, who are essentially in the best position to end illicit financial flows, are precisely the ones who are most profiting from them.

As mentioned in chapter 10, the ENABLERS Act, which amends the BSA by imposing basic due diligence requirements on gatekeepers in the United States, would address many of the concerns associated with the professions seen as responsible for enabling corporate secrecy. Although a necessary step forward in promoting financial transparency, the effort to curb the circulation of dirty money ultimately needs to be a global one. Therefore, other jurisdictions, particularly those identified as having weak AML controls, must act as well. Otherwise, illicit funds will always find another route and, like water, flow along the path of least resistance.

RED FLAGS ASSOCIATED WITH GATEKEEPERS AND INTERMEDIARIES

Red flags associated with the gatekeeping professions are indictors that individuals may be attempting to misuse a professional intermediary's services for money laundering or facilitating other financial crime. Because each of these professionals offers different services, red flags relating to the gatekeeper professions may differ based on the particular services undertaken.

Furthermore, red flags can also be grouped into categories that relate to the client, the source of funds, and the nature of the retainer or fee arrangement, among others.[10] Some common red flags relating to these professional services include requests for unusual, atypical, or overly complex legal, business, or financial arrangements that otherwise don't appear to make sense or have a logical explanation or a legitimate or economic reason; requests for frequent changes to legal structures or business arrangements, such as changes related to the officers and directors or the replacements of nominees; and discrepancies, inconsistencies, or an absence of documentation relating to the client's stated business, financial, or legal situation. A comprehensive list of red flags can be found on the FATF's website.

WHO'S WINNING THE BATTLE?

If money launderers always seem to be a step ahead of law enforcement, that's because they are. Not only is the success rate for asset seizures less than a paltry 1 percent but also the number of money laundering cases filed worldwide is almost as minuscule. Most money launderers never get caught.[11] In the United States, only about 0.25 percent of launderers are ever arrested. An astounding 99 percent of money laundering crimes go unprosecuted. Furthermore, of those who are brought to trial, the risk of conviction for a money laundering offense is just over 5 percent, and data from other industrialized countries show that levels of enforcement are even lower.[12] A prime example of this is the Russian Laundromat whereby billions of dollars were laundered, yet few suspects were identified. The Fin-CEN Files revelation also indicates that banks are not capable of curbing the movement of the trillions of dollars of illicit funds that enter and circulate through their institutions.[13]

Time and again, criminals have proven to be incredibly adaptable and opportunistic. They have demonstrated their ability to exploit gaps and loopholes in laws and regulations, as well as vulnerabilities in global supply chains, internal controls at financial institutions, and online networks. Shortly after banks were required to file CTRs, for example, structuring activity increased. Once free trade zones were designated, trade-based money laundering rose dramatically in those areas, and during the 2008 financial crisis, money laundering spiked, particularly at large global banks. Today, malware is a threat to many individuals, businesses, and government networks.

Criminals have long had an advantage over law enforcement because they do not feel bound by laws, regulations, borders, and legal agreements. Ignoring social and legal constraints allows them to always act in their own self-interest. Furthermore, rapid developments in new technology have added a whole new advantage for criminals, who have shown both a great willingness and an ability to adopt technological advancements.

Their adoption and use of new internet technology are reflected in the rapid rise of a host of cybercrimes—for example, the use of online money mules in laundering schemes and the growth of illegal online marketplaces on the dark web that sell everything from fake IDs and stolen Social Security numbers to drugs, weapons, trafficked kidneys, and humans. It can also be seen in how quickly criminals have exploited virtual currencies for criminal activity; they embraced cryptocurrencies long before these modes of payment became more mainstream. Consequently, increasingly more private cryptocurrencies that are used to conceal illicit transactions have developed.

In fact, the growth in cybercrime and cyber-enabled crime seems to outpace the ability of the government, and even the private sector, to counter them.

Criminals have long incorporated new technologies. Large-scale global criminal activities involving trafficking and financial crimes grew exponentially during the 1990s and paralleled advances in computer technology. In fact, technological advances and globalization, which made drug trafficking faster, more efficient, and easier to disguise, propelled the drug trade during that decade. For instance, the Cali Cartel began using sophisticated encryption techniques as far back as the early nineties and with more sophisticated methods than the Colombian government had at that time.[14]

In all these cases, law enforcement has been merely reactive, further highlighting just how ineffective efforts at deterrence are. As a result, transnational organized crime is more profitable than ever before. Clearly, law enforcement and regulation lag far behind innovation, which is likely to further link technological development to illicit activities.

ADDRESSING MONEY LAUNDERING

The United States has a long history and a global reputation as a police nation. It is known to have the toughest AML enforcement in the world and one of the strongest AML regimes.[15] Yet this has not been enough to counter the threat of money laundering, as US figures for the number of money laundering arrests, prosecutions, and convictions remain staggeringly low. Thus, money laundering continues to be a huge problem in the United States and internationally. Something needs to change to successfully combat this illicit activity, but any efforts at AML reform necessitate a comprehensive and coordinated global effort.

Launderers and other criminals use international borders, which are more permeable than ever before, to their advantage. They specifically seek out and target jurisdictions with weak or lax AML regimes and minimal enforcement. As one nation adopts more stringent measures, criminals merely shift their activities. Consequently, global uniformity in AML standards is necessary to prevent criminals from capitalizing on differences in AML controls and enforcement among jurisdictions.

AML reform is not just about global cooperation and more uniform standards. An effective response to these threats also requires critical partnerships between the public and private sectors. They must involve open communication and the sharing of valuable information (including data about trends, typologies, and information contained in SARs), as well as active and regular engagement and collaboration on such things as making regulations and guidelines more effective. By combining knowledge, expertise, and even resources, partnerships where the government (including government agencies and regulators) and private-sector business leaders work together can help formulate efficient anti–money laundering strategies, promote financial transparency, and bring innovative and long-term solutions, ultimately resulting in a more powerful and successful counterapproach to money laundering.[16]

AML regulations and requirements also need to be updated and revisited regularly to account for the evolution of money laundering and the development of new laundering methods. Until the recent passage of the Anti–Money Laundering Act on January 1, 2021, the US AML regime hadn't seen a substantial update since 2001's USA PATRIOT Act (which was the only major reform since the BSA's passage in 1970). Meanwhile, much has changed in two decades as a result of globalization, improvements in communications, and huge advances in technology, leading to a vastly different world and financial system. For example, money can be transferred at a much faster rate, the sums moved are significantly greater, and virtual currencies have been introduced and are becoming increasingly common. Money launderers and their techniques have gotten more sophisticated and technical, and anti–money laundering efforts need to reflect these circumstances. Developments in both the legal and illegal economies will inevitably continue, and the global society cannot afford for AML legislation to lag behind.

More illicit funds are in circulation today than ever before, and the demand for illicit financial services is equally as high.[17] Organized criminal syndicates and professional money launderers are behind the vast majority of this money laundering activity. Observations by the FATF indicate that organized crime groups are working together and coordinating their ML efforts. Further, apparently these groups are dividing the labor according to their economic connections or financial expertise. Thus, money laundering has also become highly specialized.[18] To have any meaningful effect, AML strategies must take into account these facts, among others.

One specific regulatory reform that needs to be made is an update to the SAR process. First, SARs should be filed much sooner than the current thirty days after initially detecting a suspicious incident or the sixty days in the case when a suspect cannot be identified. Many institutions don't even meet these deadlines. Timing is critical, however, for law enforcement purposes, and financial institutions should be able to gather the necessary information to file the report more quickly than these time frames. In fact, if institutions have appropriate KYC programs in place and are conducting proper CDD, they should already have much of this information at their disposal. In the case that an institution discovers new and relevant information after filing the SAR, it can file an amended SAR.

Second, SAR narratives should be more standardized. The current free-form narrative leaves too much leeway for unnecessary, redundant, and distracting information that hinders the report's effectiveness. As a result, SAR narratives vary greatly in length, quality, and content not just among institutions but also within institutions, depending on who is writing the SAR narratives.

Finally, institutions should be provided with feedback about the value and quality of the SARs they file. Institutions do not currently receive any feedback, so they simply don't ever know what happens to the SARs they file (except in the rare instance of a government inquiry) and, more importantly, whether those SARs are of any value. Receiving some sort of input would allow institutions to fine-tune their SARs, making the process more efficient.

Regulators across the globe need to uniformly mandate greater corporate transparency. Making financial information traceable has an important deterrent effect. This is especially important in countering the various risks that anonymous legal entities pose, and that can be done by implementing and effectively using beneficial ownership registries. To address fundamental privacy concerns, such information need not be publicly available. However, at a minimum, it should be readily accessible by other financial institutions for CDD purposes and by law enforcement for its investigations. Enhancing transparency standards would further benefit institutions by increasing their reputations and ultimately bringing in more business. It would also strengthen public trust in the overall financial system. But for this to work, transparency requirements must be uniformly mandated and enforced across the globe. Otherwise, criminals will simply flock to the weakest jurisdiction.

It is not a stretch to say that many Western banks profit from money laundering. All too often, the largest global banks fail to correct known weaknesses and flaws in their internal controls and become subject to repeat fines and penalties. Clearly, they find it more profitable to disregard regulations and break the law. To promote effective deterrence, higher monetary penalties and more severe consequences need to be imposed when compliance programs are insufficient or when institutions take too long to remedy previously identified deficiencies. Although law enforcement and regulators have shown that large global banks can't escape punishment, and even though AML fines have been steadily increasing, monetary penalties still represent only a fraction of the income that the biggest banks earn. Although rarely imposed, enforcing individual liability for employees of financial institutions—particularly for directors and officers, as well as others in senior positions—would also greatly add to the deterrent effect.

THE IMPACT OF MONEY LAUNDERING

Money laundering is said to be the world's third-largest industry by value, after oil production and agriculture. Some even contend that Western banks are able to remain in business because of money laundering services.[19] Yet the seriousness of money laundering and its consequences are often underestimated, as is the urgency to counter it. If left unchecked, money laundering not only is a threat to the economic and financial stability of nations but also represents a national security issue. As such, it also has numerous serious social and political implications.

Money laundering impacts both developed and developing countries. It undermines confidence in markets and results in losses to legitimate investors. At least one notable study on the relationship between GDP growth and money laundering in a number of industrialized countries found that an increase in money laundering correlates with declines in annual GDP growth rates.[20]

However, the negative effects of money laundering are most pronounced and most immediately apparent in emerging markets, which are the least equipped to deal with them. In some of these countries, illicit proceeds surpass government budgets, impacting economic policy. As launderers seek new routes and opportunities to clean illicit funds, developing economies, which tend to have deficient AML controls, will continue to be targets and suffer the greatest repercussions. These illicit financial flows will ultimately sabotage countries' development goals. Legitimate foreign investment will turn away as the integrity of the financial institutions in those countries diminishes, further hindering the countries' economic development.

Money laundering reduces tax revenues for the government, which then generally has to increase tax rates. Funds that should be used to pay for schools, hospitals, roads, transportation, parks, and other infrastructure are diverted to undeserving criminal groups and kleptocrats at the expense of ordinary citizens. This diminishes the quality of life for the citizens of those nations. Failure on the part of governments to stop the illicit flows of money ultimately results in their overall decline.

Money laundering also leads to further crime that strengthens criminal organizations and increases their influence. For example, when legitimate local businesses are unable to compete with front companies owned by criminal enterprises, corruption flourishes. In essence, money laundering transfers economic power from markets, governments, and citizens to criminals, resulting in a corrupting effect that permeates all levels of society. Ultimately, it harms democratic institutions.

Corruption cases over the past few years illustrate how PEPs—in particular, individuals who have been entrusted with prominent public functions such as senior politicians, members of the judiciary, and executives of publicly owned corporation—have laundered vast amounts of criminal proceeds. In these cases, the negative impacts of money laundering are most pronounced where PEPs come from countries with already high levels of corruption and subsequently move money overseas for laundering in more stable economies. This results in capital flight, which has devastating consequences for innocent citizens. The siphoning of government funds by Angola's ruling elite, the theft of billions of dollars from Malaysia's 1Malaysia Development Berhad fund, and the funneling of Russian funds through intricate networks of shell companies are just a few high-profile examples of these harmful financial flows.

Corrupt funds must be cleaned to conceal their source and enable their subsequent use, creating an unequivocal link between money laundering and corruption. Therefore, where there's corruption, there's also going to be money laundering. Both exist in a cycle of increased costs and human suffering that becomes ever more difficult to break as those who profit get stronger and more powerful. Among those enabling these oppressive global crimes in large part are the financial and legal systems that allow illicit funds to be disguised and transferred.

The only way to combat this serious problem is through a united global effort toward greater financial transparency. In the words of the former UN secretary-general and Nobel Peace Prize laureate Kofi Annan, "If corruption is a disease, transparency is [an] essential part of its treatment."

NOTES

1. Ronald F. Pol, "Anti-Money Laundering: The World's Least Effective Policy Experiment? Together, We Can Fix It," *Policy Design and Practice* 3, no. 1 (2020): 73–94, https://doi.org/10.1080/25741292.2020.1725366; and Ronald F. Pol, "Uncomfortable Truths? ML=BS and AML= BS²," *Journal of Financial Crime* 25, no. 2 (May 2018): 294–308, https://doi.org/10.1108/JFC-08-2017-0071.
2. Edwin M. Tuman, "Drugs, Crime, Money, and Development," Remarks at the World Bank Group/International Finance Corporation Financial and Private Sector Development

Forum, Washington, DC, April 25, 2007, https://www.piie.com/commentary/speeches
-papers/drugs-crime-money-and-development.

3. Stanley Foodman, "Gatekeepers Are under a Lot of Stress!" *JD Supra*, August 21, 2018,
   https://www.jdsupra.com/legalnews/gatekeepers-are-under-a-lot-of-stress-33947
   /#:~:text=The%20FATF%20is%20an%20independent,of%20weapons%20of%20mass
   %20destruction.

4. Caribbean Financial Action Task Force (CFATF), "FATF 40 Recommendations, Rec-
   ommendation 22: DNFBPs: Customer Due Diligence," accessed November 5, 2020,
   https://cfatf-gafic.org/index.php/documents/fatf-40r/388-fatf-recommendation-22
   -dnfbps-customer-due-diligence.

5. Alexandra Cooley and Case Michael, "U.S. Lawyers Are Foreign Kleptocrats' Best
   Friends," *Foreign Policy*, Match 23, 2021, https://foreignpolicy.com/2021/03/23/u-s
   -lawyers-are-foreign-kleptocrats-best-friends/.

6. FATF, "Professional Money Laundering" (see introduction, n. 1).

7. US Treasury Department, Press Center, "Treasury Sanctions the Khanani Money Laundering Organization," November 12, 2015, https://www.treasury.gov/press-center/press
   -releases/Pages/jl0265.aspx.

8. Reuter and Truman, "Money Laundering: Methods and Markets," in *Chasing Dirty
   Money*, chap. 3 (see chap. 1, n. 27).

9. FATF, *Money Laundering* (see chap. 4, n. 2).

10. FATF, 77–81.

11. UNODC, "Estimating Illicit Financial Flows" (see chap. 10, n. 37).

12. Naím, *Illicit*, 140.

13. Elisa Martinuzzi, "The World Is Losing the Money Laundering Fight," *Bloomberg Opin-
    ion*, September 21, 2020, https://www.bloomberg.com/opinion/articles/2020-09-21
    /the-world-is-losing-the-money-laundering-fight.

14. Naím, *Illicit*, 21.

15. Reuter and Truman, "Money Laundering," in *Chasing Dirty Money*, chap. 3.

16. Lauren Kohr, "The Building Blocks of an Effective Public-Private Partnership," *ACAMS
    Today*, July 7, 2020, https://www.acamstoday.org/the-building-blocks-of-an-effective
    -public-private-partnership/.

17. Naím, *Illicit*, 137.

18. FATF, "Professional Money Laundering."

19. John McDowell and Gary Novis, "Consequences of Money Laundering and Financial
    Crime," *Economic Perspectives* 6, no. 2 (May 2001): 6–8, http://www.ncjrs.gov/App
    /publications/abstract.aspx?ID=191327.

20. Peter J. Quirk, "Money Laundering: Muddying the Macroeconomy," *Finance and Devel-
    opment* 34, no. 1 (March 1997): 7–9, https://www.imf.org/external/pubs/ft/fandd
    /1997/03/pdf/quirk.pdf.

SELECTED BIBLIOGRAPHY

ACAMS (Association of Certified Anti–Money Laundering Specialists). *Study Guide for the ACAMS Certification Examination.* 5th ed. Miami: ACAMS, 2012.

Bullough, Oliver. *Moneyland: The Inside Story of the Crooks and Kleptocrats Who Rule the World.* New York: St. Martin's Press, 2019.

Enrich, David. *Dark Towers: Deutsche Bank, Donald Trump, and an Epic Trail of Destruction.* New York: HarperCollins, 2020.

Findley, Michael G., Daniel L. Nielson, and J. C. Sharman. *Global Shell Games: Experiments in Transnational Relations, Crime, and Terrorism.* Cambridge: Cambridge University Press, 2014.

Garner, Bryan A. *Black's Law Dictionary.* 7th ed. St. Paul, MN: West Group, 1999.

Mehlman-Orozco, Kimberly. *Hidden in Plain Sight: America's Slaves of the New Millennium.* Santa Barbara: Praeger, 2017.

Naím, Moisés. *Illicit: How Smugglers, Traffickers and Copycats Are Hijacking the Global Economy.* New York: Doubleday, 2005.

Robinson, Jeffrey. *The Laundrymen: Inside Money Laundering, the World's Third-Largest Business.* New York: Arcade, 1996.

Safire, William. *Safire's New Political Dictionary: The Definitive Guide to the New Language of Politics.* New York: Random House, 1993.

Shelley, Louise I. *Dark Commerce: How a New Illicit Economy Is Threatening Our Future.* Princeton: Princeton University Press, 2018.

Sullivan, Kevin. *Anti–Money Laundering in a Nutshell: Awareness and Compliance for Financial Personnel and Business.* New York: Apress, 2015.

Tucker, Ola. "Understanding the Risks and Challenges of Shell Companies in Managing AML Compliance." *Journal of Financial Compliance* 3, no. 4 (June 2020): 340–58.

INDEX

ABOUT THE AUTHOR

Ola M. Tucker is an experienced compliance professional whose work includes the implementation and oversight of international and domestic corporate compliance programs, as well as the design and delivery of compliance training. She is an adjunct instructor at Widener University Delaware Law School, where she teaches classes in the Graduate, International, Compliance, and Legal Studies Department. Tucker holds a JD from Syracuse University College of Law and a BA in English from Boston University. She is the founder of Compliance Notes, a boutique consultancy providing writing and training services with a focus on financial crime compliance and risk management. She has done a number of presentations and has published several articles on various compliance-related topics. Her website is www.compliance-notes.com.

CPSIA information can be obtained
at www.ICGtesting.com
Printed in the USA
JSHW031038130622
26981JS00001B/7